PREMATURE BIRTH

PREMATURE BIRTH
The Baby, the Doctor, and the Psychoanalyst

Catherine Vanier

Translated by Lindsay Watson

Routledge
Taylor & Francis Group

LONDON AND NEW YORK

For ease of reading, "he" is used throughout for the baby, the child, or the patient, and "she" is used for the caregiver, the therapist, or the analyst, but, at any point, the opposite gender can be used.

First published in French in 2013

First published 2015 by Karnac Books Ltd.

Published 2018 by Routledge
2 Park Square, Milton Park, Abingdon, Oxon OX14 4RN
711 Third Avenue, New York, NY 10017, USA

Routledge is an imprint of the Taylor & Francis Group, an informa business

British Library Cataloguing in Publication Data

A C.I.P. for this book is available from the British Library

ISBN-13: 9781782201212 (pbk)

Typeset by V Publishing Solutions Pvt Ltd., Chennai, India

CONTENTS

ACKNOWLEDGEMENTS

First of all, my thanks to the team at Saint-Denis, with whom I shared the work that has made this book possible. The path we have travelled together has been a learning experience, but they have also inspired my admiration. Over the years, they have shown unremitting engagement, interest in the babies, and have been prepared to take risks beyond the purely medical care of their little patients.

My thanks also to Dr. Jean-Marc Retbi, who agreed from the outset to make a place for me in his team, and to Dr. Pascal Bolot, to whom we owe the concept of "co-resuscitation". Over the years, we have been able to make further and further advances, primarily thanks to them, but also of course to the doctors, nursery nurses, nurses, and auxiliaries in our unit.

I wish to thank the directors of the Hôpitaux de Saint-Denis for their support, and also all the teams involved in our work: maternity, paediatrics, and child psychiatry.

My thanks are due also to my colleagues at the Centre de recherches psychanalyse, médecine et société at the Université Paris-Diderot. It was most valuable to me to be able to work and reflect within such a high-quality group of researchers. My thanks also to Bernard Golse, Bruno Falissard, and Jean-Christophe Thalabard for their support and friendship; and to Lisa Ouss and Luis Alvarez for their expert collaboration in our research project.

Thanks also to Françoise Bienfait, Jacques Sédat, and Myriam Szejer for their attentive reading of my manuscript.

And how could I not thank Alain Vanier, without whom nothing would have been possible.

ABOUT THE AUTHOR

Dr. Catherine Vanier is a practising analyst, and a member and former President of the Espace Analytique Association in Paris. She also works as a psychoanalyst in the neonatal unit at the Hôpital Delafontaine in Saint Denis and is the President of Enfance en Jeu, an association for research in paediatrics, psychoanalysis, and pedagogy. She has written numerous articles and books, including *The Broken Piano: Lacanian Psychotherapy with Children* (Other Press, 1999). In 2010 she received France's highest award, the Knight of the Legion of Honour.

ACRONYMS

AP-HP – Assistance publique—Hôpitaux de Paris: the public hospital system of the City of Paris.

ART – Assisted Reproductive Technology.

CAMSP – Centre d'action médico-sociale précoce: a social welfare centre for early detection, diagnosis, and treatment of preschool children presenting cognitive and other difficulties.

CMP – Centre médico-psychologique: a state-run outpatient therapy centre.

CMPP – Centre médico-psycho-pédagogique: an outpatient therapy centre for children and their parents.

CNRS – Centre national de la recherche scientifique: the French National Centre for Scientific Research, a governmental research organisation.

ICU – Intensive-care unit.

INSERM – Institut national de la santé et de la recherché médicale: the Institute of Health and Medical Research, a biomedical and public health research institution.

MIRE – Mission Recherche Expérimentation: research department set up by the French Ministry of Health in 1982.

NICU – Neonatal intensive-care unit.

NIDCAP – Neonatal Individual Developmental Care and Assessment Program.

PCO2 – evaluation of carbon dioxide level in the blood.

PGD – Pre-implantation Genetic Diagnosis.

PMI – Centre de protection maternelle et infantile: a mother and child social welfare centre.

PREAUT – a research protocol developed by the French PREAUT team (Prevention of Autism), offering a range of tools to identify early disturbances in communication that may be predictive of a serious developmental disturbance.

SCBU – Special care baby unit.

UAME – Unité acceuil mères-enfants: an outpatient perinatal psychiatric service.

TRANSLATOR'S NOTE

France (at least in Paris and other major cities) has been far more open to co-operation between psychiatry and psychoanalysis than has been the case in the English-speaking world. Indeed, in France the disciplines frequently overlap or merge in the person of the psychoanalytically trained psychiatrist. Collaboration between medicine and psychoanalysis, however, has been considerably less widespread, even in France, although ironically the work of the (Hungarian-born) British psychoanalyst Balint is still used there as a reference where it exists.

It has been a delight to translate Catherine Vanier's book on a very particular collaboration between medicine and psychoanalysis, involving the tiniest and most fragile human subjects—that of the *co-resuscitation* of premature babies. Her book is written with psychoanalytically informed heart, soul, and intelligence, and at the same time is lively, unstuffy, and refreshingly free of jargon and acronyms. She has a gift for expressing complex and subtle thinking with elegant simplicity and profound humanity. I have striven to do justice to the original, and to transmit the spirit of the book, remaining true to the fact that she is writing specifically about a French experience, and in particular one that unfolded in a socially deprived area of northern Paris.

Although the French and UK medical systems do not exactly map on to each other, I have endeavoured to take into account recognisable parallels within the English-speaking medical world (mainly the United Kingdom's National Health Service, in which I myself worked for fifteen years, though neither in a medical service nor with premature babies, and not with the official title of psychoanalyst but of "psychoanalytic psychotherapist").

Because acronyms tend to drain the life out of ideas, I have kept to a minimum those such as NICU (neonatal intensive care unit) and its little sibling SCBU (special care baby unit), even though they are common parlance in English, preferring to refer to "neonatal resuscitation services" (or "intensive care") where it felt more appropriate. Resuscitation (*réanimation*) is a key concept in this work, and the repetition of the word seemed to convey its spirit more vividly than the acronym.

And then there is the time-honoured conundrum of *le bébé*. In French, babies (and children) are all subsumed linguistically by the masculine gender, so there is no need for the clumsy and distracting he/she and his/her that besets the translator who sticks rigidly to that particular singularity, or the less than felicitous use of "the baby" accompanied by the possessive pronoun "their". I have done my best to use "the baby", "a baby", and "babies" in ways that are not pedantic, but reflect what works best at given moments in the book. The use of "babies" should in no way be seen as undermining one of the core assertions of this work—and indeed of the wider field of psychoanalysis, and specifically the Lacanian field—which is the singularity of the human subject caught up in the network of signifiers. To quote Catherine Vanier from these pages, "The medical knowledge of doctors, which applies to all babies, is not the same as the truth of a history which is different for each individual patient."

The internet has facilitated the translator's work in so many ways, and enabled it to become more accurate and better informed. It also means the reader can look online to find out more about any concepts that may be unfamiliar and are briefly glimpsed in the pages of this book, while underpinning its ethos—Lacan's notion of jouissance, his object *a*, the Other and the other, the paternal function, and the registers of the Imaginary, the Symbolic, and the Real (you may notice at certain points in the text that the Real and the Imaginary are capitalised, to distinguish them as signifying the Lacanian registers). But still, in spite of the marvellous advances in technology, translation can do no more than offer a version of the original from a subjective position.

Let us hope this inspiring work can help to breathe new life into the possibility of fresh collaborations between medicine and psychoanalysis.

Lindsay Watson

*To all the babies who have been in too much of a hurry
to come into the world*

On being premature: babies, their doctors, and their psychoanalysts

On a November morning in 2011, the doors opened to our new premature baby resuscitation service (neonatal intensive care unit, NICU) at the Hôpital de Saint-Denis.

The incubators entered one after the other in silent single file, still hitched up to their machines, and took their places in the new resuscitation wards,[1] intensive care wards,[2] and neonatal wards,[3] which had been waiting to receive them. The new service was not far from the old one, but moving such fragile babies required infinite care. Every movement, every intervention of each member of the team had been expertly planned by the team leaders, and everything unfolded in an atmosphere of calm and concentration.

We were changing buildings and floors to move in to the maternity unit, which had just been completely rebuilt. It is a large unit, dealing nowadays with almost 3,500 births per year. Meanwhile, the resuscitation service had been classified as "Tertiary",[4] and was taking in an increasing number of smaller and smaller babies. From being in a rather small unit where we had been used to working very closely with one another, we found ourselves in a brand-new and comparatively vast centre. We were now right next door to the newly modernised labour wards, close to the children who were being born, so that we would no longer waste any time, we would be there right away. In a resuscitation service, every moment counts if we are to save a baby's life. Running along corridors, moving from one place to another, constitutes an additional risk which the doctors hope to avoid. This unit was much bigger, much newer, much more modern and sophisticated, and pretty impressive. It would take us several months to get used to it.

The décor had something about it that reminded us of NASA, something "aerospatial". In any case, it felt very secret, very protected. To get in, you had to perform very precise rituals. There were long corridors to walk down, security badges to open doors, intercoms which were used to allow only the parents to come in. Visitors were immediately plunged into a strange atmosphere of hygiene rules, appropriate dress, the particular form of silence that reigned, and filtered light. It was almost a "religious" atmosphere, some people said, as if it were a place of worship. Others said it was like being in a laboratory straight out of a science-fiction movie.

I found out that my office was to be at the entrance to the service. My name was on the door, and below my name: Psychoanalyst. As I was standing there slightly perplexed, key in hand, a doctor said to me in passing, "You know, they did prepare the babies in advance, they told them all about the move. I hope they're not going to be too overwhelmed by the majestic new premises!"

When I asked him what the team thought about the new unit, he replied, "We're pretty overwhelmed too, at having such a beautiful unit; I suppose that's why we wondered what effect the new setting would have on the babies."

While the physical journey from the old service to the new one had been fairly short, the road travelled since I arrived in the unit, up to that moment, that day, suddenly seemed a great deal longer.

This all happened in the same month that I was asked to work on a new edition of the book I had written on neonatal resuscitation fifteen years previously. I had agreed to do the new edition, but so many things had changed since I arrived there that it seemed difficult not to deal with recent advances as well. It was impossible not to try to pass on what we had learnt from the babies themselves during the last few years. Extremely premature babies, or very low birth weight babies, as they are now called, have a great deal to teach us. There are more and more studies on their capacities from birth onwards, their sensorial capabilities, their reactivity. But for psychoanalysts, beyond these very interesting experiments, these tiny babies cast an essential light on the metapsychology of the earliest days of life. How will subjectivity be constituted in the depths of an incubator? The contribution from working with very premature babies, which is essential for child analysis, is even more so when we work with children who are psychotic or autistic; and it is also a very rich source of learning about the archaic phase of our work with adult analysands. These babies are remarkable teachers, however little attention we may pay in class. The number of premature babies is increasing. Advances in science, as well as medically assisted procreation, in some cases of which there is a separation of sexuality and reproduction, have caused a revolution in the field.

Progress in technology, with units that are ever more sophisticated and care that is ever closer to perfection, together with smaller and smaller babies, have changed the ground rules. When I started working in the field, only babies weighing more than 1000 grams, and at least at thirty weeks' gestation, were resuscitated.

These days, while the World Health Organization (WHO) sets the limit of viability at twenty-two weeks gestation and 500 grams, most French and European centres do not resuscitate babies at less than twenty-five weeks.[5] Let us remember that a normal full-term birth occurs between the forty-first and forty-second week of pregnancy. The babies are smaller than in the past, the resuscitations and time spent in neonatal units go on for longer, and the expectations regarding the prognosis are more disturbing.

How do such tiny babies give a sign to their parents? What can we expect of them? What can we do for them? One mother said to me, "There I am next to the incubator, and I spend hours waiting for this baby to give me a sign, just to let me know I'm his mother." But how could such small babies give their mothers the feeling that they exist, given that they are at the bottom of an incubator, overwhelmed by heaviness, machinery, smells and sounds? Nor is the position of the doctors the same any more. They feel an ever-increasing responsibility to take on the resuscitation of such small babies, as well as having to decide from one moment to the next to move to palliative care, as the

Leonetti law (see Chapter Four) now obliges us to do, in order to avoid what we no longer call *"furor sanandi"* but "unreasonable obstinacy". The risks facing very premature babies add to the unease. Those who carry out the resuscitations certainly wonder whether our society, at the same time as maximising the use of contraception, therapeutic terminations, and investigations of all sorts, might not be creating severely impaired children through the intervention of neonatologists. And how could they not question the norms proposed by our modern world? Doctors do not carry out resuscitation for its own sake; they are constantly questioning why they are doing it, and only ask to be allowed to speak about it, however little they may be listened to. A new head of service, Dr. Bolot, was appointed. Like many neonatologists today, he was very attentive to the "developmental needs" and the well-being of the babies, and from the start he was interested in what the presence of a psychoanalyst could contribute. He enabled me to continue to develop the work set up fifteen years previously by Dr. Retbi.

The current head of service speaks of our collaboration as of a project of "co-resuscitation": that is to say, resuscitating babies and, at the same time, their desire to live.

It is a vast project, which puts me in the position of both psychoanalyst and resuscitator. It is not an entirely straightforward project, raising the question of the unconscious and of the subject in a neonatal resuscitation service. The question of desire arises not only for the babies and their families but also for the doctors and their teams. So who is being resuscitated?

Faced with such a demand, my place in the unit today is no longer the same as it was. The questions asked of me are in a different register, and the effects of transference are altered, not only with the doctors but also with the families, and of course, with the babies. The pages that follow are a testament to work done, to progress made, and to questions encountered since the first version of this book was published (Mathelin, 1998).

Notes

1. For babies receiving artificial respiration in order to maintain vital functions.
2. For babies who are still very small, and needing respiratory support and intravenous feeding.

3. For babies who are beginning to find their autonomy in breathing and feeding.
4. Tertiary, or Type III: a Perinatal Centre comprising a Maternity Unit which deals with high-risk pregnancies and a Neonatal Intensive Care Unit (NICU) which takes care of very premature babies.
5. At the time of writing, it is only in Japan that a few babies are resuscitated at less than twenty-five weeks.

CHAPTER ONE

Psychoanalysis and neonatal resuscitation

Neonatology: a recent specialism

Since the dawn of time, human beings have tried to resuscitate newborn babies; yet neonatology as a medical specialism is relatively recent. The main elements of its history were broadly outlined in the paper given by François Duchatel at the Société française d'histoire de la médécine in 1979 (Duchatel, 1926), and are as follows.

He observed that the first reference to resuscitation of a child (in this case an older child) can be found in the Old Testament, in the Second Book of Kings, chapter IV, verses 32 to 35:

> And when Elisha was come into the house, behold, the child was dead, and laid upon his bed.
>
> He went in therefore, and shut the door upon them twain, and prayed unto the Lord.
>
> And he went up, and lay upon the child, and put his mouth upon his mouth, and his eyes upon his eyes, and his hands upon his hands: and he stretched himself upon the child; and the flesh of the child waxed warm.

1

> Then he returned, and walked in the house to and fro; and went
> up, and stretched himself upon him; and the child sneezed seven
> times, and the child opened his eyes.

Other methods of resuscitation followed, some of them rather original. In 1601, Louyse Bourgeois (1563–1636), a midwife and pupil of
Ambroise Paré, who attended the childbed of Marie de Médicis, wrote
a treatise (Bourgeois, 1926) on the birth of the future king Louis XIII.
After a long labour of twenty-two hours, the baby was born in a state
of considerable weakness and there was a risk he would not survive,
so she put some wine in her mouth and blew it into the baby's mouth:
"At that very moment," she wrote, "he rallied and savoured the wine I
had given him."

After that, many other methods were invented for starting a baby's
breathing. In the 1880s, newborns were manipulated in all possible
ways, pressed and compressed, to provoke a forced inhalation and
exhalation. They were held upside-down by their ankles and shaken,
and smacked on the bottom a few times in order to bring them to life
(and this method was used for quite a few years!).

It was soon observed that premature babies (who were referred to as
"sickly" infants[1] at this time) were at risk from the cold, and so those
caring for them came up with the idea of wrapping them in cotton
wool, and surrounding the cradle with hot water bottles. In the 1890s,
it was the incubators used for hatching chicks at the zoological gardens
that gave doctors the idea of putting premature babies into warm glass
boxes (Tarnier, Chantreuil, & Budin, 1886–1901). At first the boxes were
shared, and later individual (unlike those used for chicks), and were
warmed by paraffin lamps. During this era there were also numerous
precursors to artificial respiration, "insufflators", and other methods of
mechanical breathing.

But real progress in neonatal resuscitation came with advances in
medical research. There was certainly a need for better understanding
of physiological mechanisms, and for more sophisticated equipment. It
was only in the early 1900s that endotracheal intubation for adults was
invented, and not until about 1950 that it was used in neonatal resuscitation. We just had to wait. Wait, for example until J. F. Kennedy's
premature son died in Boston in 1963 at thirty-four weeks and 2.1 kg,
of hyaline membrane disease.[2] Wait for progress in the resuscitation

of adults—until finally, in 1965, the techniques of intubation and ventilation could be applied in neonatology.

Neonatal resuscitation, then, is a very recent discipline. It was Professor Alexandre Minkowski who opened the first major centre for premature babies in France in 1967 at Port-Royal. Premature babies in life-threatening distress are routinely taken to Port-Royal. And whereas before 1970, eighty per cent of newborns weighing less than 1.1 kg would die, after 1980, eighty per cent survived (Bétrémieux, 2010).

Between 1980 and 2000, considerable progress was made. Corticotherapy even before birth, surfactants,[3] and sophisticated ventilation techniques became available. Extraordinary machines were perfected and enabled the limits of what was possible to be pushed further and further. Attempts were made to resuscitate ever-smaller babies. In 2000, it was reported that a baby weighing only 350 grams had been resuscitated in Texas. But some doctors started to worry, concerned about the consequences of such extreme resuscitations, and wondering if they might risk leaving these children disabled for life. At this point, ethics committees were set up. In France, in 2002 the Kouchner law and in 2005, the Leonetti law, raised new questions for those responsible for the care of very low birth weight babies. Just how far should they go? Is it possible to know how resuscitation will affect a baby? And even if the baby survives, will there be psychiatric or psychological sequelae as he grows up?

It was necessary to wait again, and take a step back, to observe the development of older children who had been born prematurely, so that the scientific community could engage in research on the psychological outcomes for these babies. Studies were undertaken focusing on the development of children who had not suffered obvious neurosensory or neuromotor sequelae. Their findings included social, emotional, and cognitive disturbances, behavioural difficulties, and problems in keeping up with their contemporaries at school that were significantly more severe than in the non-premature population. In order to keep such iatrogenic effects to a minimum, proposals were put forward for programmes of "developmental care", the best known of which nowadays is NIDCAP (Neonatal Individual Developmental Care and Assessment Program).[4] Developed in 1986 by Heidelise Als, a behavioural psychologist and lecturer at Harvard, who also worked in the

Boston Children's Hospital, the programme aims to put in place an environmental and behavioural strategy, to facilitate the children's development by minimising stress on them when they are babies. Its fundamental hypothesis is: children are the main agents of their own development. Among other things, the programme involves a series of observations at regular intervals—every seven to ten days—in order to work out a programme tailored to each baby, which will take into account the baby's reactions and behaviour before, during, and after an intervention. The particular manner of the caregiver can thus be modified for each individual child in order to reduce any stress to a minimum, in relation to the child's capacity to adapt and degree of sensitivity. The environment can be modified, and stimulations—sound and light levels—can be reduced.

The incubators themselves are made opaque, using a cover that is only removed when interventions are made, or when the parents visit. Interventions can be reorganised, and periods of rest are respected. The way the babies are positioned in the incubator ensures a natural, flexed posture. Swaddling, gripping, and non-nutritive sucking are all enabled as much as possible. The baby's behaviour is explained to the parents, and contact with them, especially skin-to-skin ("kangaroo care"), is encouraged and strongly recommended during their visits. On the other hand, the caregivers are not involved, beyond imparting these fundamental principles, in the child's development. Their task is limited to helping to avoid unpleasant overstimulation.

There is no denying that the changes proposed by NIDCAP are important. Limiting aggressive interventions as far as possible, taking the babies' reactions into consideration, ensuring their general comfort and taking care over their positioning in the incubator, encouraging the parents to have physical contact with them—all seem like common sense, and in our view are absolutely essential when working with newborns.

By themselves, however, they are not sufficient. Behavioural methods and observations, however refined, miss the point unless another type of support is offered concurrently. How can you resuscitate babies without taking their history into account, and that of their parents, and the babies' desire to live? How can you engage in this process without taking into account the elements that might make it possible for something "subjective" to emerge inside the incubators? Over the years in our unit we have certainly tried to think about developmental care, but in a different way.

Saint-Denis: the neonatology service of the Hôpital Delafontaine

In order to follow the development of this work in progress, we need to look back at the way things were when I joined the neonatal resuscitation unit of the Hôpital Delafontaine, towards the end of the 1980s.

I was in a meeting in the paediatric psychiatry service (within which I still work)[5] when the phone rang. Dr. Abram Coen, the head of service at the time, told us that the head of neonatology of our hospital was asking if a psychiatrist could go to see a mother who was being treated in his service, and was "really not at all well". But that morning, all the psychiatrists were busy, and so I was asked to go. When I arrived, the doctors explained to me that this woman's reaction had thrown the service into complete disarray. She had just refused to take her baby home.

By telling this mother that her baby was recovered, cured of prematurity, and with no apparent risk of further problems related to prematurity—this fine baby, such a success for the unit—the doctors were hoping to cure her of the symptoms she had complained of from the day the baby was born. She suffered from insomnia, anxiety attacks, dark thoughts. When the baby came out of hospital, they were absolutely certain, she would dry her tears, and the baby would cure his mother of her depressive state. But now there she was saying she didn't want anything more to do with her baby: "You keep him," she had said. Assuming she was mad, they had searched the hospital telephone list for the extension where they might hope to find a psychiatrist—paediatric psychiatry, since our hospital does not have an adult psychiatry department. But instead of the psychiatrist they were expecting, on that occasion a psychoanalyst turned up. That is how I began my work in neonatology. The team took me into their service under the aegis of liaison psychiatry, so that I would make this woman see reason, and get her to rejoice in the birth of her baby and be grateful for the good care that had been given to him. And indeed, after a few sessions, she did agree to take him home.

From time to time over the next few months, there were further calls from neonatology: other mothers in difficulty. These sessions taught me how difficult it was for all these women to have any sort of relation with their babies in a neonatal resuscitation unit. From them I learnt of the trauma that the premature birth represents, and the violent shock of receiving the prognosis: "We can't tell you yet whether your baby is going to live or die." Suddenly I was aware of the radical difference between the point of view of the mothers and that of the doctors.

Babies born looking as if they are dead, or in danger of death, immediately trigger a protocol of action for the intensive care doctors. The doctors have to make an immediate assessment, according to certain very precise criteria, of whether a child can be "saved". What a doctor decodes as a series of signs necessitating a certain number of well-rehearsed interventions according to that protocol, is decoded by the parents in quite another way. They have just brought a baby into the world who may not live. Sometimes, they overhear that their child "appears to be dead". In all cases, what immediately "appears" to the parents is the signifier "dead".

Now the family drama is in the foreground, and straight away the little inert body takes its place in a scenario where each individual has his or her role to play. The roles are already inscribed in the family history, and sometimes have been that way for generations.

The baby becomes the locus of all their projections; guilt is the prime mover, and all the fantasies we hear expressed at this time only feed into it: "You gave him his life", said this mother, who wasn't mad at all, "you keep him. All I could give him was death, I'm a danger to him." This mother whom the team deemed to be "bad" was in fact a good mother, who was concerned to protect her baby. It was only by allowing her, as the sessions progressed, to speak about her history and about the family drama that had made a prisoner of her, that this mother had eventually been able to allow herself to take her child home.

Listening to these mothers, I was rapidly coming to the conclusion that everything happened as if treating a case of prematurity was equivalent to responding at the level of the symptom, leaving aside any problematic of the family in relation to life and death, which at this juncture is centred on the newborn. Babies do not "speak" to their parents in the same way as they "speak" to the doctors—luckily for the babies, who would otherwise be firmly caught up in the progress of medicine! Sickness does not represent the same thing for the doctors as it does for the families; we can say that they do not even perceive the same sickness. And neither does the treatment have the same significance for the caregivers as it does for the parents. Lacan spoke of this in a lecture he gave to a group of doctors: "When the patient is sent to the doctor, or when he approaches him, you cannot say that he is just expecting purely and simply to be cured. He puts the doctor to the test, seeing if the latter can get him out of his state of being a patient—and that is quite different, because it can involve the fact that he may be absolutely attached to the idea of remaining in that state" (Lacan, 2003, p. 302 [translated for this edition]). On the basis of this observation, we can see how a dialogue of the deaf can ensue between doctor and patient on the subject of a possible recovery, and the profundity of deafness is far greater than in any ordinary dialogue. This is one reason why doctors complain that in spite of their efforts to explain, the parents do not seem to understand what they are saying. Indeed, more often than not they do not understand.

So there I was at the beginning, an unsettling sorceress, situated outside the service, where my role could be summed up as dealing with the parents. The parents, and above all, the mothers: they seemed to be the ones who caused the most problems. The ones who were referred to me were those who did not behave as the team expected a "good mother" to behave. They needed treatment, and if necessary, would have to be referred to a psychoanalyst if no psychiatrist was available. But whereas, at first, the members of the team expected me to make the mothers see reason, they gradually realised that these women were not just questioning them, but medicine as a whole. It is quite understandable that doctors who had worked so fervently to "repair" a newborn baby would be astonished and disappointed if the mother no longer wanted anything to do with the baby; this would raise the question of whether their efforts had any point at all. It would certainly have been easier, or at least more comfortable, to consider these women mad; but psychoanalysis, as we know, has never really favoured easy or soothing answers.

So now another reading of the situation was put to the team. While these mothers were not insane, we had to admit that during the long months of hospitalisation, they had found themselves unable to invest emotionally in their babies. If the team recognised that they were not mad, then they also had to question what had been going on during this separation. Even if the baby had been "saved" physically, it was clear that something had been missed in another dimension, as when you miss a train and find yourself stuck on the platform at a railway station. Thanks to what I had learned from the mothers for whom I had been brought in, I was soon able to propose to the team a quite different way of working.

It was no longer a question of rushing to the aid of the caregivers each time a baby or a baby's family were having problems, but of meeting each baby and his parents, as soon as the baby arrived in the service. So now it was not a case of piecemeal "treatment" of mothers made ill by the separation from their babies, or of babies made ill by the separation from their mothers, but rather of working together on a common project which would enable the babies' lives to be saved "differently". In order to do this, I had to understand how the process of resuscitation worked in the unit. I had to meet not only with the mothers at the time of their discharge from hospital after the birth, but also with the fathers, throughout the entire period of the admission. To bring this project to fruition, it would be necessary to be near the babies, listening to them, and at the same time to help the doctors understand what was going on in their own minds while dealing with these difficult cases.

The analyst, then, was no longer there just to repair the damage that might be caused by long admissions, but to work alongside the resuscitation team in a different register; it was no longer just a case of being called in when things were going wrong in the family, when the parents were unhappy or aggressive and the doctors' work was suffering as a consequence. If that had been the case, we would have been there not to help the patients, but to help medicine itself.

It was a project that needed the full support of the entire team in order to be implemented.

And it was accepted by the unit.

Léa

Léa was a little girl born at thirty weeks and who weighed only 950 grams. Her mother came in to the service the very next day. The doctors could not say whether the baby would survive; they needed time to see how she would develop. They were neither optimistic nor pessimistic; they were just waiting. But the mother was not waiting. She did not need to wait to know that Léa was going to die, and she told everyone about it. But the caregivers were amazed: "How can you be so sure, when we're not?" The fact that she was so sure, and so obsessively determined, really unsettled the team. "How can she possibly not hope that her daughter will live? Does she really love her child?" they would ask.

But this mother was not asking the question in quite those terms. As far as she was concerned, the die was cast; it was as if she were laying claim to her child's condemnation to death. With a combination of prescience and reconstruction, mothers can sometimes pinpoint a fundamental truth linked to desire, in whatever it is that their child's body represents for them.

Indeed, death is inscribed in certain cases as the fatal end-result of the realisation of a desire. This is precisely what is so difficult for doctors to understand, and may lead them to call in liaison psychiatry.

We have to look beyond the trauma of the actual child. The baby, lying in the bottom of the incubator, plugged in to machines, is reduced to a little piece of the Real, an object of science, and becomes the privileged locus of inscriptions of the discourse of the Other.[6] These signifiers can sometimes be picked up in the mother's discourse, but also in that of the doctors. I proposed to the team that we should base our approach on this clinic of the signifier.

Léa's mother was sterile, and she would say so: "I'm sterile. And just because they made me a baby in a test-tube, it doesn't mean I'm not sterile any more." Léa was born following a number of attempts at *in vitro* fertilisation (IVF). The piece of flesh with which the mother identified her child's body, and which had emerged from the field of her relation to death, could only die. She had told me a dream she had had as an adolescent: her mother flung herself at her and slashed her belly with a knife. One day when she was a little girl playing with her doll, her mother had said to her, "Stop playing that stupid game, leave that doll alone; in any case you'll never be able to have a baby." This phrase, repeated several times during her childhood, had taken on the value of a prediction. She had never been able to separate from her mother. While she was at the mercy of her violence, she was also fascinated by her, and indeed was never able to let her go.

The necessary *"ravage"* between mother and daughter, which enables them to separate, had not been able to run its course.[7] This maternal excess had not been tempered by the presence of a man. As a child, she had been her mother's only erotic partner. No man had come in to the picture, and this mother–daughter relationship that lacked nothing weighed heavily on Léa's mother, both as a woman and as a mother. Nor had she ever had a man in her own life: when she became an adult, she never had any luck with men. She said she could never "exorcise this curse".

The doctors confirmed that she was sterile. She would not be able to have a child without medical intervention. The only possible chance of becoming a mother might be through IVF. So she decided to ask a male friend. She spoke of the man who had agreed to donate his sperm, Léa's biological father, as a kind, docile person who had agreed to the donation without asking to have his paternity recognised, and without ever having attempted to have sexual relations with her. "That's just how it was, he just did it as a friend. He wanted to make me happy, because he knew how much I wanted a child," said the mother. "There'll never be anything more between us. I like him a lot, he's a good mate, but he's not my lover."

Léa stayed alive in spite of a host of problems she encountered during the period of intensive care. But what would have become of her if no one had been able to listen to her mother during that time, and been able to listen in a rather different way from the caregivers, who said she was "bad"? These women who have just given birth will only be made to feel more guilty if that is how they are spoken of. It is also true that mothers have been made to bear a great deal of guilt in our time. And yet, during all my years of practice in hospitals and elsewhere, I have never come across a truly guilty mother, but only women who are victims and have been prevented from forming a bond with their babies. These were mothers who did not deserve to be accused, but rather helped to understand what had gone on during the birth. In hospital, these mothers, who may be aggressive with the staff or with their own babies as a result of fear or despair, are very difficult for the teams to manage. That is doubtless the main reason why the doctors ask us to intervene.

At the beginning, when the doctors saw how the sessions with the parents were changing their attitude to the team and to the babies, they assumed that I was succeeding in "conditioning" or "convincing" the mothers to be happy, and sometimes in "reassuring" the fathers, helping them "adapt" to the situation. How could they come to understand that my work was in fact quite different? How could they come to realise that these parents, by speaking about themselves, could grow to understand something of their own history, and of the place this child and the premature birth now occupied in their history?

Knowing that I did not prescribe medication, they said they imagined that I provided a reassuring presence and would lavish support and good advice on the parents of the premature babies. So far then, all was going fine. "Oh well, it can't do any harm," they were thinking.

However, once they had the impression that something else was happening, when the parents really seemed to be asking different questions, and above all, once they started to register "clinically" the effects these sessions were having on the babies' bodies, on their state of health, the caregivers began to feel strange and unsettled. My work started to look rather more serious. The hardest thing for them was to accept that words could actually have an effect on a baby's body. When a baby reacted to something I said in the presence of the parents, and his physical state would alter, the doctors would say jokingly, "But it's just not possible, speaking can't have that sort of effect on the body, it's sorcery!" They suddenly became rather mistrustful. And yet, as Caroline Eliacheff (1998) reminds us, we realise very quickly that for a baby who cannot yet speak, the body is the locus of language. But it is easy to understand the doctors, too: having a sorceress working in a high-tech medical service is not altogether reassuring! In the end, since I found the idea of casting spells quite appealing, I stayed in the unit, and tried to set up meetings to speak with the team. Dr. Retbi, the head of service at the time, was very supportive in helping organise these get-togethers. He was doubtless quite suspicious himself, but also very curious and intrigued by what I might contribute, so he decided to attend the meetings himself, and asked all the doctors to participate. Week by week, year by year, after speaking about theory, and bringing along papers to read, I was able to encourage them to work differently.

Co-resuscitation

Many things have changed since the days when babies were restrained in their incubators so that their lines did not come out, or their monitors become detached, and since the days when parents were not allowed inside the service. The mother of Medhi, who herself had been premature, told me she had spent two months in a NICU. When her parents visited her, they had to stay behind the window in the corridor. Nobody was allowed to go in. She also told me of the difficulties that followed her discharge from hospital, and how she was put in foster care by social services a few months later. Her mother, although she had had other children, was never able to take care of her in the way she took care of the others.

The parents' attitude to the baby, and sometimes also that of the siblings, now has a significant place in the way services operate. With the proliferation of studies showing the impact of the parents' projections on the development of their children, teams have rethought their protocols; and nowadays parents are invited to spend as much time as they wish with their babies. They are also strongly encouraged to take part in caregiving. When they seem disorientated or depressed, or if they cause problems of one kind or another to the team, they are offered a session with the service psychologist (the presence of a psychologist in a tertiary service has become a legal obligation in France).

But in our unit, we chose another option. When I arrived, I was working "on demand", as everyone did at that time, but soon this method appeared to me to have little to contribute to the success of the project. So it was agreed that I should be introduced to all parents, as soon as their baby arrived in the service, as the psychoanalyst who was responsible for the psychical and emotional development of their baby. It was on this basis that all parents met me to talk about their baby. From then on, I was involved in the process of resuscitation, and became part of the service, participating in the way the parents and babies were received into the service, and in the babies' progress. That is how it came about in our team that we now talk of our project as being one of "co-resuscitation".

After the first meeting with the parents, I would often find them beside the incubators, throughout the period of the admission. In some cases, the first meeting was very superficial, but at least it enabled the parents to realise that a psychoanalyst in the service was listening to their baby. From these initial meetings, a demand might arise. This is how we have proposed a framework for working with the parents, creating a space for psychoanalysis within neonatology. It is no longer a case of the parents coming to me because the team finds them "weird", but because they really want to speak with me. I give them an appointment in my office, and these sessions may continue for as long as they wish. While the formal meeting is routine and according to protocol, the parents will only "follow it up" if there is a demand. It is this demand for psychoanalysis which will make it possible for real work to be done.

Experience shows us that following these initial meetings, many will ask for further sessions, sometimes long after the baby has been discharged. "Co-resuscitation" signifies that in the team we have agreed that we place equal value on the medical resuscitation and the psychical resuscitation of babies.

Transference

Since several different transferences have to be taken into account, how do we work with these specific types of demand? With the passage of time, the caregivers have agreed that it is right to question the impact of premature birth on a baby, on the team, on the family, and also on themselves. Nowadays, our service is able to offer a particular way of working which is psychoanalytic in orientation, and differs from that of the majority of other NICUs. The work is carried out at three levels— that of the parents, that of the baby, and that of the team—taking into account the different problematic of the transference at each level.

In psychoanalysis, transference can be defined as the link that reactivates the demand for love in childhood. Freud spoke of the displacement of archaic imagoes transferred on to the person of the analyst, during the early stages of analysis. It is a story of love and of desire. It is a reactivation, a re-kindling which takes place without the knowledge of the subject and which is central to the analysis, being both its motor and the chief means of resistance to it. Even though the analyst is neither the father nor the mother, nor any other actual person linked to the history of the patient, the analyst can occupy the place of each of those figures in turn. The analyst will most certainly work with the transference, while keeping in mind that it is not him- or herself who is involved. Enabling the analyst to "not believe he or she is actually in that place"[8] is one of the aims of what used to be called "training analysis". But this position is not always an easy one to maintain, even if the analysand supports it.

Freud, speaking of the Rat Man, admitted that he was extremely upset when his patient saw him as the cruel captain of his memories: "He repeatedly addressed me as 'Captain', probably because at the beginning of the hour I had told him that I myself was not fond of cruelty" (Freud, 1909d). This displacement on to another person, beyond the bounds of reality, does not occur only within the framework of analysis; it is present whenever one person addresses another by formulating a demand. It is common practice in any human encounter to confuse the representation one makes of the other with his reality; the most obvious example of this is love at first sight, where the other, without our knowing anything about him, unleashes an inexplicable passion. What is captivating about this stranger is more a reflection of the subject, who is captivated himself, than of the other. In the case of psychoanalytic treatment, the transference becomes the analyst's tool in the work of analysis. Positive and negative transferences and resistances are forms of "data" which allow analysts to take their bearings in the direction of the treatment. The transference is closely linked with the compulsion to repeat, and with a certain way of being in the world and articulating one's being with the object of one's desire. Within the framework of analysis, transference neurosis is produced as in a laboratory experiment so that something of the subject can come to be articulated differently. So it is not just a repetition but also an invention, a creation which, if the analyst uses it skilfully, and avoids falling into the many traps which will be set for her, will allow the patient to change subjectively. One of the definitions Lacan gave of the transference, in 1951, is as follows: "In other words, transference is nothing real in the subject if not the appearance, at a moment of stagnation in the analytic dialectic, of the permanent modes according to which she constitutes her objects" (Lacan, 1951, pp. 183–184). In the course of analysis, the subject of these "permanent modes" may come to know something about them. But an analyst who makes forays into the world of medicine will be confronted with various types of transference which will require particular ways of working; in each case the response will have to be reinvented, because we are no longer working within the usual analytic framework.

Working with the parents

The work with the parents begins the moment the baby is brought in to the unit. When they arrive, appointments are given automatically, one with the doctor who will be responsible for medical care, and another with the psychoanalyst who will follow the baby throughout the entire admission. After this first routine appointment, parents can ask for more as often as they wish. All the mothers feel so guilty about giving birth to a premature baby that for some of them (though not all), asking them to request appointments with a psychoanalyst only makes them feel worse. One mother said to me, "I'm already feeling terrible about giving birth to such a sick baby, who's so fragile that he's hovering between life and death. And now the doctors have decided I'm crazy and are asking me to make an appointment with you!"

The fact that all the parents are seen from the start alters the tenor of the transference. From the start, the analyst is not there as a figure in the parents' imagination, to judge them or put them on the right path, but rather as the one who is supposed to know something about the development of their baby. From the first session, the analyst listens differently. It is not a case of medical questioning, nor of a psycho-medical investigation. Nor is it a case of the analyst being empathic, but rather of listening in the way informed by analytic training to whatever the parents have to say. And it is because the analyst does not respond to their demand with scientific knowledge or even with psychologising knowledge about the psycho-affective development of their baby, that they are able to speak to her, and then can feel free to ask for more appointments. It is also because the analyst does not tell them the "right attitude" to have towards the baby, nor the best kind of behaviour to adopt, nor even the reasons why they are so upset by the birth, that some true speech can emerge; something of the family drama that has surfaced as a result of the birth can be traced, revealing the web of fantasies in which this prematurity has been inscribed. It is the distance between the position of the analyst, who has everything to learn from the parents, and that of the resuscitating doctor, which allows the analyst to hear the articulation of whatever the parents project on to the body of their child, this "real" little piece of their own bodies, and the baby the doctors are going to take care of. In these times of extreme anxiety the whole web of family fantasies is mobilised, because life and death are at stake. The medical knowledge of the doctors, which applies to all babies, is not the same as the truth of a history which is different for each individual patient. As Lacan emphasised, it is this distance which makes the difference in the position of the analyst: "The question of the psychoanalyst's knowledge is nothing to do with knowing whether it is all articulated or not, but rather with knowing in what position he needs to be in order to support it" (Lacan, 1971). The fantasies and the family history can be worked through using the effects of transference. This will involve the deciphering of a discourse and its effects. The process of deciphering is of interest to the doctors, too, and enables them to work somewhat differently themselves. It is important for them to realise that their patients have a view of their illness which is not the same as the doctor's scientific view. Prematurity does not mean the same thing to a resuscitating doctor as it does to the parents of a 500-gram baby. For the parents, the baby is revealing an entire family drama concentrated around the event of "prematurity". They are at a loss, often trying to make sense of the birth, trying to find a cause for this irruption of the Real into their lives. But for the analyst, it is not a question of looking for cause and effect, but of finding points of articulation of this illness "prematurity" with the history of the parents, so that they can experience this birth a little differently, and can begin to bond with their baby. In order for this to happen, the analyst needs to be able to take on board the violence and the effects of the death drive. The transference to the team psychoanalyst and the type of listening that she offers allows things to be said that could never be said to a doctor. It is not a question of taking the parents into analysis, but only of defusing the fantasmatic traps they are caught in, which stop them from making a place in their lives for the baby.

From the very first session, the parents speak of their anguish, of the trauma that this encounter with the Real has represented for them. It is important for them to be able to symbolise what has happened, so that they can continue to imagine a future for the baby, and so that the baby does not become a mere object of medical care, but can remain a child, their child.

A mother who has just given birth, whether prematurely or not, to a baby who is immediately taken away from her because the doctors think the baby is in danger, finds herself overwhelmed by a drama which is so violent that she loses her bearings and becomes disorientated. Time is suspended, and she can only count the days according to the baby's weight, as the baby continues the pregnancy outside her body, in an incubator which nurtures the baby she was incapable of holding on to, in her place. A mother will often ask us: "When will his birthday be? The day he came out of my belly, or the day he came out of the incubator? You're lucky, he doesn't move about much in your incubator; when he was in my belly, he really hurt me!"

This baby was so painful for her and so easy for us. Quite often, mothers will not be able to look at their babies, talk to them or give them a name. What is waiting to happen is the possibility of the mother's libidinal investment of the baby. How can these babies be assigned an ideal place in which "phallicisation" will be possible? How can these tiny, sick babies make mothers of these women? For these mothers, "His

Majesty the Baby", to use Freud's words, does not look anything like a premature baby. They cannot recognise themselves in these babies, who cannot recognise themselves in these mothers.

Yet this stage of phallicisation is indispensable for babies; they will never make themselves into a fetish object for their mother, imprisoned in her fantasy, if she turns towards another person, allowing the child in turn to be promised to another man or another woman. But if the mother's look is turned away from the child, if the child is too weak and too distant to make the mother feel that he or she is interested in her, the investment of love between them will become problematic and the baby will have nothing to hold on to, in order to enable the development of a sense of self.

But how can a mother invest in a child she experiences as monstrous and persecuting, a child who signifies her own powerlessness and failure? Work with mothers is always the work of mourning, loss, and separation. Once they can symbolise this lack, they are then able to separate the child from the horror of the Real, and begin to project a possible future on to him.

Day by day, the rituals of coming into the service, of taking the baby out of the incubator, are put in place as so many attempts at symbolisation. As the weeks go by, the team, who gradually withdraw from the position of "the good mother who keeps the baby alive", ask the true mother how she is feeling. "You're the one who knows your baby better than anyone, how do you think she is this morning? Maybe you can help us understand her, so we can find out how to help her."

This invitation—or perhaps it is an authorisation—to look at something other than the read-out on the monitors, to project something on to the child, to look ahead, helps the mothers to "create" their baby, while at the same time allowing the babies to create their mother. The team, in its capacity of other, has two functions:

1. to separate the child from the mother;[9]
2. to authorise the woman to become her child's mother.

This function is all the more important in cases where the father is absent and there is no family to support the mother. This is the work that allows the mother to keep in mind that her baby has a life ahead of him. During the period of the admission, while the babies are being restored to health, the mothers also need to be restored to health, otherwise they will be incapable of looking after them when they leave the service.

How can a mother in this situation come to believe that if the child is alive, it has had something to do with her? Most of the women we see in our service would not have become mothers if it had not been for scientific progress. Their babies could not have lived without it, and so they believe that they themselves are the carriers of death. So the hospital, acting as a third party, can protect the baby from the mother and the mother from the baby.

Working with babies

How can we begin to imagine the suffering of a premature baby in a resuscitation service? Current research highlights the astonishing capabilities of newborns. How can premature babies, who are even more immature than babies born at term, make something of the world from the depths of their incubators, according to what they perceive or feel? They are too weak to give any sort of sign, and too weak to decode the signals that are made to them; so surely this must mean that they need an even greater level of attention and availability than others.

But does the workload in the service allow for this level of availability? Babies come into being as human subjects partly thanks to the mother's capacity for reverie. They anticipate their mother's reactions, expecting a response that they quickly learn to trigger, in the game of "peek-a-boo", in which the paternal function plays a role. But how is it for babies in hospital? Some say that premature babies suffer from a lack of stimulation, others, that they suffer from overstimulation.

Once a week, at the team meeting, we are able to think of the children as human subjects above all else. From the moment children are admitted to the service, we try to welcome them not just as bodies that need fixing, but as small human beings, each one carrying a history that was already being made long before the admission to hospital, even if that admission happened at the moment of birth. The stay in the neonatology service will be just one episode in their continuing history, provided nothing happens to bring it to a halt.

We go beyond the measuring of milestones, and far beyond mere observation, putting the emphasis on the place that needs to be created for a child, and on truthful speech, because speech has a degree of power over the body. The care of doctors, whose desire is to prolong life, is not always sufficient; in order to live, human beings have to be inscribed within a system of speech, otherwise they will die. If they become inscribed in a mad system of speech, they may become mad.

Two babies born at the same term and with the same birth weight, presenting similar symptomatology, will not necessarily develop in the same way, even if they are given the same quality of care. It is impossible to generalise, and that is what raises questions for us. Each body, inscribed in a different speech system, differs from every other body. Medical knowledge is concerned with the body in general. Confronted with the truth of the bodies of different babies, we may question that knowledge. That is what analysts, working in medical services, put into question. It is a truth of a different order from medical knowledge, and it entails the questions of desire and of fantasy. Both the birth and the hospitalisation will have different meanings for each family and each baby.

The mother of Pierre, caught in a trap of repetition, could not hear what the doctors were saying. "It's obvious," she told me tearfully, "my mother had a child that died at birth. It doesn't matter what they say, those doctors, Pierre won't be able to live. How could I possibly do better than my mother did?"

On the contrary, Julie's mother, when her daughter was not at all well, would reassure the nurses. "I was premature too. It's like that in my family, all the girls are small and born early. If Julie had been any different, I wouldn't have recognised her. I'd have been really surprised. She wouldn't have been my daughter if she hadn't been premature."

This is the kind of discourse that carries babies along, but they may also be trapped in it. In order for human subjects to find a place in a discourse, they have to be detached from it. It is during the sessions the parents have with the psychoanalyst that work can be done on the fantasy.

In the case of such tiny babies, how can we speak of transference? We can hardly imagine that they are repeating their childhood demand for love. It is also difficult to speak of an "intersubjective" relation, even though the babies I work with very soon recognise my voice and look at me when I walk up to the incubator.

I think it is reasonable to say that this type of transference is established in the same way as when we work with autistic children. Indeed, just as in sessions with autistic children, or with some psychotic children, analysts have to take the risk of showing their desire, an analytic desire, the desire that is at the heart of the transference, as Lacan taught us. While in the case of neurotic patients analysts have something to hear, when the patient is not neurotic, analysts have something to say. As Lacan said, the fact that autistic people don't speak doesn't mean there's nothing to say to them (Lacan, 1989, p. 19).

While in the usual analytic process, it is a question of progressing from the Imaginary and the Symbolic registers towards the register of the Real, when we work with autistic patients, the direction is reversed, and we try to lead the child from the Real towards the Imaginary and the Symbolic. Working with these tiny babies seems to me to be of the same order. In the transference, the analyst will lend a thought to the baby, a psychical existence, a history linked to the analyst's desire. On the basis of psychoanalytic theory, the analyst will give thoughts to the babies, thus enabling them to construct themselves as subjects. This is often the case when we work with children who are in great difficulties. It involves assuming children possess a knowledge that supports the theory. Alain Vanier put it thus: "A theory is a pathway in language. But gradually it ceases to surprise us, to amaze us, its effects are exhausted and it starts to feed the resistance. In treating autistic children, however, theory is strangely less prone to this wearing-out process, perhaps because the theory functions in an immediate way like a fiction, to help articulate structure" (Vanier, 1993, p. 33 [translated for this edition]). The essence of the link which is instated between the child and the analyst seems, here too, to be inscribed in this "supposition". When the mother is present, she is "drawn in" to this movement and the child is integrated into a signifying chain. But sometimes it takes a long time for the mother to be able to approach the incubator. It is during this "blank time", the period when time is suspended, and the resuscitation is "in waiting", that the team needs to be all the more present for the baby.

Working with the team

The work with the team means that the problems encountered on a daily basis can be revisited again and again. How can they bear the anxiety triggered by certain babies? Or the aggression of certain families? In these circumstances, a more personal questioning cannot be avoided.

This was certainly not the approach used by the doctors who were the first to request the collaboration of analysts. Their questioning was related more to scientific progress.

The more that medical technology was perfected, the more babies were saved; but the price was paid in long and difficult hospitalisations for all concerned: the families, the babies, the doctors; and so the medical services started to wonder if, while prolonged admissions saved lives, they did not also create psychotic children. Did they not play a role in the children's development, in the destiny of the drives? Did they not make those children, so accustomed to suffering, into masochists? Did they not make those babies, cut off from the usual structuring stimuli, into depressive or backward children? Might it not be better to abstain from these interventions; are we sure we are not doing harm when we intend to do good? Caught up in these difficult questions, modern medicine has called upon psychoanalysis in order to become more efficient, more knowledgeable, and to be able to repair the potential damage done by scientific progress. But is it really a question of repairing the damage? While psychoanalysis can bring new light to bear on these problems, it certainly cannot respond to the anxiety or soothe the unease aroused by these technical innovations, any more than it can help to perfect their methods. On the other hand, what does appear to us to fall within the domain of psychoanalysis is the process of questioning with which it confronts medicine, regarding the place offered to the human subject, and the place of doctors.

Many analysts are keen not to risk working in medical services. And indeed, the presence of an analyst in a medical service is seldom easy for the staff to accept initially. It is not a case of trying to impose a different knowledge on them, nor of taking over a patient from them, but simply of allowing speech to circulate differently in the team. It aims to allow the staff to question the way they work and explore their own transferences to their patients. It offers them groups in which they can speak of the difficulties they are encountering and can understand what they have been experiencing. Where very difficult decisions are involved, such as stopping resuscitation, or having to tell the parents that their child will be disabled, many doctors appreciate being able to come and speak about them.

When I presented this project to the team, I used the work of Ginette Raimbault to support my proposal; she was one of the pioneers in the field of analysts working with doctors, in the 1960s. I asked her to supervise me when I went to work in neonatology. She organised groups for doctors in medical services, of the type proposed by Michael Balint (1964) at the Tavistock Clinic in London in the 1930s. The participants would bring clinical cases, and would be encouraged to free-associate to them. It taught the participants to listen to others and to themselves, without it becoming psychotherapy (Moreau-Ricaud, 2000). The participants learned to recognise the particularity of the other. "The efficacy of this recognition, which is a major dimension of medical action, is based on the theoretical supposition that nothing can exist unless its existence is first recognised" (Raimbault, 1982, p. 29 [translated for this edition]). In my turn, I proposed to the team that we should have meetings based on this outline. The transference which emerges in relation to the analyst who runs the group enables the doctors to get a fix on what is happening in the transference for them, for their patients and for the families. Since time immemorial, doctors have been the ones who know. From being sorcerers or high priests, they have become "scientists", and their scientific knowledge reinforces the patients' belief in them. These days, we believe in "scientific experts", and we attribute all the knowledge to them. Therefore, demand and the effects of transference are reinforced. In his paper given at the Collège de Médecine, Lacan emphasised this: "At the extremity of this demand (the sick person's demand), the function of the relation to the subject-supposed-to-know reveals what we call the 'transference', to the extent that the myth of the subject-supposed-to-know finds more support than ever. This is what enables the existence of the phenomenon of transference, in so far as it refers to those aspects of the desire for knowledge that are most primal, most deeply rooted" (Lacan, 2003, p. 302). Progress in science makes patients believe that medicine is omniscient and omnipotent. In our service, for example, medicine has the power to decide whether or not to resuscitate a newborn baby. Medicine also has the power to decide when to withdraw life-support and to move on to palliative care, when it believes that continuing with life-support would be a matter of "unreasonable obstinacy". Medicine, as far as the parents are concerned, has the right to decide whether their baby lives or dies. This can mean that if a baby is not cured, it is because of pure ill-will on the part of doctors.

The doctors, for their part, run the risk of serving only medicine, or rather advances in medical technology, hiding behind protocols, medical imaging, and sophisticated machinery, to the point of leaving aside the truly clinical dimension of medicine, which does not shy away from encountering the patient at close quarters. It is true that the babies we work with are so tiny that it is easy to ignore them, to the point of not even recognising that they exist. Rather than being at their patients' bedside, doctors in neonatology run the risk of being stuck beside these life-giving machines. They are the ones that need to be kept in good working order, that need to be constantly examined. There is now a tendency to install an IT centre in neonatal resuscitation units, where rows of computers are built into a sort of control tower, pouring forth graphs and numbers, constantly updating on the condition of each patient, so that the doctor never needs to go near the incubator to find out how the babies are doing. But that still leaves the problem of the parents, who have to be dealt with face to face at some time or other, because they want to hear how their baby is progressing.

This avoidance of contact is one of the things an analyst addresses in a medical service. In our service, the doctors have agreed to take the risk of contact with the babies as well as with the parents. It is certainly not easy for them. The caregivers are caught up in the parents' transference, without knowing what is expected of them. Beyond reassuring the parents that their baby is not going to die, doctors do not know what role has been assigned to them. They do not know what has fed into the parents' demand, and they do not realise that the parents attribute a great deal more power to them than merely saying whether the baby will live or die. Caught up in this drama they are living through, they are also bringing to the doctor the question of their "being" parents, looking for the truth about a whole range of issues about their family, which have been raised by the distress their baby is in. It is not easy to understand the demand behind the symptom; how can one respond to such questioning? Surely it is easier to limit oneself to "scientific" answers, about the baby's body; answers which above all reassure the doctors. If doctors have to give bad news to the parents about their baby's prognosis, whether they tell the truth or only the partial truth, they will inevitably be confronted with anxiety about their own death, and the death of others.

Recent research has shown that the more desperate the situation of a baby is, the more doctors will address the parents using complicated, incomprehensible technical words. Caregivers will try their utmost to protect themselves by falling back on what they know about the body and its organs. Sometimes, telling the parents the whole truth, as is widely recommended to doctors nowadays, can be tantamount to an attempt to get rid of the transference and the subjective effects of giving the news. When I joined the service, one of the team doctors confided in me: "When I have to give a poor prognosis to the parents, when I have to tell them something awful, such as that their baby is about to die, or there's a risk of serious impairment, I speak very fast and in a very matter-of-fact way, as if I was saying: 'OK, now I've told you everything, I don't know any more than you do, so just leave me alone.'" A clear attempt, certainly, to block any demand, and to annul the transference.

Doctors would prefer language to serve merely to communicate scientific facts; but it carries a great deal more than that. The team is always astonished when a mother, who has been told over and over again what the situation is with her baby, seems unable to understand what is being said to her, and persists, for example, in believing that her baby is going to die, when the doctor has told her that he has pulled through. It is very hard for a practitioner in resuscitation to realise that the parents do not always ask for their baby to be saved, or that a mother might not necessarily demand that her baby be saved. So what is the best way to speak to parents? Doctors are inevitably influenced by their own prejudices and their own history. They are caught up in their own unconscious discourse, which determines their response to the patient. The whole team will be devastated when parents say they do not want their baby to live; and a mother who is considered a bad mother will be rejected by everyone. So it is the whole unit, the institution, that needs to be listened to as one listens to a patient. Confronted with danger, the team will produce a system of defence against anxiety which will also need to be decoded, and the staff in the service will become a sort of organism which will reject the mother it cannot bear to listen to. From that point on, the analyst will need to work with the institution; meetings will be set up so that the team can reorientate itself.

These kinds of meetings and groups for doctors lead us to think above and beyond caring just for the baby's physical development, above and beyond the protocols already in place regarding the well-being of the baby or the mother–baby bond. They make us reflect on the impact that each one of us has, each member of the resuscitation unit, on the development of the newborn baby who has been given into our care. In this set-up, the psychoanalyst is no longer a specialist called in to resolve a specific problem, but takes part in a real team project, in an orientation that sustains the desire of the caregivers to work differently. That is another reason why we can now speak of "co-resuscitation" in our unit.

Working with doctors

When I first joined the service, there was no mention of my working with the doctors. My mission at that time was rather to work with the "problem" parents to help them "adapt" to the situation of "prematurity". The problem parents were those who were not full of joy at the birth, those who were not happy that their baby had been resuscitated, or who did not seem grateful. I agreed to listen to the parents, but in a different way, and I also proposed another way of working with the doctors. Because of the effects of transference, and of the increasingly overwhelming malaise they were experiencing in their day-to-day practice, they agreed to this. I offered them working groups in which they could speak about themselves as well as their practice and the effects it had on them. They agreed to explore the impact of premature birth on babies and their families, and what was going on for them when they were faced with these families. We also decided to have large-group meetings for the whole team, in which we could think beyond developmental care, beyond the protocols we already had in place covering the babies' well-being and the mother–baby bond.

These protocols are full of good intentions—which is one reason to be suspicious of them—but they cannot possibly take account of what actually goes on during the period of a baby's hospitalisation, and they rather entail the risk of making it impossible to ask the question of what is going on for the team during this time. There was a sense of "protocol followed: mission accomplished". But "trying to put the babies into their mothers' arms", for example, is completely inadequate, unless work is done in parallel on the questions of separation and the fantasy, giving the mother time to protect herself, time to speak about violence and trauma and her ambivalence, which is often caught up in a family history in which repetition is at work as a sort of deferred action. No protocol could possibly take account of this particular aspect of the problem.

Of course, it is perfectly understandable that the technical achievements represented by such resuscitations are essential to a medical team, but in the course of these meetings it became clear just how many other things were important to them. When doctors speak about the moment when they are summoned to the ward to make the decision (in less than three minutes) whether or not to resuscitate, they can certainly give the medical reasons why they made the decision one way or the other. But even nowadays, it is impossible to know if a baby who presents all the signs favourable for resuscitation (gestational age, weight, vital signs measured on the Apgar scale) may not be severely impaired a few years later. Practitioners of resuscitation would like to have the most "objective" criteria possible. But because science can offer no guarantees, it is inevitable that it is the subjectivity of the doctor that takes command, and that immediately brings guilt and anxiety to the fore. Walter Benjamin spoke of the incredible value that society places on human life in our times. Far more than in earlier days, to live seems to have become an imperative.

One doctor said to me, "When I am faced with a baby, I say to myself, 'He's got to live'; it's as if I'm saying, 'Live, baby!' And I start all those resuscitation techniques I've learnt. I realise I'm just working like a machine at that moment, without really thinking. Beforehand, sure, I think. I certainly think when I'm called in by the maternity unit. I think about the consequences while I'm in the corridor, as I'm running to the labour ward. But once the baby's there in front of me, once the decision has been taken to resuscitate, that's it. I get the lines in, I start ventilating as precisely and as soon as possible." Once a baby has been admitted, even if it takes all night, the resuscitation will continue, and start again and again: giving another cardiac massage, increasing oxygen supply, adjusting dosages. Around the doctor, the team is on alert, fascinated, caught up in the jouissance of the spectacle of resuscitation. There is jouissance for the doctors, too, who are fascinated by the power they have at that moment over the body, fascinated by an illusion, which is often proved to be precisely that by the babies who are "lost" or who "escape" the doctors' ministrations. But during those nights, in the heat of the resuscitation, nothing counts more than the extreme tension of the moment. What doctor could fail to be terrified by that jouissance?[10]

During the hours of resuscitation, time ceases to exist, and will only start again when the digital read-outs on the machines are stabilised, when the infant starts to breathe. The fear of not achieving this, of having made a mistake, having made a false move or a wrong evaluation, of not having been vigilant enough, and of being responsible for a baby's death, is constantly present. But the fear of not achieving the resuscitation is certainly doubled by the fear of succeeding, because once the baby is stabilised and the doctors remove their masks, they start to wonder, "Will there be sequelae? Did I do the right thing in trying everything to save this baby?" But on the other hand, how could we possibly refuse to resuscitate a baby, since we know how to do it, and we can never really know how things will turn out. It is impossible to know in advance, but a few weeks or months later, the MRI scans will offer a sober evaluation of the sequelae and the likely state of the baby as he grows into childhood. At this stage, there are further complicated and painful decisions for the doctors to make, because now they have to decide whether to withdraw intensive care and implement pallia-tive care, and agree to accompany this baby they brought back to life, towards death.

However little we may listen to them, doctors do speak about these things. One of them said to me one day, "Working in a NICU, it's enough to drive you crazy. I wouldn't advise anyone to stay there too long!" Who in that position would not be tempted to believe in their own power? Every aspect of their daily work appears to support the view of them as omnipotent. The parents see them as gods who may be generous or cruel, according to what has happened on a particular day, who are able to decide whether a baby should live or die. Even the teams need their doctors to be all-powerful. If a doctor shows any signs of doubt, the team panics. In order to be able to do their work, the caregivers need to see the doctor as the one who knows, the one who will give them the order to carry out the intervention that will save the baby's life. As Joseph Gazengel describes so well in his book (Gazengel, 2002), everything is set up in the resuscitation unit so that doctors have no choice but to believe in their own power. And the greater the risk of death, the greater the need to believe in that power.

The word used, resuscitation [translator's note: in French it is *réani-mation*], means giving back the breath of life, bringing back from death to life. "Every time I resuscitate a baby," said one paediatrician, "I feel as if I'm snatching it back from the claws of the devil."

But a resuscitation service is also a place of transgression. The transgression can take various forms; for example, one may find one-self looking at babies who really should not be looked at. In spite of progress in the field of echocardiography, we still cannot really see or touch such tiny babies while they are still in their mother's womb. And yet in a way, neonatologists can do that. Recently I heard a doctor lean-ing over the incubator of a minuscule baby and saying, "But what are you doing here, baby? I shouldn't be looking at you yet, you should still be inside your mum's tummy." Peering at, or touching the contents of the mother's womb, must surely have an effect on doctors; battling to restore a baby who will satisfy a particular mother, restoring the phallus to the mother; you can hear a great deal of this in the doctors' words. And of course there are also links with and effects of the fantasy of each individual doctor.

But the ultimate transgression, the one they speak of most, is connected with the option that is sanctioned for them so that they do not risk "unreasonable obstinacy"—transgressing the commandment not to kill, and simply switching off the life-support machine. The more this transgression is possible, the more the doctors strive to resuscitate, surrounded by their teams who support them and assist them in ways that go far beyond mere medical intervention. Deciding to withdraw life-support, or not to resuscitate, seems to equate to a transgressive power that is absolutely terrifying. And when doctors are told they must not be too obstinate, they then try not to make the decision alone; they try to get the agreement of the parents (which has its own problems), they ask other teams for their opinion, take the decision to a consultative commission, rely on ethics committees and sometimes on the work they have done with a psychoanalyst.

Grégoire

Grégoire was admitted to the service as a result of acute foetal distress and prematurity. He had appeared to be dead when he was born in the thirty-first week of pregnancy, weighing 1.85 kg.

He had certainly suffered even before he was born. The first ECGs of his brain caused concern to the doctors, who feared there would be sequelae and probably a risk of impairment.

The mother had been warned about the baby's critical state at the time of his birth.

In our first session, she explained to me that she was sure this baby would die. The doctors had spoken of a risk of impairment, but had not at any time said that he would not survive. And yet she was absolutely certain he would die.

It is this certitude in the mother, this knowledge that differs from that of the doctors, that is played out again and again in the history of many children. This mother knew that losing Grégoire was the only possibility for her.

She had hoped to become pregnant by a man she had just met, and with whom she had fallen in love. But this man wanted nothing to do with her. She hoped to entice him into marriage by telling him that she was expecting a child. He was not convinced. Now not only did he continue to reject her but, she said, now she had a child with problems, it was definitely "off". He had no desire to see mother or baby.

She also told me how, a few months after she was born, her own mother left home and never came back. Her father left her in the care of a female cousin of his, and she grew up in her household, although she never felt accepted there. Her mother-substitute did not want to keep her. From the age of fifteen, she was put into care.

And now this man she loved didn't want her either.

In her fantasy scenario, her son could not live. It was impossible for this mother to think that a relation of love and desire could come into being for her, since she had never been loved herself. This narcissistic wound was going to be repeated with her son. This child set the seal on the loss that the mother could not rid herself of. She had never been the object for another, so she could only ever be deprived of her own object.

"Prescience, reconstruction," wrote Ginette Rimbault, "or is it not rather recognition by these mothers, in this otherness represented by the body of their baby, of a fundamental truth linked to desire and to the female sex which restores the status of delusion to the equivalence baby = penis? The baby, who for her represents something impossible to have, a difference which is radical, real, and cannot be symbolised, would as such be dedicated to death. The baby's body, entering the scene as a fragment of the Real, in the place where the signifier is lacking, would be caught up in the death drive" (Raimbault, 1982, p. 173).

The child as object can only be lost, he embodies the object *a* in the maternal fantasy, at the same time a delusion and a lost object.

The lack which Grégoire's mother had been unable to fill for her own mother was not now going to be filled for her by her son. In spite of the prognosis of the doctors, who did not think the little boy's life was in danger, his mother remained absolutely certain that he was going to die.

A few weeks later, the baby's condition became much worse. He was now suffering from hydrocephalus and needed an operation to insert a shunt. The baby survived the operation, and the team started to feel quite hopeful in the days following surgery. The mother, however, continued to predict that the boy would not survive.

"In any case," she said, "I'm not strong enough to look after him. If he survives, he'll have to go into an institution, when he comes out of hospital."

The nurses on the unit were beginning to worry about how withdrawn the baby was. He was less and less reactive to our attempts to care for him, and seemed to become more distant as the days went by. In the weeks that followed, his medical state worsened, too. The doctors who had saved his life once already were very active around his incubator, "he had to live", so great was the temptation to show the mother that we were not wrong. "He can't do that to us!" said an intern. It was terribly painful for the team to consider the possibility that Grégoire might die; they did not want to give up, even though the spectre of "unreasonable obstinacy" was appearing on the horizon. As if it was the team's purpose to prove the mother wrong. It was only once we had had a number of meetings, in which we were able to speak about the effects this much-feared death would have on us, that the situation calmed down, and the doctors were able to pursue their thinking about this baby in a new direction.

Some time later, I had stayed on late, and tried to take advantage of the calm of the evening to speak to Grégoire again. But already he seemed to be too far gone; he had become even worse in the last few days, and the team had begun to come round to the mother's prognosis. It seemed there was no doubt now that he would not survive.

He died that night. The following day, a woman doctor from our service told me: "I told Grégoire everything I could think of to tell him. I told him about his mother again, about his history, about how much the whole service wanted him to live. But did he understand me? What could my stupid well-meaning words do in the face of death? When I realised the kind of discourse I had fallen into, I started to speak to him differently. I told him that he seemed to me to be exhausted by having to battle for hours on end with suffering and loneliness, and that he had every right to leave us. I think he tried to look at me at that moment, and I felt terribly alone, too. I don't think I'd ever said anything like that to a baby before. A few hours later, he became very unwell, and this time I couldn't save him."

Developmental treatment and the "supposition of the subject"

While the baby's well-being, the reduction of painful or disturbing stimuli, and the involvement of the parents, are all clearly essential elements in the care plan, we were hoping to be able to set things up in our own way, based on our experience: our day-to-day experience and our theoretical references. Our objectives were refined over a long series of meetings: we wanted to reduce noise levels, to take account of the baby's pain levels, and to set up protocols for sedation. With the invaluable help of the nursery nurses, we also created opportunities for contact with the babies, both while they were being cared for and at other times, and to be more alert and attentive to the slightest signals the babies might make. We learnt within the team to take account of their calls, to communicate without losing sight of our main concerns, to listen to the babies without forgetting to listen out for the alarms of the machines going off. And we learnt to speak to them truthfully, not just out of habit or following a protocol, but to speak about them, about the story of how we met them, in an exchange that enabled us to take account of their response, too. Our aim was to be as present as possible for the babies, and only to cover up the incubators when the babies really needed rest and quiet, rather like when you close the curtains in a baby's bedroom. In our view, the total, full-time covering-up of the incubators, as prescribed by NIDCAP, would hinder us from being in contact with the babies when they were awake and seeking to communicate. By systematically covering up the incubators, we end up losing sight of the babies' presence. Furthermore, in certain cases the parents would not visit at all, or only very seldom, meaning that the babies were left alone in the dark, day and night, except when they were being treated. We felt that their development would not be encouraged if the only contact they had with human beings was when they were receiving treatment, which was often painful.

Our team was joined by a psychomotor therapist. Using her very specific approach, she helps the nurses to spot signs of discomfort or pain. She evaluates the babies' state of wakefulness, alters their position to increase the level of comfort, and gives sessions to enable them to relax, physically and psychically. She helps parents to make contact with their babies, to get to know them, to start to notice the signals they are making from the depths of their incubators, snuggled in the cocoons we have prepared for them. The psychomotor therapist intervenes as a third party between the babies and the team or the parents, so that there can be special moments when they can touch, carry, help with toileting, bathing, and have some skin contact. When the babies who were born prematurely leave the service, they are given regular appointments to monitor their psychomotor development. On these occasions, she will also see the parents again, and they will be able to tell her how they are managing at home since the baby became part of the household. The psychomotor therapist also takes part in team meetings and contributes to the individual care plans the team puts together for each family.

In order to be "mindful" of these babies, I referred to the hypothesis proposed by Alain Vanier in 1989 of "the supposition of the subject" (Vanier & Pelletier, 1989; Vanier, 1995; Vanier, 2002). In order for the little person to become a subject, it is necessary for an Other to suppose that the baby has a degree of subjectivity. It is the care and attention, and the words which accompany the supposition of a subject, that will give the baby the sense of existing. The "I" of Piera Aulagnier is also linked to the pleasure of the mother, the father, and the social group, in other words, the symbolic register. But above all it is a moment in a historical process, and it comes initially from the Other. The mother, as spokesperson, has an anticipatory function, and it is from her that comes "a shadow, an outline, the matrix for the I, which shows that before speaking, [the subject] is spoken of in outline" (Vanier, A., 2000 [translated for this edition]). According to Piera Aulagnier, this journey, this maternal anticipation, is constitutive of human subjects, and also constitutes their history and their very existence, which is fundamentally historical. So subjects emerge from the Other, the Other who supposes them, embraces them and represents them as separate entities. Experiments in "turn-talking" bear witness to this. The mother interprets her baby's babbling, speaking for the baby and saying "I" in his place. The emergence of a phonemic difference leads her to consider what the baby says as a statement. Alain Vanier emphasises that above all, the mother has assumed that she has received a sign from a subject, a sign Freud demonstrated in the *Project*, which can precede all other forms of address, the supposed sign of a supposed subject, before she even assumes that the subject has any knowledge. At birth, babies only exist in and through the mother; through the mother or any other person who addresses or names them, who tells them who they are, whether they are a boy or a girl, what they are feeling, what they are thinking. The subject is in the Other. If a mother does not speak to her baby at the time of birth, the baby cannot become her object. If the baby does not encounter the mother's desire, and has no idea what might satisfy that desire, he will not offer to become that object, because the mother will show no lack. The baby will have nothing to give her, and will not immediately occupy the place of the imaginary phallus which will open up the pathway to separation. It is this cut which will allow the creation of a space in the Other, a place which will summon the subject into being. In a neonatal service, machines respond in an omnipotent way to the vital needs of the babies. The baby is left with nothing but machines, the setting in motion of the circuit of the drives may become problematic. All babies identify with the world that surrounds them. For premature babies, the world of machines is purely real, and they cannot make any sense of it. There is a serious risk that a baby, during this period of resuscitation, will have no choice but to identify with the machine, this absolute Other, if no one comes to take up a position between the baby and the machine.

But by "taming" the machines, and continuing to suppose something of subjectivity in the babies who are hooked up to them, it becomes possible to enable the babies to become constituted as human subjects.

It is because an Other can experience a baby as interesting and actually existing that babies, in turn, can know that they exist. To put it another way, we can say that an intrinsic part of being a baby is being the object of jouissance for the Other. Without that, the baby does not exist. If all goes well, a third party will eventually intervene to prohibit this jouissance. At that point the child will be able to experience desire, be able to become a subject and eventually make sense of the world. But there will still be nostalgia for the object he has been. The child will use fantasy to try to recuperate the lost object. It is only by recuperating the object he has been for the Other that it will be possible to separate from it and regain a modicum of freedom. This is the trajectory of the later stages of analytic treatment.

But what happens when the parents are prevented from looking into the cradle, and the baby is nothing but the object of medical care? Can that baby make itself the object of jouissance, and if so, of what type of jouissance? This is the question that challenges us above all in a resuscitation service. Surely it is important that we do our best to enable a baby to be an object for someone?

Because a baby is too sick and unable to create something of a mother, it is also the case that this baby cannot allow the mother to "suppose the subject" in him. Sometimes this creates difficulties for the doctors, who are wary of making the babies into "objects", their own objects, in so far as it makes them doubt their own capacity to save their lives, or worse still, their capacity to want them to live when the risk of sequelae is too great. If all of a sudden the question of withdrawing life-support is put to the team, the relation of the caregivers to the child is immediately altered. The baby becomes a problem for the doctors, and they would rather forget that he exists. Speaking about the baby may trigger new conflicts in the team, or revive old ones; speaking about the baby is unsettling, and the team will stop speaking to the baby, limiting themselves to medical interventions only. It becomes impossible to "suppose a subject", impossible for the doctors to come between baby and machine, impossible to respond to what the baby expects. The work of the entire team is now focused on the idea of the "supposition of the subject".

This, then, is how we have been led to intervene "differently". We have been obliged to make major changes in our ways of working, thanks to our exploration of the question of the birth of the subject, our awareness of the different transferences that are formed within the team, and the constant putting into question of our clinical practice.

Based on the notion of the "supposition of the subject", we have worked on our ability to communicate with the babies. We have also looked at the question of the fantasy, the place the baby will come to occupy within the family, linked to the premature birth, and the impact of all these aspects on the service. For our team, the history of the babies and their families has to be integrated into the very process of resuscitation, and this means we are involved as a third party: our function is a symbolic one. In *Therapeutic Consultations in Child Psychiatry*, Winnicott relates how one of his little patients, Bob, pleased with the work they had done in the session, thanked him by saying, "It is a thing you put in a word" (Winnicott, 1971, p. 87).

Transforming things into words even during resuscitation itself—that sums up how our unit functions. We try to approach, and to "tame", the question of the Real.

It is far from being a question of the psychoanalyst working in isolation. The analytic work informs all that is done by the caregivers, it is not "extra" work; it is part of the care given by the service as a whole.

These elements seem to us to be an integral part of "developmental care". It means that we need to ask questions in addition to those that inform all the current programmes, including NIDCAP.

Notes

1. Before 1950, the label of "sickly" infant was systematically associated with prematurity. Referring to an "incomplete" child, they would write in the notes, "premature/sickly".

2. A pulmonary disease very common in premature babies which can cause severe respiratory complications.

3. Surfactant: a tensio-active film that coats the inside of the pulmonary alveoli and facilitates respiration. Because the lungs are not sufficiently mature, the newborn at less than thirty-five weeks does not yet produce surfactant and is at risk of developing respiratory distress, known as hyaline membrane disease. The lack of surfactant is treated by administering exogenous surfactant. Following the discovery of surfactant, the resuscitation of very small premature babies made considerable progress.

4. This is an individualised neonatal programme for evaluation and developmental care. Recent studies have been carried out to attempt to evaluate the NIDCAP programme. Some indicate very positive results with regard to the cognitive and psychomotor development of the babies concerned (Als et al., 1994) and others (Maguire et al., 2009a, 2009b) show rather poorer results, with no improvement in the infant either neurologically or in respiratory functioning. Whatever the case may be, all the studies evaluating NIDCAP are rated as being of "fair" quality by the scientific community, because they are limited to a very small number of children. So for the time being, the results remain unconvincing and the studies of little significance. In any case, the programme is difficult to implement and entails specific training and a large budget in order to learn to use the observation grids. Only two services in France are currently accredited by NIDCAP: Brest, and more recently, the Centre Hospitalier Universitaire of Montpellier.

5. Section of the paediatric psychiatry department of Seine-Saint-Denis. Head of service, Dr. Hervé Bentata.

6. Following Lacan, we distinguish the other, that is to say, the fellow-being, the imaginary partner, from the Other, in the symbolic register, the Other of language, a place that cannot be mastered and on the basis of which the subject is constituted; hence the formula "The unconscious is the discourse of the Other."

7. In *L'Étourdit*, Lacan uses the word *"ravage"* to describe the daughter's ambivalent relationship to the mother, from whom she expects "more substance than from her father". However, her hopes are necessarily disappointed since the mother is in no position to reveal the mystery of femininity.

8. An expression for which we are indebted to Moustafa Safouan.

9. We will explore this later.

10. This paragraph includes extracts from Vanier (2012).

CHAPTER TWO

Working with families

She gurgles ... and then in her voice most tender
Gazing on the child God illuminates with splendour
Seeking the sweetest name that she can share
With her joy, her budding angel, her nightmare:
"So you've woken up, you horror", says her mother.

—Victor Hugo

The mothers

Maternal ambivalence

From time immemorial, the vision men have of the mother–child relationship has been imbued with sentimentality. This myth, supported throughout the millennia by religion, literature, and poetry, is an evocation of perfect bliss. For the whole of humanity, it is the myth of paradise lost. There is such nostalgia for the "whole", the dream of melting into the Other to the point of being one with her, of completely satisfying her, and being completely satisfied by her; it is as if an unthinkable anguish were linked to the loss of this archaic relation of the baby to the mother. Mankind has never succeeded in mourning this loss, this quest for the absolute—it recurs in various forms, from the agonies of love to the dream of perfect harmony. It is what Jacques Lacan called "the obscure aspiration for death".

One wonders whether this idea of a perfect mother–child symbiosis, this image of plenitude and infinite radiance, is born retroactively or is a reflection of reality.

Some psychoanalytic theories have broadly supported this blissful conception. It often appears, as for example, in the expression "mother–infant dyad", that psychoanalysis has contributed to the myth of the father thought of as absent. Elsewhere, theories of "attunement" foregrounded the training of the mother: by adapting herself perfectly to her baby, she would be beyond reproach, and this perfect mutual happiness would allow the child to grow up in complete tranquillity.

It is quite strange to hear psychoanalysts talk about happiness, and even more peculiar when they speak of mutual happiness. Don't we realise that, once the baby is born, he is no longer in the mother's womb? That at the very moment of birth, something is lost, a lack appears in the register of the Real? That violence and trauma preside over every birth? Do we not realise that the mother is not alone with her baby? She is marked, whether the father is present or not, by her own woman's desire for him, just as this man's desire is inscribed in her. Have psychoanalysts forgotten how babies are made? Jacques Lacan reminded us: it is that very desire that mothers need to make plain, in order to escape the madness of being a mother who is totally satisfied by, and satisfying for, her child. Surely it is more a question of a *folie à deux* than of mutual happiness, if the child inexorably becomes the mother's object, as she is destroyed by the child just as much as she will destroy him. That pious image, so often reproduced, of the mother and child in a state of ecstasy and plenitude, should raise a few questions for us.

And yet these days the myth remains a resilient one, while it seems most others can be destroyed. The last bastion of the "repressed" in our society appears to be contained in this image. It is an image of purity if ever there was one, the virgin totally fulfilled by her child-king, while bodies and desires are set aside. No need for a father to make babies, a test-tube can do that. What matters nowadays is maternal love, which must at all costs be secured for the baby, who in turn will reciprocate it, being a perfect baby. Being the fruit of science, he cannot possibly fail, and will provide a perfectly fulfilling love relationship. And yet no one can be unaware that passionate love, animal love, carries within itself a promise of murder.[1] Entailing such a degree of fusion, it is closer to death than to life: it is a ravaging possessiveness. Through love, it becomes possible to kill and devour the other. Is it perhaps this memory that feeds the anguish some men experience when faced with a woman's desire? And is it not this memory that makes the Giaconda's smile so strange and so disturbing?

In *Leonardo da Vinci and a Memory of his Childhood*, Sigmund Freud evoked the mother–child relationship thus: "It is in the nature of a completely satisfying love-relation, which not only fulfils every mental wish but also every physical need; and if it represents one of the forms of attainable human happiness, that is in no little measure due to the possibility it offers of satisfying, without reproach, wishful impulses which have long been repressed and which must be called perverse" (Freud, 1910c, p. 116). He goes on to speak of perversion in relation to Leonardo and his mother. And in the smile of Mona Lisa, he would find all the ambivalence of a relation to the woman who was loved so much that she could prohibit him, as a child who had become an adult, from ever asking for such tenderness from the lips of other women. On the subject of Mona Lisa's smile, Freud says that it expressed the mother's ambivalence: "If Leonardo was successful in reproducing on Mona Lisa's face the double meaning which this smile contained, the promise of unbounded tenderness and at the same time sinister menace … then here too he had remained true to the content of his earliest memory. For his mother's tenderness was fateful for him; it determined his destiny and the privations that were in store for him" (ibid, p. 114).

In the conclusion to his account of the study days on child psychoses in October 1967, Lacan warned against this fascination with the mother–child relation: "Here, we should point out the irreducible prejudice that burdens the reference to the body as long as the myth that covers the child's relation to the mother has not been dispelled. An elision occurs that cannot be noted except through the *object a*, while it prevents us from grasping precisely this object in any exact way. Let's say that this elision can only be understood by opposing the idea that the child's body corresponds to the *object a* […]" (Lacan, 1984, p. 255 [translated for this edition]).

Lacan denounces the myth, Freud speaks of perversion and ambivalence. It seems that there is enormous resistance to the idea of ambivalence these days. I chose the title of my first book on psychoanalytic work with premature babies, *Le Sourire de la Gioconde* (*The Smile of the Mona Lisa*), in order to highlight this idea.

If, for example, we examine the work carried out in maternity units or in paediatric services for newborns, we find that everything is aimed at preserving the image of sweetness and maternal love, at all costs. One gynaecologist working on a labour ward told me, "These days, epidurals mean that labour is completely painless. From our point of view, this means progress, in that the mother–baby bond is reinforced. Mothers don't hate their babies any more, they don't get aggressive in the first few days any more, they can love their babies straight away." When I asked the doctor how we could explain why some mothers didn't become immediately "attuned" to their babies in spite of the epidural, he replied, "Oh well, those ones are abnormal mothers!" Those "abnormal" mothers, the ones who have a psychoanalyst called to their bedside, spoil the harmonious atmosphere of the maternity unit; they are ambivalent, and they do not get much support from the doctors.

Ambivalence is not flavour of the month, and yet how can we envisage motherhood without ambivalence, whether it comes from the mother or from the caregivers looking after her and her baby? Because the caregivers are supposed to love their patients just as much as the mothers are supposed to love their babies.

We only need to make a detour via the work of Melanie Klein to be unavoidably reminded that all relations are based on ambivalence. The good contains the bad, just as love contains hate; to preserve and to destroy, to give and to receive, are opposite sides of the same coin. Jacques Lacan reminds us: "Doesn't the extreme of love, true love, reside in the approach to being? And true love—analytic experience assuredly didn't make this discovery, borne witness to by the eternal modulation of themes on love—true love gives way to hatred" (Lacan, 1999, p. 146).

In Greek mythology, we find the theme of infanticide during orgiastic festivals. Mothers who are possessed by mania, half-goddesses, half-women, tear their children limb from limb, and hack them to pieces. They kill them, but they do not eat them; only the Titans have that privilege.

But this is not the case in the Euripides tragedy, where the Bacchantes are mothers who kill their babies and devour them. They then suckle wild beasts, and in their turn are devoured by them. Throughout this tragedy, the theme of animality is foregrounded, while the link between animality, motherhood, and devouring is found throughout the Ancient World.

There is an African myth—"The calabash and the ram"—that Denise Paulme (1976) explores at length, which takes up the idea of devouring. The calabash represents a mother-plant sprouted in the ashes of a woman who has killed and devoured all the children in the village. The gourd, which fattens too quickly on such fertiliser, becomes stifling and luxuriant. The mother who lives again in this terrifying plant catches and devours all the children in the village, especially those who try to escape. A ram is summoned; he uses his horns to break up the calabash, setting free all the children who are trapped inside. Everything can get back to normal, thanks to the ram and his horns, and order is restored. But it is nevertheless the same calabash that both devours and gives life.

Wherever there is love, there lurks the idea of devouring, the animal idea of devouring the baby: "That one's good enough to eat", for example. "I've just been eating him up with my eyes ever since he was born, I can't take my eyes of the cradle." Since the earliest times, however, because they are not ogresses, women have abstained from the pleasure of devouring their children. But it is not that they do not have the urge to do so. What they do not have, what they lack, is somewhere else, and it is precisely because of this lack that they do not do it. This animal position is prone to see-sawing, thanks to the fact of castration, in the register of the human and of what can be symbolised.

It would be just as extreme to think that maternal love could exist without violence, without hate, without ambivalence, as it would to deny the existence of the unconscious, that unconscious in which the forces of life and death reign and influence every aspect of our lives without our knowledge.

Fantasies of devouring are at work in mothers just as much as they are in babies. The more babies experience terror at the idea of their own desire to devour their mother, the more they will experience her as cruel, living in constant dread of fusion and death. The strong and violent physical contact between a newly delivered mother and her baby brings to the fore the most animal of fantasies. Later in life, children who draw monsters with terrifying teeth are still testifying to this archaic and terrifying link to the mother. "To speak of the sadistic oral stage," Lacan emphasises, "is, in fact, to remind ourselves that life is fundamentally nothing but a devouring assimilation. At the oral stage, the theme of devouring is situated in the margin of desire; it is the presence of the gaping jaws of life" (Lacan, 1991b, p. 242 [translated for this edition]).

Thanks to Freud, we know that newborn babies, beyond the demand for nourishment, beyond need, only want to satisfy their hunger. Babies want to devour their mother; they want all of her, and from this moment on a sexual meaning is given to the notion of cannibalism. "For the human being, feeding is linked to the good will of the Other […] and it is not only on bread and the good will of the other that the primitive subject feeds, but on the very body of the one who does the feeding" (ibid, p. 239).

Sometimes mothers speak about their fear of being destroyed, of the feeling of being "emptied out" by their babies. "He's exhausting me, I can't go on like this." Babies are experienced as vampires, with their never-ending demand which the mothers can never satisfy, and the babies' passionate and exclusive love makes them feel as if they are being devoured. This "gaping mouth of life", this violent libidinal force emanating from the child, becomes unbearable.

"My little brother is eating my Mummy up," said a little girl of three, watching the greedy baby suckling.

If a mother does not feel supported, if her history has made her narcissistically fragile, if by becoming a mother she can no longer be a woman, she is in a dangerous position. With or without an epidural during labour, she will resent the baby who is making her suffer so terribly.

In the early days, she will be the perfect mother, she will make every possible sacrifice: a masochistic position. It will be a perfect love, where everything is given to the other so that he does not lack anything. But that is where the trap slams shut. The Imaginary is master of the game, and symbolisation fails, because no possibility of loss is opened up for the mother. So it becomes either a case of a mythical mother, sacrificed to her child, or of a child who is sacrificed, devoured by the mother's love. How could it be otherwise in a "dual" relation, in which, as its name suggests in its etymological closeness to "duel", one of the pair will die on the duelling ground?

According to Winnicott, however, mothers need be neither mythical nor devouring, neither sacrificed nor sacrificing, but could be "good enough", by sublimating these quite normal aggressive impulses.

We were always taught that when a mother found herself unable to care for her baby, she had been "prevented" from being able to do so, rather than being guilty.

Winnicott often reminded us: a mother is naturally good. If she fails at being a mother, it means she is carrying within herself a much older wound that has never healed. Sometimes it stems from severe maternal deprivation in her own childhood. For her, there is not even any question of "animality", she seeks neither to devour nor to satisfy her child, and she does not want to be perfect. This baby is literally dropped; she can no longer carry him either physically or psychically.

Where animality is concerned, Seay's (Seay, Hansen, & Harlow, 1962) astonishing experiment shows that out of fifty-one female monkeys separated from their mothers at birth, only nine went on to have young when they were adults. Out of these nine mothers, five left their babies to die with the greatest indifference, and four showed aggressive behaviour that led to the death of the newborns.

Can the maternal instinct be caused to fail in animals, too? As the experiment showed, their behaviour can become aberrant; it would be wrong to place confidence in their instinct to nurture babies in spite of everything.

An emotionally damaged woman may become mortifying, and lose all her bearings, falling into madness at the moment of giving birth to a child. But can we speak of a maternal instinct in human beings? One word can suffice to ruin everything between a mother and her baby, a family curse which she bears without even knowing it: "You will be a bad mother, you will be a child killer."

From the very beginning of our work in the neonatology service, we became convinced that medical intervention is capable of undoing the power of words, of lifting a curse.

In a resuscitation service, the mothers who have just given birth to a sick or premature baby are confronted more than anything with the image of the bad mother, which is the image they have of themselves: a mother who has been unable to carry her baby, who has given the baby a life that is too fragile, and who maybe wants that baby to die.

While ambivalence is always present during pregnancy, a problem-free birth boosts the mother's narcissism by presenting her with a beautiful, healthy baby who reassures and gratifies her.

Whereas when a sudden and unexpected birth takes place in a state of panic and emergency, when the doctors are unable to reassure the mother, and the baby is really in danger, reality merges with fantasy, and trauma arises.

"It's quite true, I did want her to die," said one mother of a premature baby, who also blamed herself for having wanted to get rid of the child throughout her pregnancy.

Trauma is outside speech, there are no words for it because by definition it is impossible to think about. Guilt may become a way of "thinking about" it.

Women whose babies are taken away from them at birth try anything to find an explanation, a causality; they want to find a psychical link. There is a force that drives the human subject to seek the causality of an event. The event has to be given a signification, a status. It is an attempt to reconstruct historical reality. This working through is indispensable for new mothers. We can see how the consoling words of the family or the staff only serve to depress them further. Indeed, attempts are made to stop the mother from saying certain things, to speak of the possibility that she might wish for the death of her child. The team cannot accept anything a mother says about her sense of guilt, and will go to great lengths to make her listen to reason, with reassuring words and medical explanations. Yet sometimes she has a great need to speak of her guilt, and to believe in it for a while, so that she can succeed in going beyond the trauma of the birth.

Most of these mothers will feel bad when the baby is born, and the child will become persecutory. When the baby leaves hospital, the woman will have to live with a child who is only alive thanks to others, a child who has wounded her narcissistically, who has given her a taste of failure. She will be aggressive towards her baby, just as she will feel as if the baby is being aggressive towards her.

During the hospitalisation, the team will take up the position of being "bad" in her place, in order to spare the mother and the baby. In any case, the team is there to protect the mother from the baby, and the baby from the mother.

I can remember the relief of one mother, who had had a very difficult pregnancy, when one of the doctors on the team said, "You can rest now, I will look after your baby." She told me a few days later that she finally managed to sleep that night; she was no longer the only one responsible for the baby. "I knew," she said, "that he would make him stay alive, so I was reassured." Relieved by the immense effort the team was making to force her baby to live in spite of himself—or in spite of her—she could finally take a rest.

The service may also be in the position to authorise a mother to stop being "mythical", to release her from responsibility for the baby who, at this moment in her life, constitutes a danger to her.

It seemed to us that insisting on maintaining the mother–child bond at whatever cost was not always the best way to support the development of a bond between the parents and the baby.

The service, protected both by its entry vestibules and rituals, and through the confidence and authority of the doctors, operates to prevent the mother and baby from devouring one another.

On the one hand there is scientific knowledge, and on the other hand, the fantasmatic scenario in which the baby and its parents each have a designated role. Scientific knowledge makes a difference to the casting of the scene, and to how the baby's body is "directed" in it. The mother is now able to speak about a different history, and a different kind of knowledge. But it is a history that is impossible for the resuscitation team to hear or understand. This knowledge, the mother's prescience, marks the baby's body as the privileged locus of an inscription. It is the inscription of the signifiers of the Other, and it is there that we find what needs to be heard in the maternal discourse.

This inscription goes far beyond the "talking to the baby" that has become widespread, although that is certainly indispensable and to be encouraged; it needs to be used as the basis of an orientation that may allow the mother and the baby to find a different place, and even to be dealt a different hand of cards. These days, in most neonatal resuscitation services, the majority of the psychologists' efforts seem to be aimed at maintaining the mother–baby bond at all costs. Supporting the mother, allowing her to endure her primary maternal preoccupation in spite of the electronic screens and the interference of the powerful doctors. Catherine Druon (1996), one of the first psychoanalysts to work in neonatology—at the Hôpital Port-Royal—said that this position should be "grandmotherly", in order for things to work out well. Skin contact, the mother's benign listening, the incorporation of the baby into speech, as a human being in a world of humans, are all certainly indispensable. But over the years, they have come to appear to us to be quite insufficient.

What struck us in our work at Saint-Denis is something quite other than the position of grandmotherly authorisation and reassurance; it is rather a paternal position, that of a third party, the team, intervening to protect the mother and the baby by separating them.

In this period of cutting, the analyst will have to work with the question of loss, the symbolisation of the birth that, in its status as emergency, with its drama and the unbearable presence of death, has been impossible to speak about. In *Civilisation and its Discontents* (1930a), Sigmund Freud emphasised the fact that a part of this drive (instinct) can be placed in the service of Eros when it is turned towards the external world to destroy something animate, instead of destroying itself.

Premature motherhood

The mothers who are referred to us share a sense of injustice, and feel trapped. They feel that they are victims, and most often say they are overwhelmed by the ill-fortune of this birth. However, they are often also convinced that it could not have been otherwise, that there was no other possible outcome. They say that they feel that their chance of being a mother has been invalidated. At the moment of a premature birth, as we have seen, there is considerable disorientation. Women feel let down by their bodies, which they no longer understand. They start to question their relationship with their husband or partner, wonder whether they are capable of becoming a mother, and bring up the question of their own mother. At this point of irruption of the Real, it is often the woman's mother who is at the forefront of the fantasmatic scenario.

The baby who has just been born has nothing to do with the one she had imagined. And yet it is vital that she can make the passage from the imaginary baby to the one she has in reality. While this is true at every birth, it is more particularly the case when the baby is in mortal danger.

The dream baby, the one she had been expecting, as Danièle Brun has observed, is the one linked to her own mother. "The woman's life includes the representation of a baby that will be born, but also that of a child she will have to give up. It's the one that she, like every child, from the very earliest age—and of course she has absolutely no memory of this—wished for, imagined she could make, with her own mother, or receive from her" (Brun, 2011, p. 29 [translated for this edition]). This disappointment will only be greater, and the wound more painful, in the case of prematurity.

They find themselves violently thrown back into the archaic and anguishing world of their own early childhood, and they are already more vulnerable than other mothers because of the manipulations, the transformations of the body image, the alterations in self-perception and sense of identity that are inherent in all pregnancies. There are no words truly to mediate this world and its lost memories. If they are to survive and to imagine that their baby is capable of living, everything will depend on what they can retrieve from this time deeply buried within them, from their primary narcissism, from the very first connection with their own mother. Everything will depend on what there was at that time to make a separation between the woman and her own mother. Following the separation, what subsists is the parents' speech. What is "said" is what is inscribed for the child. It is on this basis that the signifiers are constituted.

How was the mother inscribed in language when she was a baby? In order for the signified to become signifying, the primary object, the object of primary satisfaction, has to be lost. It is not the loss of the object that causes anguish for the child, it is not that the mother is absent, but rather that she is too present. She cannot let go, she cannot look at anything other than her baby.

If the baby is a girl, the bodily contact between mother and baby takes on a different dimension. The baby will not be able to become a speaking being if she does not have a body that is separate from the other. The future subject can only begin to emerge if this fusional mother–daughter body-to-body is given up. And giving it up is not easy. The little girl can be captured in the illusion of being one and the same that this erotic complicity gives rise to (Lessana, 2000). It is a phenomenon we can liken to Russian dolls. We will see later on how this passion between mother and daughter can be orchestrated throughout several generations. The various actors in the play are from past generations; there are deaths, births, love stories, and their conscious or unconscious resonances, a whole family constellation that constructs a web of signifiers. Like a puppet manipulated by thousands of invisible strings, the mother will act, or rather be acted upon, at the moment she brings the child into the world. Thus we may say that all mothers are victims when their chances of giving life in their own turn are hindered.

It is on the basis of this separation from their own mothers, whether it happened too early, too late, or not at all, that the terrible experience of premature separation from the baby they have just brought into the world will be constructed.

At the moment of a premature birth, the mother's body will refuse this separation. This is confirmed by Françoise Loux, in the fascinating narrative of her own experience of having just given birth prematurely to little Valentin: "We are not separated yet. Why can't he go back inside me? We'd be back in another place, a wonderful place!" (Loux, 1991, p. 13 [translated for this edition]). In reality nothing is wonderful about this birth any more. So the mother prefers to dream that she is still one with her baby. How could he be separate from her, if she cannot touch him? Sometimes the monitors can be disconnected simply by allowing a caress. It is difficult to speak to him through the noise of the machines, through the closed covers of the incubators. Does a baby really exist if you cannot touch him, cannot breastfeed him, or soothe him? It is too much to expect a mother to "suppose" that this "mechanical" baby[2] has some "subjectivity".

The thought that a baby is not yet born, or that he is already dead, is fed from the same source. Such mourning-in-anticipation, which makes any emotional investment impossible, often take place *sotto voce*. It is only once the baby goes home that the complications arise, when the mother has to face the fact that the baby she had given up in order to avoid terrible suffering, is actually alive. Again, everything will depend on how she is supported by the team, how she is listened to, and how the team desires not only to make the baby live, but also to be alongside the parents, to be attentive to their distress which may not even be apparent. They will need to be vigilant about the impact of the interventions they make, and not just on the babies, because these interventions can have iatrogenic effects on the parents, too.

In every case, the narcissistic wound is huge. The mother, who has suffered a terrible blow, cannot accept the cut. In order to lose something, you have to have actually had it in the first place. The baby who is gradually weaned from the mother's breast, from her presence, from her caresses, will lead the mother at the same time to give up her own stake in this interdependence. Françoise Dolto speaks of "symbologenic" castrations which are carried out mutually (Dolto, 1984). Renunciation takes place on both sides, at the same time. The breast, the look, come to signify a lack. The child will differentiate himself from the mother and will become able to make an object of her. The object is created only in order to be lost.

Becoming a mother prematurely involves mourning something that has never existed. Mixed in with this mourning are the confused, archaic memories of subtle exchanges, emotions, and disturbances in her relation with her own mother. This latter is also something that weighs on the identity of all subjects: memories from the period before they could speak, of the time when they were only spoken of and to.

For a full-term mother, the birth of her baby can be a wonderful and unique moment of amazement and discovery. At this time, the baby will be phallicised, and will satisfy the mother and be satisfied by her. In order for the mother to introduce the baby into the symbolic order, in order for her to name him at the same time as she recognises the father, she will also have to experience the lack of the baby. This will only be possible for her if she has had the baby all to herself at the beginning.

When the mother of a premature baby comes out of hospital, she realises that something has been "confiscated" from her, and that when the baby is discharged from hospital, three or four months later, she will reclaim what she is "owed". Everything will be out of synch, it will be impossible to start again from zero. The rhythm will have been disrupted. Life will have gone on, the baby will have grown, she will have gone back to work. Neither of them will be available to the other in quite the same way as they would have been. The magic will have gone, and it will be very difficult to find a way back to this baby, who is no longer newborn, and yet is a new arrival in her own world.

It is through learning from these mothers, from their sufferings and those of their babies, that we have been able to orientate ourselves and set things up in our service.

As we have seen, there is no medical prescription for treating the distress of these parents who are troublesome to the doctors. Rather, what we do is to work alongside the team and all the parents in getting to know the premature babies. We offer a special kind of listening to babies who are thirsting for communication. The ones who are "extremely premature" are the most demanding of all human beings we have ever encountered in terms of needing some kind of access to meaning. The service does not position itself as an all-powerful agency that is capable of repairing babies while consoling the mothers, who feel lost; rather it is a space in which, throughout the hospitalisation, difficulties of motherhood or fatherhood can be spoken about, as well as the babies' hesitations between the desire to live or to die.

In each case a different way has to be created for the particular mother to find a way of investing emotionally in her baby, of taking him on. It is a question of inventing a space for play or a meeting between parents and babies, within the team, in the rhythm of everyday life, where it becomes possible to set the parents' imagination free.

During the period of hospitalisation, which is nowadays becoming longer and longer because of the low birth weights of the babies, the babies will be in a position to "construct themselves". At the same time, it is important that they can be offered the chance to construct their mothers.

Most mothers and babies succeed in building a relationship. There is no one way to achieve this; there are as many ways as there are mothers and babies. It is not possible to create a protocol; the team has to create anew in each case.

Not all babies discharged from a neonatology unit are at risk. We have already mentioned the extent to which we were convinced that for certain babies, the period of hospitalisation would have an effect of "prevention". The medical discourse can have the effect of erasing what had felt to the mother to be of the order of a curse. It is like "a new spell" that can undo the bad magic.

In the normal course of things, the period of wonderment, the time of the mother's jouissance when the baby is identified with the maternal phallus, does not last. It is transformed into phallic jouissance, mediated by the beneficent loss represented by castration. If this moment is prolonged unduly, if the mother is unable to "let go" of her little child, if she cannot find her bearings as a woman and her desire for a man, then the baby will not be able to give up being the one who satisfies her. He will be at the mercy of the Other. The phallus will remain an imaginary object, and the baby will be coupled with the mother. In these circumstances, phobias may erupt. As Jacques Lacan pointed out in the case of Little Hans, the child becomes identified with the mother's desire. For him, the ego ideal is, passively, to become the mother's ideal.

This imaginary captivation seems to be encouraged by the narcissistic wound provoked by premature labour and precocious separation.

Frances Tustin (2003) explains how when babies and mothers are separated too soon, the baby loses a part of his body; the baby's affects may be frozen if the mother fails to stick the pieces back together. So it is important that depression does not hinder the mother from fulfilling this role. But sometimes, as a reaction to this depression, the mother throws herself into an attempt at reparation that is far too intense. This leads to an overwhelming excess which triggers fear in the baby. And the role of phobia is precisely to protect from too much protection.

Deprived of her baby at the moment of birth, and terrified by the weeks she has just lived through, the mother expects a great deal of the baby; she is also afraid. If her history draws her back to her own mother, if there is no man beside her, or at least someone who can fill that place, then phobias will quickly appear. There may be impulsive phobias, fear of touching the baby, fear that he will die a sudden death; as we have seen, such phobias may well erupt during the period of hospitalisation. The violence of the bond is reinforced, and an imaginary couple is constituted, like the one formed by Hans and his mother, or Hans and the children he was going to have: "He will have the children [...] structured according to the model of the maternal phallus, which he will finally make the object of his own desire" (Lacan, 2014b, p. 293).

From mothers to daughters

The mothers who have the greatest difficulty in recovering from the traumatisation of premature birth are those who have a particular type of history with their own mothers: that is to say, those who, because they have not experienced the "ravage" that Lacan spoke of as being necessary between a mother and daughter, remain in a state of "ravishment". These are women who have experienced passion and ambivalence in the mother–daughter relationship, where feelings run so high that they are able to become mothers in their turn only with the greatest difficulty and pain. In such cases, guilt comes to the fore. The premature birth brings the drama of past conflicts back to life. Daughters will retain a fear of their own aggressivity from this past. Often, signifying words come to be inscribed in these histories of failure, the words of mothers and grandmothers that prohibit the realisation of the desire for a child. The birth thus becomes a threat to the mother; and the daughter feels that she is carrying a persecutory baby, that she is transgressing a terrible prohibition. The birth becomes the affair of two women between whom there is no distinction, as in the religious engravings in which Saint Anne, the Virgin Mary, and Christ are often depicted together.

The cult of Saint Anne is directly linked to sexuality, since it emerged at the same time as a critique of the idea of the Immaculate Conception. How could sexuality be completely eradicated from the scene?

From the years 1480–1485 onwards, all the religious representations of the Virgin and Child became trinities: no mother and child without a grandmother participating in the scene. In such scenes we no longer know whose mother Saint Anne actually is. A particular example of this can be seen in the beautiful wooden statue from the workshop of Hans Geiler, *Sainte Anne trinitaire*, which dates from 1515, where we see Saint Anne holding the Christ child in her right arm, and the Virgin, who is also portrayed as a child, in her left; one mother for two children (Guillot de Suduiraut, 1998, p. 98).

It is not a case of "holding the holding", of supporting the Virgin so that she can support her own child, but rather of taking the place of the mother for both of them.[3] "Holding the holding" is a notion developed by Claude Boukobza (2003) on the basis of D. W. Winnicott's work, which would involve supporting the mother, mothering her, so that she in her turn can mother her own baby. She illustrated this idea in numerous articles and in her clinical practice at the reception unit for mothers and babies at the Saint-Denis hospitals. But what we are talking about here is not supporting the mother, but taking her place, becoming one with her.

In the painting by Leonardo da Vinci in the Louvre, Freud noted specifically the second character blended in with the Virgin's body, as if these two women's bodies were indeed only one, forming a double mother. There again, it is not a question of giving support, but of fusion. Two mothers mingled for one baby, or one mother for two babies: in either case, it invariably means that the place of the baby's mother becomes impossible, has been stolen from her.

We can imagine the dramatic consequences if the baby, whose place between these two women has perhaps been assigned even before birth, comes to be born prematurely, in danger of death, and is taken away from the mother. In this configuration, the role of the neonatology service is essential, as long as it agrees to situate itself in the position of third party, if it takes on its role as "separator" and does not take itself for Saint Anne, confusing itself with the "absolute mother" for the baby.

In *Totem and Taboo*, Sigmund Freud reminds us that in human history, maternal divinities preceded the gods in the position of Father. The mother-goddess transmits the link between death and life. Throughout the whole of Freud's work, maternity and death are associated. For the man, the woman has three faces: that of the mother who gave him life, that of the mistress, and finally, that of the earth-mother who will take him back into her bosom (Freud, 1913f).

In a first phase, the mother will be "everything" for her baby, while at the same time he will fantasise that she will want to take "everything" from him. The castrating mother will be experienced as dangerous by her son. He will continue to defend himself from this fear and this love, sometimes for the rest of his life, failing in his encounters with other women.

"Before desire learns to recognize itself [...] through the symbol, it is seen solely in the other" (Lacan, 1991a, p. 170).

It is the residue of this particular desire that will remain terrifying. The daughter, as we have seen, is immediately caught up with her mother in the ambivalence of love–hate. It is her first love object, she will not let go of it easily. In an early phase, she wants to make a baby with her mother. In a second phase, when she turns towards her father, rivalry, hate, and aggression will take centre stage. But the transition from homosexuality to heterosexuality is not always straightforward. Sometimes it is difficult to give up the mother in order to turn towards the father or towards any other man later on.

Women who have just given birth sometimes mention long periods of sterility, miscarriages, and premature labour, which seem to re-enact the little girl's terror of her own body with its lack, and the rage she feels towards her mother. Doesn't becoming a mother entail the risk of being hated, too? How can you authorise yourself to be a mother if tender feelings towards this first love object were missing? If separation from the object was made impossible? How can you make a narcissistic investment in yourself as a mother; how indeed can you love this body that resembles the detested one so much, how can you love the fruit that issues from it? The mother's violence is equalled only by the narcissistic despair in which the daughter finds herself plunged. If her narcissism has been constructed in such a fragile manner, carrying a child in her turn will be very painful. It is these mothers whom we see collapsing when they give birth, voided of all substance, emptied out. As Lessana (2000) comments, what could be worse than having a mother? Unless perhaps giving birth to a girl?

Wounded, castrated, the girl discovers that her mother does not have a penis, and is furious with her for having made her in her own image. Her protests and aggressivity will be turned inwards into aggression towards herself, and self-harming; girls will attack their own femininity.

When Sigmund Freud spoke of feminine sexuality (1931b), he explained how the pre-oedipal link to the mother will come to organise the oedipal link to the father. Before the girl enters the Oedipus, in the way one sails into a port, she will pass through tempests, waves of protest and aggressivity, before she will be able to "devote" her love to a man. Sometimes, she will feel she is prohibited from having a child, the equivalent of a penis according to the Freudian equation, which would place her in a position of direct rivalry with her mother.

When she discovers her mother's castration, her aggressivity is transformed into anxiety. The lack that the girl had become aware of is then transformed into a lack of love, and via protests and furious rage, which may or may not be expressed, she will turn towards her father. In order for everything to fall into place, it will again be necessary that the primary relation to the mother has not failed. The source of the child's narcissism is in the tender and eroticised exchanges of this relation. In a first moment, the girl will seek for the lost object in herself (autoerotism), then in her father, and finally in each of her encounters with other men. As she grows up, she will look everywhere for something to fill the lack: coquetry, make-up, seduction. She will want to be perfect; she will be successful at school, and will try to please her mother by all possible means. She will try to be forgiven for her new-found taste for her father by seducing her mother, and seeking reassurance from her mother that she will still love her and always will.

If the first love relation was insufficient and if, at the end of the Oedipus, she finds she is faced once again with a rejecting mother, she will feel a failure. Her mother's words will plunge her into despair, make her feel ridiculous, and will prevent her from moving not only towards her father, but also towards any other man. She will feel confused and abandoned. If the girl is rejected by her mother, her body will freeze, and she will find that she is trapped yet again. She will either feel worthless, or will throw herself into a terrible rivalry with her mother, which will end in self-destruction; or—another solution she has in reserve—she will take refuge in a relationship that is too fusional, but thanks to it she will be able to fend off the mother's condemnation. As Françoise Dolto said, the only way to escape from a lion is to cling on to its back. By now the feminine path of identifications is closed off.

The all-powerful women have to remain together. The girl will protect herself by protecting her mother from castration. The baby will be made by parthenogenesis; there will be no need for a man, as the women are now capable of self-fertilisation. Parthenogenesis is a fantasy we sometimes come across: it is a fantasy of a feminine power capable of self-fertilisation and self-generation. We can always discern the trace of pre-oedipal fantasies as well as the question of omnipotence. We find love, hate, and envy, as Melanie Klein (1975) pointed out. The mother remains the only valid love-object, the one with whom the girl forms a unit, since, into the bargain, they are "the same". The ferocious energy of the drives is at work in the history of every birth.

Noëlle

Noëlle was born prematurely at twenty-nine-and-a-half weeks, weighing 1 kg; her mother had had a long and difficult journey to reach that point.

She had tried everything—from appointments with doctors to consultations with clairvoyants. When she was thirty-seven, she had been told she was infertile. She had been considering approaching the adoption services to apply to adopt a child, when she had found herself pregnant after a further attempt at IVF. She had already been in analysis for two years at this point, and tried to understand what was happening. Why had it taken so long for her to finally become a mother? Why did she keep encountering all these obstacles, all these difficulties? She had told her story, session after session.

She had spoken of her childhood, and of the violent bond that held her tightly to her mother. She had very little to say about her father, who was self-effacing and discreet, or indeed about the man with whom she had made the child. "This baby," she said, "I didn't necessarily want it with him. It could have been him or someone else, I really didn't care; I just wanted to be a mother."

During one session, the story of "Tom Thumb" came back to her. The woman in the story says, "I want a child, even if he's only as small as a thumb." Her wish was granted, and Tom came into the world. He was minuscule, cursed by his mother's wish, and literally fulfilling it. Mothers have always been fearful of having the last word on how their foetus should develop, terrified as they are of their own omnipotence.

This analysand said, "Noëlle's birth is magical, it's wonderful, like a real Christmas story." She had wanted a child at any price, and Noëlle was born. Now she was paying the price: the stay in the NICU, the fear that the baby was about to die, the risk that the baby would be disabled, the team's judgements about her capacity to be a mother. She felt guilty, constantly under observation by the nurses and doctors, who she felt were always ready to point accusing fingers at her for the slightest failing, the most banal comment. "They're spying on me, I know exactly what they're thinking, that I'm a bad mother. I sometimes think they agree with my mother, that it'd have been better if I hadn't had a baby." The curse had been pronounced when she was just a child herself; her mother had predicted that she would never have a baby because she was too "naughty", she broke her dolls and did not like children.

She was an only child, and her mother's anger towards her had been occasioned by the late miscarriage of a little brother. "It's your fault," said her mother. She was five years old, lively and wild, and often disobedient. One evening, she had run away from home because she was afraid, but she could no longer recall of what. She had run straight out through the countryside that surrounded her parents' farm. Two days later, she was found by the inhabitants of a neighbouring village, who took her back home. In the meantime, her mother had lost the baby she had been expecting. There were no further births in the family, and her mother was never the same towards her again.

In myths and fairy tales, it often happens that as a result of a curse, an innocent young woman is struck by infertility, or gives birth to a monster. Such witchcraft is usually a form of revenge. A mother, a wicked stepmother, a mother-in-law, or even a wicked fairy can spit out murderous words, often motivated by jealousy. The bewitched young woman is to blame. Her guilt, linked to repressed infantile desires and to sexuality, calls for punishment. It presages a terrible narcissistic blow for the mother-to-be. The baby will either be abnormal, or simply will not exist. The baby is threatened and at the same time is a threat to her. In classical antiquity, when there was a risk of the wrath of the gods descending upon mankind, the baby would presage infertility. It might be in the form of vegetal sterility: failure of crops, with its social consequences in the form of plague, famine, and death; or it could take the form of animal sterility: no more babies, no more descendants; the disappearance of the human race, the risk of annihilation. It constituted paying for a misdemeanour, for an irreparable crime.

An abnormal child was the sign of a transgression, as was a child of incest (Gelis, 1996). In fairy tales, the fault is often a relationship where there is a risk of incest. The young girl who has grown up to wisdom and beauty unleashes the fury of a mother who refuses to risk having to give up her own position. The Sleeping Beauty is plunged into a death-like sleep. Snow White is banished on the day the mirror announces to the stepmother that she is no longer the fairest in the land. Donkey Skin is sent off into the forest in disguise, so that she will no longer be seductive. Cinderella, without the help of her fairy godmother, would have been left with nothing but the cinders of her burnt-out life, prevented from existing by her wicked, tyrannical, and jealous stepmother.

It's the mothers who lead the dance. The girls need time to allow themselves to come back to life: they certainly can't do it prematurely. The latency period is absolutely necessary. Sleeping Beauty has to wait, half-dead, half-alive, until finally a prince comes and wakes her with a kiss. Snow White has to sleep, poisoned in her glass coffin, until Prince Charming arrives.

Freud speaks of the latency period in the *Three Essays* (1905d). It is a time for a pause, a suspension of development. It is the time necessary for the working through of the Oedipus complex, for the putting in place of the barriers against incest; it is what will allow the girl to escape a "catastrophic destiny". A young girl growing up becomes a threat to another women and there is a risk that she will take her place. She is "banished" to the forest or "put to sleep" in order to get away from her. The woman rejects the girl and demands that she be put to death; the girl is initially rescued by a man who does not carry out the sentence. This first man shows the woman that she cannot do what she wants to this child, that she does not have the right to do everything she wants. By disobeying the queen's orders, he responds to the girl's appeal, which is an appeal for protection from harm within the maternal field. This first man takes on the function of the symbolic father: putting some distance between the child and the mother, he sets her on the road towards life. Later there will be a second man, strong and bold, who will not hesitate to kill dragons in order to save her life. When she has become a woman, he will fall in love with her and make her his queen. All little girls dream of a Prince Charming. And all of them will have to make this long journey that will lead them from the loss of the first love object to the encounter with a man, and then other men, bringing into play the desire to seduce and the jouissance of a sexuated body, which is now the source of desire and not merely of punishment and hate.

Noëlle's mother was no longer a little girl, and yet she had not yet made this painful journey. She was still tightly bound to her mother; and although she said she hated her and wanted her to die, she could not live a single day without her. For all those years, it had been too soon for this woman to want to be a mother herself. Did she really want to become a mother? Or was it that she wanted to give her mother the baby she had, in fantasy, taken away from her all those years ago?

Given this configuration, Noëlle had done well not to be born any sooner. It took her mother a considerable amount of analytic work to establish a loving bond with her own mother, beyond mere hate. She needed to establish what it was that her child's prematurity was replaying in her own history, so that she could finally extricate herself from the curse that had imprisoned her. It is this hate that needs to be worked with in the treatment in order to find the love that lies at its root. Noëlle's mother was left with very painful memories of the three months of hospitalisation in the NICU. She felt guilty, useless, a danger to her baby. She did not dare to touch her: she was afraid she would do her harm, or even that she would go mad and try to kill her.

Terrified by impulsive phobias, she sometimes feared she would hurl herself at the machines and pull out the lines that were keeping Noëlle alive.

To destroy in cold blood; to hurt for the pleasure of hurting; to kill for the pleasure of killing. At times this child unleashed the most appalling horror in her. At those times she would run away from the service, walking straight ahead, pounding the streets for hours on end, unable to return. She would run away, she would run away from herself, just as she had run away from home when she was little, on that famous evening when her whole life had been thrown off balance.

Only the nurses knew how to look after Noëlle, she thought. And yet she was glad to realise, day by day, that they were doing so with gentleness and sensitivity. Gradually she found she was able to speak in the session about this "suspended" time when her baby had been taken away from her, as a beneficial time. "It was too early for me to take care of her properly."

Noëlle would not have survived without resuscitation, and the fairy tale would have turned into a nightmare. Without this time for the mother to overcome what had trapped her in her relation with her own mother, nothing could have come into being in her relation with her own child. The service came to "wake up" Noëlle. The team's desire for her to live functioned for the mother as an authorisation to take charge of her in her turn. Can we say that medicine intervened there to undo the curse?

She told me, "In the unit, they won't let my mother in, I don't know why, but I find it reassuring. Last night, I dreamt she stole her from me."

The fact that the grandmother was forbidden to visit gave authority to the mother. Thanks to the doctors, there was no risk that the grandmother would try to come and recuperate her "due". Everyone in the team knew who the baby's mother was, and they put it into words for her every day: "We were waiting for you to give her her bottle, she always cries when you go away." Words such as these gave her a growing sense that the baby really belonged to her.

Noëlle's mother, in common with all those who are impeded from becoming mothers, was the victim of a history that weighed too heavily, so that becoming a mother in her own turn, identifying with this woman who was both loved and detested, could not happen without considerable problems.

She said that up to that point she had never been able to love anyone. She had left Noëlle's father two months after the baby was born. She met another man when Noëlle was three years old.

As is the case in any problematic of hysteria, she was expecting love to provide the miracle cure. She was bruised, she felt she was made only to be abandoned, betrayed, neglected. There were moments when she felt beautiful, seductive, likeable. She could feel powerful, capable of attracting a man or of fascinating women. At other times, everything would collapse, and once again she would be lost, alone, sterile, and humiliated. What she called her "terrible lucidity" would then make her completely insensitive to those around her. She would turn in on her desolation, absent from others and from herself, in a state of complete numbness.

The demand for absolute love that she addressed to her mother meant she could not possibly be open to meeting other men. None of them could be as phallic as this mother, none of them could stand up to her. If one of them did stand up to her, it was a provocation to her to put them down, to castrate them, to dominate them. "But where are all the real men?" was her endless refrain.

She was not really able to create any bond with her daughter, whom she experienced as a tyrant and a rival. But this new encounter with a man she thought to be different from the others, gave her hope.

She was certainly afraid. She was afraid of ridiculing him, afraid of being destructive all over again, afraid of falling back into the wretched state she was so familiar with.

It was the same "all or nothing" situation she had described during her pregnancy, during the month before the baby was born. Should she keep this baby or reject it? Love it or hate it? Be brilliant or hopeless? It took a long piece of analytic work for her to be able to find her bearings again, delineating what it was in the passionate link with her mother and in the failed encounter with her father that had left its mark on her life, and made her into this premature mother. She was able to loosen the grip of the vice that imprisoned her in this position of victim, where she felt both persecuted and persecuting, in a world that left her feeling solitary and frozen. She achieved this by rediscovering in herself both the fear and the love with which she was confronted, and by giving up the jouissance of unhappiness, which she gradually tried to reconstruct, session by session, in a story which she started again and again from the beginning, like a fairy tale that alters each time it is retold.

Traumatic births

"The day he was born," one mother told me, "I had no idea what was happening. It all happened too fast. Time stood still at that point. I only remember a few things—flashes, images all jumbled up, sensations, the stifling August heat in the waiting room, the doctor's furrowed brow, words I couldn't make any sense of. 'Emergency, danger, danger to you, danger to the baby, a caesarean straight away.' I didn't understand what was happening to me, or even whether they were actually talking about me. Where was my mother? I wanted them to call her, I wanted her to come and take me away from it all. I just wanted to get away, I don't think I was capable of thinking of anything else. It's for the good of the baby, they said. But which baby were they talking about?"

While we know that giving birth can always be traumatic,[4] premature birth takes place in conditions of such violence that the effects on the mother are particularly pronounced. Giving birth to a baby who may weigh less than 500 grams, in the fifth month of pregnancy, without being prepared, is literally horrifying. It is impossible to know if the baby will live or die. Initially, the doctors simply cannot say. For these mothers, the brutality of the delivery, which is usually completely unexpected, represents a violent intrusion into their pregnancy, and time seems to stand still at the moment the baby is born. In the days following the birth, the mothers may feel stupefied and flabbergasted. The violence of the delivery is made even worse by another form of violence—the emergency hospitalisation, involving a very precocious separation which in the best case will last three to four months, and much longer if there are complications. In the days that follow, the mothers have to endure yet another form of violence—and this is by no means milder than the others—when they have to face the grim prognosis which today's doctors consider it their duty to give, because they are obliged to be "transparent": they tell the "service users" all the possible disabilities their tiny baby is at risk of. But for each mother the consequences are different, and the impact of this real life event can only be interpreted and understood in the light of the individual mother's fantasy. The trauma of the delivery inscribes itself in a particular fantasmatic history, even if it has just disrupted this history, and at the same time it takes up a certain place and a particular meaning. The signifying value will never be the same for one subject as for another. As we know, the same accident never has the same impact on two individuals. For Freud, there are only two types of trauma: the trauma of birth, and the trauma of the discovery of sexual difference, which is subject to primary repression. The lived trauma of the delivery will reactivate the primary structural trauma retroactively; and this lived trauma, as we understand it today in our societies, will depend on the way the trauma (the trauma that psychoanalysis speaks of) is handled.

For some mothers, there will be anguish/anxiety (*Angst*). In most of these cases, the mother will have been prepared for a possible premature delivery. For example, there are those who have been hospitalised for some time, because of the danger of premature delivery. In such cases, the doctors and the family members, who are all expecting that the baby will be born too early, will have spoken with her about it. Then there are others whose personal history makes it easier for them to bear the shock. For other mothers who are unprepared and more fragile, the delivery will be experienced in reality as such a violent scene that the only affect will be horror (*Schreck*). This encounter with the Real will be impossible for them to symbolise. Because the level of excitation will be so high, they will find themselves in a situation of absolute distress and will lose the capacity to think. In the face of this brutal separation, this subjection to the desire of an omnipotent Other, they will be immersed in a state of panic that they cannot process.

Joséphine

This was the case for the woman who did not know which baby the doctors were talking about. She spoke to me at length about her history. She had been a baby with no problems, she said. At the age of three months she had been adopted by an attentive, loving family, and her childhood, according to her, had been unclouded. They had even told her that she had come out of the tummy of a very nice lady who had wanted to give her parents a present, and so had given her to them. When she was three years old, her mother gave birth to a mixed-race boy. Since her mother and father had white skin, just as she did, she recalled wondering very soon how it was that her little brother was this lovely caramel colour, which her parents seemed to like so much. Whoever could he be? Where had he come from? Why had he come out of her mother's tummy, when she knew she had come out of another lady's tummy? She remembered that she had decided that babies must come out of the mother's tummies either caramel coloured or white, according to the day of the week, and did not ask any further questions. A childhood without problems, she had said.

Sexuality, sexual difference, different colours: as a very small child, she was brutally plunged into a sea of questions to which she could find no answers. Later, she was a good student; she studied biology, and became especially interested in genetics. She married a man who was a friend of hers, and whom her parents had recommended she should marry. During the year following the marriage, she discovered she was pregnant, and everything was for the best in the best of all possible worlds—until the day of the appointment for a check-up, when the doctors decided that because of hypertension and risk of eclampsia, they would perform a caesarean. "He'll be better off in an incubator than in your womb," they had said. These words, which were harmless to them, threw her into a state of panic and confusion, which she still cannot explain. Since the birth, she had not wanted to come in to the unit, and was afraid to see her baby son, or to touch him. She just wanted to run away and leave him in the good hands of the doctors. "I don't feel like a mother at all," she said. "Giving birth doesn't mean you're a mother. Anyway," she added, "it's a boy. I wanted a girl. I think it would be easier to love a girl." It took this woman a long time to be able to get close to her little boy. During this time, she spoke a great deal about her birth mother, her biological mother, and her brother. The presence of her father, who was both self-effacing and benevolent, puzzled her.

There were many sessions during which she would go over her memories of childhood, the enigmas of sexuality, and the working-out of her own infantile sexual theories. As the weeks passed by, a displacement took place of the real scene on to her psychic life, and allowed her to make sense differently of what had happened, introducing something of her own subjectivity into this traumatic life event. "I'm just starting to realise," she told me one day, "that all this actually happened to me."

Even if the effects of the delivery are less dramatic for some mothers, all of them agree that the birth is a shock. The baby is torn away from the mother by the emergency paediatric admission. There is no question of placing the baby to rest on her belly, no time for words, and sometimes it is impossible for the parents to know whether their baby, who looked dead at birth, is actually alive or not. Only the doctors can say anything about it, but they are too busy intubating, ventilating, transferring the baby to the NICU so that he can be connected up to the machines, catheterised and perfused.

Most mothers speak of wanted pregnancies. The baby was hoped for, and they often have happy memories of the early stages of pregnancy, and like to speak about them. It is not the status of being pregnant that is problematic for them, but that of being a mother. Recently one of them put a question to me which I thought was very pertinent: "I saw a TV programme about women who are in denial about being pregnant. I can't understand how something like that can be possible. I knew very well that I was pregnant. It was only when my baby was born that I couldn't understand that I was her mother. It felt really strange when I arrived in the service and they said to me: 'Are you Lise's mum?' I wondered who on earth they were talking to."

For the mothers, beyond the trauma of the delivery, motherhood itself can become traumatic. Once a baby is admitted, the incubator becomes a sort of artificial uterus, which is designed to replace the mother's womb for as long as is necessary. The mother, now separated from her infant, feels excluded, useless, not daring to intervene between the doctors and the baby. But just as Winnicott said, "A baby doesn't exist", so we can say that without her baby, a mother does not exist either; she is prevented from constituting herself as a mother. Being prevented in this way, and the mothers feeling they are very much to blame for it, only compounds the trauma of the delivery. How can this thin little baby, in such danger, in such pain, restrained in the bottom of the incubator, be in any way in a position to make "something of a mother"? In this situation, it is difficult for the mothers to allow themselves to suffer from the sickness that Winnicott called "primary maternal preoccupation". It is difficult for them to imagine their babies, difficult sometimes even to give them a name. These women were not yet ready to separate from their babies, and the delivery alone seems not to have been sufficient to detach the babies from them. When they arrive in our service, everything happens as if their babies had not yet been born, and many of the mothers, terribly upset by the birth, will say to us, "I don't feel as if I've given birth. It's as if I can still feel him moving inside me."

This double separation cancels itself out, as if the delivery has not actually taken place. The mothers are prevented from feeling like mothers, not because they are separated from their babies, but precisely because they have not separated from them, because the real separation has prevented the symbolic separation. The fact that the babies need to be resuscitated throws these women into an overwhelming state of guilt and ambivalence. The narcissistic blow is so massive that they immediately lose all their bearings. "I'm no good for him," some of these mothers tell me. "I've given him death; it's the doctors who've given him life. I wasn't even capable of keeping him inside me long enough for him to be out of danger."

Each premature birth puts the mother's narcissism to the test. For these traumatised women, the possibility of libidinal investment in their baby is in a state of suspense. The necessary illusion comes up against the violence of the reality and there is a risk that the baby will be reduced to pure Real, as long as no symbolisation can occur to allow him to be phallicised.

So how can a place be found for the baby alongside the mother? Unless we bring this question into the work, it is pointless to try to encourage mother and baby to bond. Doctors are impatient ... but still, maternal love does not always emerge spontaneously. Analysts know about violence and hate, they are used to hearing about the mother's desire for death and the strength of the death drive at work in the baby.

One young woman who had just given birth had enormous difficulties coming into the service to take care of her baby. The team in charge, as usual, found it very difficult to bear a mother who did not show any interest in her baby. It was only after a considerable number of sessions that she remembered the following story. When she was seven years old, she pushed her brother's pram down the stairs outside their house. The baby fell out and rolled on to the lawn. He was not hurt by the fall. But the mother, who had witnessed the scene from a distance, had rushed over, terrified. She had started to scream at her eldest daughter, "You'll be a child-killer one day!" So of course, it was not possible for this young mother to come into the unit, not because she was a bad mother, as the team thought, but because on the contrary she was a good mother who wanted to protect her child from this curse. "Forcing" her into motherhood before she had had a chance to work through her history would have had catastrophic effects on her.

Most often it is violence that presides over the birth of a premature baby. Following closely on the violence of the delivery is the violence of words: "We don't know if he is going to live, there may well be complications, we will only be able to tell in a month's time."

Whether it is an emergency medical decision to save the life of the mother and of the baby, or whether it is a delivery that begins suddenly and brutally, without any control, all plans are thrown into disarray, all the things the parents had dreamed of to prepare for the calm and serene day which would welcome their child into the world, are blown apart. And then this child, born in a state of panic and unpreparedness, is snatched away from them by the doctors.

And then there is the baby, tiny and fragile, curled up at the bottom of the incubator. But more often than not, the mother is not there. Having become a mother prematurely, she cannot allow herself to be there, experiencing this birth as a trauma without a name. This impossibility to name is found again in the inability to give the child a name, so that the baby will sometimes stay in the unit for several days with just a number written on the incubator. This brutal interruption of her pregnancy will leave the mother with a feeling of unreality, of "not being there".

The "still face"

The reactions of a newborn baby in the presence of his mother have been studied, filmed and measured. The "still face" experiment is well known today; many researchers have studied it (Brazelton, Stern, Tronick, and others).[5]

The scene unfolds like this: the babies are aged between three and six months. At first, the mother is asked to play with her child, talk to him, smile at him, engage with him, and react to his attempts to get her to engage with him. It has been established that by three months, a real exchange is possible between the baby and his mother. When she has played with him for a while, she then has to turn her back on him, and then move back towards the child, brutally putting on a fixed, impassive face, a "still face". The baby seems not to understand what is happening, and is visibly perplexed. He furrows his brow, expects a response and then tries to elicit one, trying to re-establish communication. But since nothing happens on the mother's side, he tries smiling at her, gurgling, wriggling, smiling even more, holding out his arms to her, doing everything he knows how to do at the time of the experiment, in order to see his mother's face show interest in him again. He visibly wants to get her to react. But there is no reaction. So he gets angry, starts to yell, to flail around, crying louder and louder, still without getting the slightest reaction. And then, in despair, realising that nothing is working, that she appears not even to see him any more, and that she is no longer speaking to him, he gives up, abandons the whole thing, stops looking at her, and slumps down, his face showing the most profound sadness. He is defeated, withdraws into himself completely, and at the end of the experiment, unable to attract his mother's attention any more, he completely "switches off" from his surroundings. It is notable that the mothers say they have great difficulty once they are asked to re-engage with their child, and that there is a mirroring of the baby's distress that has been caused by the experiment. "I felt as if I were deserting my baby. I felt torn away from her, and I felt as if I were losing a part of myself. I felt sad, angry, desperate in turns. I never want to do it again" (Brazelton & Cramer, 1991, p. 109). The mother takes time to recover and to be able to speak to her baby again. It takes her time to send his own image back to him—the specular effect that is essential prior to the mirror stage. This mutual adaptation is absolutely necessary, otherwise the baby collapses. He seeks the mother's desire, and she seeks his. She acts as a mirror to prove to him that he exists; without that, the baby has no "being". He is plunged into despair and distress. He falls "infinitely", as Winnicott puts it, and takes time to allow the relationship to be re-established. When the experiment is stopped, and the mother is asked to take care of her baby again, he takes a very long time to accept renewing contact with her. Brazelton, and later Stern, seem to be the only ones to have noticed that it is a real problem for the baby, and that after the experiment, the mothers often complain of difficulties in their contact with the baby in the days that follow.

These studies have certainly thrown light on the importance of the mother's psychological availability in the mother–child relationship. But do we really need scientific studies to prove it? It is certainly true that a mother who is preoccupied with something else, anxious or depressed, has difficulty in being present for her child. She may well take care of him, do all the necessary things, change him, feed him, but she will be prevented from showing him the pleasure she gains from taking care of him.

I remember an experiment similar to the "still face" that made Françoise Dolto furious: "Children are not laboratory rats!" she said to me. "It's playing Sorcerer's Apprentice. How can they possibly know what the long-term effects will be on the relationship between the mother and her baby, of this sort of amusing game that seems to give scientists so much pleasure? Taking risks to demonstrate such obvious things is absolutely out of order!" She was certainly not wrong about this, but everything goes on these days as if we can only believe in the effects of the mother's psychical state on the baby if they are "scientifically" proven to us. So long as the "experts" have not given "evidence", anything that is of the order of good sense and everyday experience is given zero value. My own view is that these experiments create another problem, in that they serve to make the mothers feel even more guilty. Once it has been demonstrated scientifically, it is easy to assume that everything is their fault. As if a woman was responsible for her own incapacity to be present for her baby!

I have encountered innumerable "still-face" mothers next to incubators. And how could it be otherwise? Their baby has been torn away from them; there is no possibility of dreaming or imagining. They are petrified, overwhelmed by the risk of mortality and by their own guilt. Is this baby really theirs? Has he really come out of their womb? When they first come to the unit to see the baby, they are usually distant, absent. The effects of "still face" are often unavoidable in these cases.

The final months of pregnancy, when the belly is well-rounded, when the baby can be seen, and the mother can feel the baby moving, and get to know him, is an extremely important time in the construction of the child, but also in the construction of the mother.

Mothers who are victims

One woman was just on the point of beginning to feel her baby moving inside her when she was delivered prematurely. She had just begun to be recognised as a pregnant woman by the people around her, as a "mum-to-be".

This crucial period of acclimatisation allows the baby to "become incarnate" not only literally, in the mother's womb, but also in her fantasy.

Preparing the layette, beyond merely assembling clothes, creates the image of the baby's body, its arms and legs, in the mother's imagination. Buying the cot, arranging the baby's nursery, allows her to begin to conceive of a representation of her child.

These final months allow her time for imagination. This one kicks her—he's going to be a footballer. Another calms down when they are listening to music or reading poems—she'll be tranquil and contemplative, maybe even romantic, according to the type of music she seems to like. At the same time as the mother is learning to dream of her child, society starts to recognise her as a mother. She acquires a special status; often she will feel stronger and more important. As Françoise Dolto points out in *La Sexualité féminine*: "Because fertility is experienced as being conditioned by the phallus, the mother about to give birth becomes, for herself and for others, the image of the indigenous phallus, not only while she is pregnant but also when the baby is suckling, and before the baby reaches the stage of expressive mobility of his body in relation to the world around him" (Dolto, 1996, p. 133 [translated for this edition]).

This image of the mother destroyed by premature delivery seems to make the necessary phallicisation of the child impossible. The baby is disappointing, in so far as the mother feels disappointed in herself for not having been able to carry the child to term, and give birth to a beautiful, healthy baby. Remember the mother who said to me: "It's you in the service who gave him life, all I could give him was death, so you'd better keep him." While the mourning for the imaginary child always takes place at the moment of birth, in the case of premature babies, this mourning seems to be made even more difficult, if not impossible.

How can a woman feel that she is the mother of a baby who does not make any sort of sign to her, who does not suck at her breast, who does not look at her, who in no way reassures her, and therefore cannot "make something of a mother of her"? The mother thus finds she is still carrying the imaginary child, in an attempt to fight against the disappointment and the inevitable guilt. All at once—no baby blues, and it is the Real, in all its horror, that calls the shots.

The premature delivery foregrounds the mother's sense of being a danger to her baby. While it is true that by giving birth to a baby, you are also giving death, a normal delivery will keep this representation at a distance, and the more so if the baby is strong and vigorous. Where prematurity is concerned, life and death are too closely mingled, and telescope into one another. The mother, seized by the Real, is unable to accept reassurance. Premature babies cannot be of any help to their mothers, partly because of their own weakness, but also sometimes because of the way things are handled by the resuscitation team. The babies leave their mothers alone to face their own anguish; they are not able to encounter them in an act of reparation.

D. W. Winnicott insists on the extent to which primary maternal preoccupation seems to him to be a sickness. Thanks to this "sickness", this transient madness, the mother will want to be the whole world to her child. He compares this necessary symptom "with a withdrawn state, or a dissociated state, or a fugue, or even with a disturbance at a deeper level such as a schizoid episode […] a woman must be healthy in order both to develop this state and to recover from it as the infant releases her" (Winnicott, 1975, p. 302).

How can a woman be in good health when her child, who is in danger, has been taken away from her at birth?

As we have seen, the final stages of pregnancy inevitably evoke the relation of the mother-to-be with her own mother, as well as her entire oedipal problematic, however well or badly she may have come through it. Where repetition dominates, mothers may lose their footing to the point of suffering episodes of delirium or states of severe depression.

Agnès: the trauma of birth

Born at thirty-four weeks, Agnès had spent two months in the NICU of a hospital in Paris, because of her prematurity.

When she was referred to me, she was twenty-three years old and had just given birth to a gorgeous little girl who weighed 3.25 kilos.

It was while she was in the maternity unit that this young woman suffered an extremely serious *post partum* psychiatric episode, during which there were times when she lost her identity completely. She had run away from the hospital three days after the delivery, in an acute confusional state, asking passers-by if they knew where she was going. Was it a dissociative fugue state? Or a transient psychotic disorder? Or a *post partum* psychosis? The hospital's psychiatric department suggested several diagnoses, and referred her to me after they had prescribed some medication.

"I am seriously ill," she kept repeating, and nothing made her cry more than her family's well-meaning attempts at consoling her.

Agnès had always been in excellent health. She had been easy to bring up, and had never caused any problems—until now.

As a baby, she had been adopted by a family when she was discharged from the premature baby service. She knew almost nothing of her birth mother or her history. The social worker at the hospital had only given the adoptive parents a few pieces of information from the file.

The parents regularly went to see a psychologist in the service. They scrupulously followed all the advice they were given, and hid nothing that they had been told from their daughter.

When she was very young, she already knew that her birth mother had chosen her name, and that she had come to visit her regularly during the first eight days after she was delivered. But before she had been discharged from the maternity unit, the mother had asked to sign papers giving her up for adoption, and then she had disappeared, leaving social services with a fake identity and a false address. Nothing more was known about her, except that the staff at the hospital thought she was very unwell, but no detail were given as to what her illness might have been.

The adoptive parents, following the advice of the psychologist, had told her everything they knew, and even things they did not know. They had to "make the relationship positive" at any price. They had to tell her that the mother's abandoning her was an act of love, that her adoptive parents were very grateful to her and thought she was a good mother. This is what they said, but it was not what they thought. It was not so much the advice they were given that was at the root of this derailment, but rather the misrecognition of what the violence of an adoption represents for the adoptive parents.

This "soft" version of events suited Agnès, who grew up without any problems, to the great satisfaction of her parents.

When she realised she was pregnant, shortly after her marriage, she was delighted. She was expecting her baby, who was very much wanted, in an atmosphere of happiness, cheerfulness, and harmony with her husband and family.

The pregnancy was progressing wonderfully well, apart, perhaps, from a few difficult days, when she heard from the doctor—whom she described as a magician who could "see inside the womb"—that the baby was a little girl. She was pleased, but felt disturbed without really knowing why. During the three days following the scan, she started to vomit, and nothing could stop her. And yet, "having a little girl, that was really sweet."

The only thing that upset her was the business of the name. She had chosen names for a boy, but so far she couldn't think of any for a girl.

The vomiting stopped, and suddenly a name came to her—she would call the baby Marie-Agnès.

In spite of protestations from the family, who considered this choice somewhat lacking in imagination rather than seeing it as a search for origins, she managed to insist on her choice, and everything became normal, calm, and happy again.

At the end of the seventh month, she started to have contractions. She was admitted to hospital; the doctors thought the baby was too small, and prescribed rest and perfusion.

At this point, she tried to refuse, and asked to be delivered prematurely: "I felt it was the moment to give birth, I don't know why." Her family and her doctor reasoned with her. It is certainly true that Agnès had always been extremely reasonable, ever since she was very little. She was never angry, never contrary, always very positive. In the end she gave in. She now accepted that she had to rest, without protesting, and she did not even seem to be sad, but maybe just a little absent. She was doubtless resigned to not being listened to.

A few weeks later, the baby was the perfect weight, the text-book weight. The doctors decided to stop the perfusion. Five hours later, Marie-Agnès was born, after a problem-free delivery, and everyone felt the satisfaction of a job well done. The baby was not premature.

For the first three days, Agnès said she was too tired to hold her baby in her arms. By the third day, she no longer knew her own name, nor why she had come into the hospital.

What returned in her analysis was her horror, hatred, and violent feelings toward her birth mother. She said to me, "How could she have abandoned me? Now I have a child, I understand that my mother was a monster."

What monster is this? Who is a monster for whom?

Her hatred had been masked by the good intentions of the adoptive parents, who had been too well advised. Torn apart by her ambivalence, while she rejected her birth mother, she also wanted to shout about her relation to this sick mother by all possible means, this mother with whom she could identify only as a monster.

Once Agnès had done some analytic work in which she had been able to recover the drama of her history and understand the meaning she could give to the symptom "threat of premature delivery", she was able to reclaim her daughter, whose grandmother had become the child's new adoptive mother, as we can expect in a story that, because it has never been heard, will not cease to repeat itself.

The work of an analyst in a neonatology service is neither to reassure nor to attempt to cover over suffering at any price. The analyst has to agree to listen and understand, because without this, some twenty-three years later, the baby within the adult will relive the violence of a trauma that she wanted to deny. We have to trust the unconscious not to forget. Time, as we know, has nothing to do with it.

The mothers around the incubators are most often suffering from an inability to think about their babies. Who does she look like? What is he feeling? Who is she? In the impossibility of putting these questions, these women are paralysed, trapped between medicine, which knows better than they do, the mourning for the last stages of their pregnancy, and the real risk of the death of their child.

Most often, everything happens as if the babies were still in the womb, as if they had never been delivered. There is never a baby blues day in a neonatology service. Paradoxically, admission to hospital seems to obliterate any chance of separation.

The essential preoccupation of psychologists who are asked to work in NICUs seems to be a project of "reparation" of the negative consequences of a painful separation, both for the mother and for the child. It is a question of supporting the bond at all costs, and of negating the effects of the distancing by all possible means. This therapeutic project surely has its source in the ever-present desire to cancel out the trauma of birth. Here too, the myth of happy motherhood, of the mother who is totally fulfilled by her child in a perfect symbiosis, is certainly at the root of this orientation.

To be sure, separation from their babies is painful for the mothers in a neonatal service; this is what they tell us. It is just as painful for the children, whose suffering, even physical suffering, we cannot deny. But is it really a case of separation? The relation between mother and baby will not develop easily; even if the team, full of good intentions, tries desperately to get mothers to cuddle their babies. This separation, which comes "on top of the other one" when the newborn is brutally and often silently admitted to hospital, seems, by doubling the cut, to annul it, to prevent it from operating properly; in other words, to prevent it from creating symbolisation. What is missing, then, is the mother who lacks.

On this basis, the orientation of our work in neonatology seems to us to take on a different aspect. The work of the resuscitation service would no longer be simply to restore the "tableau of motherhood" by making the baby viable; rather, it would be to give back a living child to a mother who is capable of taking him on, as the child is able finally separate from her. For this to happen, the trauma of the birth has to be symbolised, so that it can be inscribed.

The most precious thing the period of hospitalisation can offer is to allow a cut, a loss, the activity of a third party. It is the work of mourning that confronts us as a team, and it is also through the work of loss and separation that we will be able to support the parents so that each of them can find their way back to a subjective position.

Malika: the place in the fantasy

Malika was born prematurely, a year after her brother Malik, then aged six, fell out of a window and died. The mother was desperate, and insisted on becoming pregnant again immediately. The doctor, faced with her distress, also advised her to become pregnant again as soon as possible. For the mother, he said, it was the only way to recover. In the neonatology unit, the mother said to us that Malik had told her before he died that he would come back as a girl. Of course she had not mentioned that to the doctor.

As she stood by the incubator, she leaned over the baby and murmured, "It's me, Malik, it's Mummy, open your eyes. I know it's you, just give me a sign."

What sort of psychical development could be expected for this little girl who had no right to exist except as the reincarnation of her brother?

Freud said, "Our nurseries are full of ghosts." If it is the case that, through repetition, every birth is a re-enactment of something of the family history, orchestrated by the fantasy, then it is surely inevitable that when a child reincarnates a lost sibling, there will be a "psychical catastrophe" for the second child. The "ravage" will be even more serious if, as is so often the case in the history of lost children, the death is never spoken of to the second child. How often do we encounter a mute child who incarnates his parents' impossibility to "speak"? How many psychotic children carry within them the weight of a family secret? When parents have not had time to do the work of mourning, they cannot speak of the dead child, and the "un-said" becomes a further determining factor in the child's pathology. When family secrets are made flesh, the child who is the unconscious bearer of them may become insane or die as a result.

Murielle: the effects of belief

Murielle was born at the end of the seventh month of gestation. She weighed 1.5 kg. When she was admitted to the service, she was alive and exhibited muscle tone, and needed ventilation for only twenty-four hours. There was no hyaline membrane disease, and clinically and neurologically she was healthy; from the very start of her admission, the team was optimistic about her. "She's small," they said, "but she'll pull through all right." Several days after her birth, we had still had no sign of her parents. The mother had signed her discharge papers and left the maternity unit. The chief administrator of our service decided to telephone the parents' home to show them a sign of life from our side. It is hard for the team to deprive itself of the pleasure of giving good news. It was more than a week after the birth that Murielle's mother came to visit her daughter. She was smiling, self-effacing, asked no questions, and preferred not to become involved in caring for her baby, even though the nurse suggested she might like to help us. The following day, she had an appointment with me. Straight away, she said she trusted our team completely. Murielle was doing so well with us; she hoped we would keep her as long as possible. "Well, as long as it takes," she added, "so that she'll be well." But that was all she wanted to say during that first session. During the days that followed, I was by the incubator when she came to visit. When I asked her, "How do you think your daughter is doing today?" she replied, "Oh, well, I don't know, it's difficult to say. I don't have much of an imagination." When Murielle cried, when she smiled, her mother remained silent, as if nothing about this child was addressed to her or to us. On the first day it was possible for her to hold Murielle just for a few minutes; the baby stared at her, very attentive, very serious. But the mother, amazed at the way she was looking at her, turned away from her and said, "But what on earth is she looking at like that?" The nurse replied, "She's looking at you." "Oh no, no, she's too little. You can surely see she's not even there."

"The baby as subject is supported by the supposition of the mother, who is thus the one who initiates the baby's subjectivity. The mother can transform the baby's cry into an appeal, on condition that she supposes the baby has knowledge—knowledge of the object that he can demand" (Vanier, 2002). For Murielle, such a transformation was not possible. The supposition of the subject implies a place, the place of the other, from which she can support herself. The subject is already there, in the mother, who represents the subject as separate. That is what happens when everything goes well … But Murielle's mother had no imagination, and therefore no supposition.

A few weeks later, when the baby's state of health was becoming more and more satisfactory, the mother started to speak to me: "What I've got to tell you is a bit strange," she said, "I'm afraid you may not be able to understand. We don't come from the same culture. You're all scientists." I encouraged her to say more. She continued: "My husband and I are Haitians. For us, magic is very important. We believe in it as much as you believe in your medicine. Murielle is not going to live." She went on: "My husband was married when we met. He left his wife to come and live with me. Then this woman was furious, she put a spell on us. She came into our house and she said, 'You will be infertile. If you have babies, none of your blood will survive.' For five years, my womb was empty. But we wanted children. In our culture, the only way to fight magic is with magic. We went to see some very powerful witch-doctors, we hoped they would be more powerful than her, and we asked them for a baby. A few months later, I was pregnant, but the baby died a sudden death a few weeks after birth. The following year, we went back to see the witch-doctors. They were quite sure they could thwart this woman's spell. But a second child was born, and he also died a sudden death three months later. So when I found I was pregnant with Murielle, we came to France to try to break the spell. This is my third child. Will your doctors' magic be stronger than this woman sorcerer? I'm terrified all the time that you're going to tell me that Murielle is dead."

So it was the progeny of this couple who had had this curse put upon them. The team was shaken when they heard this woman's story—as she became more and more confident, she told everyone about it. The staff did everything they could to reassure her. It was as if we were saying, "There, there, of course we are good witch-doctors. Just because we're in France, it doesn't mean there are no good witch-doctors. Murielle will live." As the weeks went past, the neonatal team took up the gauntlet. They were caught up in a game of omnipotence. Surely science has always trumped obscurantism?

The day of her discharge, Murielle was in perfect health. She was cheerful, showed good muscle tone, and was alert; the EEG was perfect, as was the ECG, the check-up scans were satisfactory, her digestion was good—everything that could be measured using our scientific techniques gave excellent results. She was just two months old when she left the unit, one summer morning around 9 a.m. At 5 p.m. the same day, Murielle's body was brought in to A&E. She had died an unexplained sudden death during the day.

Medicine is no more capable than psychoanalysis of explaining the inexplicable. It is not a question of opposing medicine, or trying to propose a theory to the doctors that will explain everything. The analyst does not know why "your daughter is mute", any more than Molière's doctor did. It is certainly not a question of mirroring back omnipotence in the face of medical power. What psychoanalysts can share with doctors is just that—the inexplicable. Only the patients may perhaps have some clues as to the answers, and it is by listening to them that both psychoanalysts and doctors can learn something.

Murielle's mother had told us that the witch-doctors, using their magic powers, had made her pregnant. None of her three children, she had said, was her husband's. The spell cast by the jealous wife had prevented her from being impregnated by any sexual act with this man. Only the witch-doctors could put a baby in her womb. But once the baby was born, the other woman's power took the upper hand. Desire is not structured solely at the level of the individual; the discourse of the social bond also plays its part. Medicine and magic, surely, have in common that they are both based on belief systems! In our fight against a spell that had been cast, it all happened as if it required a magical response. So we had to resort to a higher agency, whether sorcery or medicine; but in order for it to work, this agency must be even stronger than the one who cast the spell, so it must be an agency with a similarly destructive power: indeed, the power to destroy as well as to create. In this case, we were surely drawn into the world of fantasy. Was it not a question of opposing the omnipotence of destiny, of creating life, or causing death, or, like Mephistopheles, promising eternal youth to Faust, for the price of his soul?

Prematurity and assisted reproductive technology (ART)

The most extreme medically assisted births allow parents who would not otherwise be able to have a child, finally to have their demand fulfilled. If a couple is infertile, is it right to go against it in this way? We even heard during the 2000s that there were American researchers who proposed cloning as a solution. The mother would have a daughter who was a clone of herself, the father would have a son who was the living image of himself. This method, they explained, would avoid the need for sperm or egg donation. The child would be the exact double of the parent, so there would be no unknown foreign elements to disturb the family. Here again, it seems we are in the realm of reproducing "the same". Is there something here to do with the negation of difference, the transgression of the prohibition of incest? Human beings are irresistibly attracted to those who are like them. Is the "drive to clone" so strong that it would look everywhere for the other without alterity, so that one could be sure of only ever finding oneself? Would that not be the means of losing oneself? No more need for seminars on identification, then, if children will be their parents' genetic twins.

The implantation of multiple embryos increases the number of children at risk because they have been born prematurely. Fantasies of omnipotence can become reality these days. Should we respond to the demand for them to be fulfilled? How far should doctors go to satisfy their patients?

"You can't just order a baby like a piece of furniture from the La Redoute catalogue," said one father who was arguing against his wife, who wanted the doctors to give her a baby "by any possible means". And then whose is the child? One obstetrician who specialised in medically assisted births was astonished to hear that children born thanks to his interventions were being named after him. He found it amusing, but did not seem to question what might be behind it. How well will these children's symbolic bearings, essential to their own construction as human subjects, be functioning in a few years' time?

Some scientists expect psychoanalysts to take up a position, sometimes they want them to "take care of" or prevent the possible complications of their medical interventions.

This was the case for Mrs. B, who came to see me on the advice of her gynaecologist. She had a little boy of seven, born as a result of IVF. Now she and her husband wanted another baby. Her doctor had suggested that, rather than starting all over again, they could implant one of the embryos that had been frozen eight years previously, at the time of the first IVF. But Mrs. B was not comfortable with accepting this offer. "I can't bear the idea that I'd be bringing a child into the world who was conceived nine years ago, a newborn baby who'd be older than his big brother." The doctor had thought there was something wrong with her. Why wouldn't she understand that this procedure would present far fewer complications? It would be far simpler, unless, of course, as he pointed out, the eight-year-old embryos fell to bits when they were thawed out. It was Mrs. B who fell to bits, however, overcome with anguish. She could not understand why her wish to become pregnant had fallen apart, and at a stroke had caused difficulties for her doctor.

"Dear Colleague," he had written, "I am referring Mrs. B to you; she is about to undergo the implantation of an embryo, but her mental state is disturbing, and there is a risk that it will cause the medical intervention to fail. Thank you in advance for doing what you can for her."

Doubtless he had no idea that I was not a colleague. Whatever I could do, if indeed there was anything, might in no way lead to a state of affairs for which he would wish to thank me. How could anyone not have understood the difficulties this woman and her children might have encountered? The older brother would become the younger brother, even though the big brother would actually look like a newborn. How would this story write itself in the unconscious? There is a perverse dimension to this which we cannot ignore. It is *perversion in vitro*.

Medicine cannot make use of psychoanalysis. This is not because of a lack of good will on the part of psychoanalysts, but rather is a question of a difference in register, a radical impossibility.

So what is it we are being asked to do nowadays? Is it a questioning about ethical positions? Explanations as to why certain attempts in the field of ART have failed? Will psychoanalysis enable medicine to understand, for example, what it is that makes women give birth prematurely? When there is no obvious medical reason, the scientists will ask questions, wondering why a particular pregnancy did not go to term. They seek the causes once they have established the effects; they want to understand. As Jacques Lacan emphasised: "It consists in thinking that some things are self-evident, that, for example, when someone is sad it's because he doesn't have what his heart desires. Nothing could be more false—there are people who have all their heart desires and are still sad [...] there is nothing that could be further from psychoanalysis in its whole development, its entire inspiration and its mainspring, in everything that it has contributed, everything it has been able to confirm for us in anything we have established" (Lacan, 1997, pp. 6–7).

Is premature delivery a symptom? The relation between cause and effect is not so clear to psychoanalysts. Each human subject is different; each human being, inscribed in a complex network of signifiers, "reacts", among other things, with the body, in or on which words come to be inscribed which cannot be spoken in any other way. What will be the meaning of a particular premature birth? It will never be the same as that of any other, each one asking a question in its own way, about life, about death, about sexual difference, linked to several generations. The clinic requires humility on our part; and it is only case by case that we can start to put forward a few hypotheses, which in turn raise further questions. The same causes do not have the same effects: that is one of the specificities of the unconscious; it is beyond comprehension.

Certainly, in each case of prematurity, we can discern something of the mother's ambivalence towards her child. But ambivalence is always present, whether or not the child is premature, and this ambivalence does not necessarily mean that the baby is born early. The death drives of which Freud spoke are indissolubly linked with the drives of life, and the death drive, as we have to keep reminding ourselves, is not the desire to murder. It is impossible to point to ambivalence as the only cause of prematurity. Nor can we talk naively about the "wanted child", which we hear about endlessly these days, as if a wanted child is protected from all possible problems. It all depends on why he or she was wanted.

When we treat children, we know very well that the parents' desire for them, while it is necessary, is not always without its risks. And what is more, premature children are often very much wanted. So another myth bites the dust.

A number of analysts, such as Bernard This and Monique Bydlowski, thought that the date of the delivery had the value of signification, as if the unconscious chose the date of birth as the anniversary of another birth, death, or other event (Bydlowski, 1983, p. 143). This may be true in some cases, but again, is it possible to generalise?

A report by MIRE[6] suggested that prematurity could be a psychosomatic phenomenon (Alexandre & Bizos Kukucka, 1993). A psychosomatic illness, by definition, affects the body while being linked with the mind. It is the third category of human illnesses: physical illness, mental illness, psychosomatic illness. But these days, can we really make such a differentiation? Do we not now believe that mind and body are always linked? Do not all illnesses concern both the psyche and the soma, so are they not all psychosomatic? According to this report, prematurity is the result of a psychical conflict in the mother. It is this conflict that is supposed to cause the premature delivery.

Looking for a "cause" for prematurity does not seem to us to be a particularly interesting question. In any case, it is impossible to isolate a single cause as such. Whatever sets off a premature delivery, it is our task to locate it on the side of the inexplicable, on the side of the Real. Whatever meaning it is given, whatever explanation is found for it, it will never, case by case, be more than a retroactive reconstruction of an event that cannot be thought about as such.

On the other hand, what is easier to identify is the fact that in almost all these histories of difficult births, the relationship between the mother and her own mother was painful and complicated. Freud said that even before the little girl wanted a baby from her father, at the time of the Oedipus complex, she had wanted to give her mother a baby. This is something we find very often in the analysis of children. The child's father is ignored, the mother's reference becomes her own mother, and her bond with the baby will be altered by this. Love or hate (the two sides of the same coin) between mother and daughter now takes centre stage. The baby will become trapped in this fantasy.

For Marie-Magdeleine Lessana, "motherhood is not transmitted from mother to daughter, as the phallus is from man to man. A girl will not be able to become a mother—though she may give birth, but that does not mean that she becomes a mother for that child—until she has passed through the 'ravage,' through a kind of uprooting, a detachment, without substitution. She has to give up hope of directly obtaining permission from her mother to give birth" (Lessana, 2000). These mothers are victims, women who are prevented from becoming mothers, who wait too long for their own mother to give them permission to give birth in their turn, and who develop phobic-type symptoms in relation to their own child *in utero*. The stay in the neonatal service and the "repulsive" look of the premature baby lead these mothers to speak of the fear the baby has aroused in them. Sometimes it even induces panic. Is it prematurity that unleashes anguish in the mother, or was the anguish already present? Is it guilt that unleashes the anguish, the guilt about a desire for incest with the mother? Could we then understand the expulsion of the baby as a defence mechanism? One thing is certain: the hurtful words of their own mothers make these women into damaged mothers, and have a severe impact on their bodies. No one these days believes that mind and body are hermetically sealed separate units. Everyone, even the scientist, is prepared to admit that life events, dramas, any suffering which is deemed to be psychical, have an impact on the body.

"Love," says Antonio Damasio, a researcher in neurology, "and hate and anguish, the qualities of kindness and cruelty, the planned solution of a scientific problem or the creation of a new artifact, are all based on neural events within a brain, provided that brain has been and now is interacting with its body. The soul breathes through the body, and suffering, whether it starts in the skin or in a mental image, happens in the flesh" (Damasio, 2007, p. xvii). For his part, Lacan might have said that man thinks with his feet! "Many people have suspected that the human being is nothing but a hand. If only that were true! There is, of course, the whole body; and the human being thinks also with his feet. I have even recommended that you do this yourselves, because ultimately it is the best thing anyone could wish for you" (Lacan, 1975, [translated for this edition]).

Speech has its effects on the subject's body, and will be as one with it to the point of leading it right up the gates of death. The unconscious moves us, it never leaves us in peace, never lets us forget, so long as we have not remembered. It shows itself in our dreams, our slips, our parapraxes, just as it does in our physical suffering. That which inscribes us differently from any other being may make our life something that is very different from what we would have wished for. It is in this enigma that we may find a clue as to what makes a baby come into the world prematurely.

There is nothing to indicate that a neonatology team would be able to answer this question, even with an analyst on board. Nor is there any question that this would be desirable during the period of hospitalisation when the baby is in danger. Sometimes, the parents with whom we have worked will choose to go through a long period of analysis which will enable them to discover what it is in their particular and unique history that has inflected the course of their lives and that of their baby in this particular way.

On the other hand, while their baby is in the unit, the support of the team and the meetings with the analyst may permit the parents to put into words what they are going through, to find a way to bond with their child, and to find each other again, as long as they are given time, without prejudice and without an agenda.

The fathers

He had followed the incubator from the labour ward right up to the doors of the NICU. He had waited outside while the doctors admitted his little daughter. Finally, someone came to fetch him and, after the rituals necessary to gain access (entry vestibule, hand-washing, putting on special clothing), this man who loathed the smell of hospitals was beside his baby. The nurse explained how the machines worked, but he could not hear her; a few minutes later, a doctor came to tell him how the baby was doing, but did not manage to reassure him.

When he left the unit, he passed me in the corridor, and asked me the way back to the maternity unit. He seemed quite disorientated and lost. On my white coat I wore a badge with my name and the name of the neonatology service. Forgetting that he needed to leave, he started questioning me feverishly: "You work here? Do you know if my daughter is going to live? Why are the doctors saying we have to wait until they can say yes or no?" Sitting down in the waiting room, he now began to relive his last few hours of panic, without understanding what had been happening to him. Every ten minutes, he would go to reception to ask them to call the recovery room to find out how his wife was doing, then he would come back and sit down, with an air of resignation. When I spoke to him, he said, "I can't go back to the maternity unit without being able to tell her something about her baby; even if she's in her room, I can't go there." He started telling me that everything had happened so quickly, there had been no warning of the sudden onset of labour. Nothing either to warn them that they would have a child so quickly. The day his wife had told him the news, he had changed colour, just like the pregnancy test. He hadn't felt ready to be a father. Even at that point in time, he had felt that they were rushing into parenthood. "It's awful," he told me, "to feel you're out of synch with your own life. Do all men feel that way? Maybe I'd have got used to the idea of being a father if she'd been born after nine months, but this, it's too soon, I thought I had more time to prepare myself. It's not enough for a woman to say to you one day, 'You're going to be a dad ...', you don't think it's going to happen, and yet it changes your whole life. Maybe she had time to get used to it, because she was pregnant ... Me, I was miles away from it ... And now? What am I supposed to do to be a father? Wait for news of the baby? Go back to my wife?"

What is a father?

Since Freud, we have found this question at work in the entire psychoanalytic theory. The seducer-father, the father of the primal horde, the prohibiting father, the real father, the imaginary father, the symbolic father. The Paternal Metaphor, the Name-of-the-Father, which for Lacan allowed the child to make its trajectory through the Oedipus complex and become "neurotised". The man who has become a father already has some idea of this place that is assigned to him by a woman. This idea certainly comes to him from his childhood, from his history (before being a father, he was a son), but it also comes from what is transmitted by tradition and culture.

In *Totem and Taboo*, Freud proposes the mythical story of the father of the primal horde (Freud, 1912–1913). An absolute male, he reigns over his sons and enjoys all the women, forcibly prohibiting them to all other males. Deprived of jouissance, the sons decide to kill the father. When the father dies, the rivalry among the brothers with regard to possession of the women reaches fever pitch. The law is enforced more and more strictly, and a totemism of the paternal function comes into being. The dead father becomes even more prohibiting that when he was alive. He no longer reigns by force, but his symbolic function now operates, and is unavoidable for the group. It is at this point that the prohibitions of murder and incest are put in place. The little boy henceforth becomes a man on the basis of the threat of castration. The threat prohibits a particular form of jouissance, that of incest. The prohibiting father therefore does not transmit the omnipotence and the unlimited jouissance of the father of the horde, but instead he transmits castration, to which he himself has had to submit in his capacity of son.

We know which aspect of the paternal function will be of interest to the mother of the child. It is she who will introduce this function, and it is what will introduce phallic signification. It is the father who, in the play of jouissance, will take care of the desire of the mother. The child will then be able to escape from the position of object of the maternal fantasy, as long as the mother gives an adequate place to the father—to him, or to any other who could fulfil this function.

Moustapha Safouan explains: "The father appears to have two possessions: the mother, and whatever it takes to possess the mother. This imaginary effect is the equivalent of a belief or a judgement of attribution. Attribution of what, we may ask? Of an object of desire ... an object that suffices to arouse desire, if not to command desire, simply put an object that has something peculiar about it—namely that no one actually has it" (Safouan, 1975, p. 130 [translated for this edition]).

Where there is the idea of a lack, of an object that could be lacking, desire can appear. If there is third party functioning, the mother cannot be in the position of playing with the child like an object, but a real space for "play" can come into being, and something of an "I" will become possible. The mother does not make a child for herself, for her own jouissance, as she would treat a piece of property. She makes a child for a man, in the name of a father. The act of making a child involves a third party. The baby cannot totally fulfil the mother, she remains lacking. It is no longer merely a case of the relation between two bodies, but involves language and a world in which sexual difference obtains. In such a space where play is possible, the mother can represent the child to herself as separate from her.

In China there is a ritual which Françoise Dolto often referred to: the day after a baby has been delivered, the mother leans over the cradle and says, "I greet you, young master, my son, or young lady, my daughter, and all the respected male ancestors of my respected husband." At a later date, the mother presents the child to the family members assembled for the occasion, and the baby is given a name. This dual presentation inscribes the child in the register of the symbolic, of naming, while the mother is inscribed in the register of lack. It is because she lacks that she can come to lack for her child, too. At the moment of birth, the child is presented to the father by the mother.

The father's position is often difficult and uncertain, and will depend to a large extent on the mother.

A few days ago, when I was passing through the waiting room, I heard two four-year-old girls talking to each other. They were waiting for their parents, who had gone in to the service to visit the little brothers who had both just been born. One of them was telling the other, quite proudly, "I know where babies come from. They come out of our mummies' tummies." The other little girl looked very impressed; she waited a moment, and then asked, "So what about daddies, where do they come from?" The reply came without hesitation, "Well, I don't know about that, but I know it's the mummies who make them."

Fathers do indeed get their bearings from a representation belonging to the mother. It is a representation built up according to what sort of man he is for her, but is also linked to what was already inscribed for her, even before this pregnancy, and is in the register of castration, since, as soon as the child is born, "it is caught up in the question of the father in so far as it is already a cultural question and present in the maternal field, since the child, at the moment of birth, becomes inscribed in the mother's problematic in relation to the question of the phallus, and thus of her fantasy" (Vanier, A., 2010, pp. 83–84 [translated for this edition]).

For Winnicott, every kind of care given to the baby up to the age of two is in the maternal register. Of course, the father, according to him, can fulfil these functions, by giving care, but he needs to know that he is in a "maternal" position in relation to the baby. This is no reason why he should not help his wife! But to be in a paternal position, he will have to occupy a different position: supporting the mother, protecting the mother–baby relationship, and underpinning her maternal authority. It is only when, as Winnicott put it, he keeps an eye on "mother's appetite, voraciousness, for the baby" (Newman, 1995, p. 195; see also Winnicott, 1991), that he is truly fulfilling the role of a father: the father allowing the child not to be completely subjected to the mother's desire.

How is this managed in a neonatal unit? The upset caused in the parents' finding of their own roles will certainly affect both the paternal function and the dynamic of the couple. The "separating" function of the father is turned upside-down in this case: he will try his utmost to facilitate contact between mother and baby. If he feels he is failing in this task, he will try to make up for his wife's inability to be present for the baby. Some fathers find themselves in the position of forbidding their wives to be with the baby, and keeping him to themselves.

Mothers then complain that they are not allowed to go near their baby, the father has taken her place in the baby's life, and has truly become an obstacle to his wife's presence. These mothers feel cheated of their place, not so much by the neonatology service, but by the child's father, who has become incapable of seeing her as this baby's mother. Faced with this "slippage" of the place of the father, who himself has become a mother, it is the neonatology service that now has to take up the paternal position.

One mother said to me, "I think he's actually pleased that I gave birth prematurely! When the baby was in my womb, it wasn't his. Now he's taken her away from me, as if she's his business and not mine!"

Motherhood is biological, it takes over through the life of the senses, above all through the two bodies. The father's true function is to allow the child not to be completely subjected to the desire of the mother.

On the labour ward, the emergency paediatrics team descends on the newborn without always having had a moment to speak to the father about how serious the situation is. The baby is installed in a transportation incubator, and urgently moved to another service. If the baby has been transferred to another hospital, the father will have had to follow the ambulance to the other side of Paris, in order to stay with the baby. But then—he does not know what to do. Should he go back to the mother? Where would he be more useful? Where is his proper place? How can he find it? What should he do for his wife?

Long admissions of babies in the service can sometimes "load the dice" from the very beginning.

In some cases, the father may become very aggressive towards the team, or he may visit very rarely, or not at all. He will say, for example, that such little babies are not really his problem, but only for women.

In order for a man to become a father, of course, he has to make a place for the mother in himself. As Winnicott said, any parental identification is based initially upon a maternal identification. Many fathers find this risk of feminisation rather disturbing; it sometimes means they will say they feel estranged from the baby. By doing this, they protect themselves from the risk of regression, via the most primal identifications, to the image of their own mother. In order to resist this omnipotent woman, with her extraordinary powers, the man needs to signal his essential virility. Anything not to be like her! It is a male fragility which needs to be respected, even though it can be hard for staff in the service to understand that the fathers, too, need to protect themselves from their babies. The teams tend to praise those men who throw themselves enthusiastically into a maternal relation with the baby. And yet some fathers have to put up defences against the desire for pregnancy that we can often discern in little boys of three or four years. When a little brother or sister is born, many boys will develop symptoms of faecal retention, both fearing and longing to have a baby in their tummy like mummy. At the moment of becoming a father, this little boy will re-emerge, and the adult man will experience his paternity linked with what he had much earlier experienced in relation to castration. It is not possible to be both a boy and a girl. While the little girl has to give up on the idea of having a penis (a renunciation which is mitigated by the promise of a baby), the little boy has to give up on the idea of having a baby in his tummy. The man, just as when he was small and emerging from the Oedipus complex, has to move from a dual relation to a triangular relation. We have already explored how difficult this can be.

The team simply has to accept that not all fathers will be able to take care of their babies. It will take a great deal of patience, a great deal of talking through, to enable a father to reach the point of being able to risk approaching his baby, without feeling that the team is being judgemental. Premature deliveries, where both mother and baby are in danger, mean that the father will be profoundly shaken, faced once again with the horrors of castration and impossible identifications.

In other cases, on the contrary, the father may be very present. He may prove to be very demanding and oppositional towards the team, as if the only way he can be of use to the mother and baby is by somehow taking revenge for what has happened. So he tries to disagree with the doctors on every count. If he is responsible for this baby, why should he have to bow down before the doctor's decisions? Being obliged to "give in" makes him doubt his capacity to be a father even more. Who is the father of this child? To get out of this impasse, he may respond by trying to identify with the doctor. He thinks that the father is the one who knows what is good for the child. So he will not "leave them be"; he harasses the medical team, wanting answers. He wants to know as much as the team members who resuscitated the baby; they in turn are often embarrassed and overwhelmed by his questions, which they are certainly unable to answer. The father who insists on one appointment after the other is trying to hide his anguish, feels he has to show how "strong" he is, wants to know how the baby is doing, wants to know whether he should tell his wife or not. He wants to protect her, and is also afraid for her:

"My wife is fragile. I'm the one you should speak to, you can say everything to me," or "She's a bit funny at the moment, I can't get through to her since the baby's been in hospital, you really need to look after her! There's nothing I can do any more. Neither can you, by the way! You're not doing anything, not even telling me how my baby is going to be!"

How can a man possibly feel like a father when he has the impression that he has lost both his wife and his baby? He cannot succeed in being a man for his wife, because he does not know how to soothe her anguish. Nor can he see how to be a father to this baby that is somewhere between life and death. He thinks that he is protecting his family by attacking us. By showing himself to be decisive and authoritarian, he thinks he is restoring his wife's and his baby's confidence in him, as well as boosting his own self-confidence.

This way of being a father is one that the team members really need to understand, when they are confronted with a man who perhaps feels that his ability to fulfil his role has been severely shaken, especially if this is his first child. The reactions of fathers in neonatology services vary according to their individual histories. The paternal function is directly linked to desire. Here again, as in the case of the mothers, the service may have an important role of offering a lifeline.

At the beginning of her life, Inès was fragile, and her mother was not very present. She needed time, but Inès's father could not wait any longer. He did not want to take care of the baby without his wife being there, but he could not get her to come into the unit to help. He kept on asking the male doctors in the service what he should do, how a father should react in this situation. This put the doctors in a very uncomfortable position.

The baby does not have the same body-to-body relation to the father as to the mother. (This raises the question of why there is nowadays an obligation, in vogue in some services, to insist on skin-to-skin contact (kangaroo care) with the father.) Sometimes a father finds his place by opposing the medical discourse. Or sometimes he will identify with the doctor. In his hope to make reparation, his need to be useful, he wants to be better informed than the medical staff, and to give his opinion on any intervention. In some cases he will be absent, in others he will be too present, he will take up all the space around his baby. It will then be important for the team to understand his distress and to accept his questioning, even if it is not always easy.

When a mother meets her baby a few days after the birth, the father may feel appeased if his wife seems to have difficulties in investing emotionally in the child. Then, rather than occupying the place of a third party, he may try to get close to the baby, setting his manliness aside, devoting himself to playing a role for the baby that is rather that of a replacement mother.

Fathers often tell us how difficult it is for them to believe it if they see things are not going well between the mother and baby. Once again, the idealisation of the mother–baby bond takes centre stage, as most certainly does the bond with their own mother, which will also be idealised. The wife's apparent lack of interest in the child is unbearable to them, as it throws them back into the phase when their own mother began to constitute a lack for them. They are also aware of the lack in the mother that this baby may give rise to. They now find themselves confronted with their own history as a newborn baby, devouring and devoured.

Trapped in a maternal identification, losing their bearings, they try again to "make reparation" by "taking on the function" of the mother for the child, and becoming a rival to her. They cannot bear the prospect that this baby is not everything for the mother; it mirrors their relation to their own mother.

But a child needs his parents to have differentiated roles, it does not need two identical mothers or fathers.

When the mother is prevented from taking her place by the extreme prematurity of the baby, the father will tell us how disturbed he is by what looks to him like indifference on his wife's part, or even aggressivity.

Fanny

"I don't understand why she's rejecting this child, it's as if she's not there. How can I get her to take an interest in her? She's not even interested in me any more!"

He kept asking the team how he should approach his wife and daughter, and complained about his wife to the nurses, who certainly did not approve of the mother's withdrawal, and thought he was a nice, devoted father and sympathised with his bewilderment, but made efforts not to take any particular position.

During this time, his wife told me in a session, "I wasn't able to visit her straight away, so obviously she became attached to her father over those first three days. When I went there for the first time, she didn't want to look at me, she only had eyes for him. I wanted to hold her hand, but she pushed me away, she didn't want anything to do with me."

Fanny was extremely premature, weighing 880 grams and born at twenty-eight weeks.

She was intubated, ventilated, plugged into machines in her incubator, and we had no idea as yet of what the prognosis might be for this fragile baby. And still her mother felt rejected by her. She had pushed her hand away, she said. Well, doubtless there was something repulsive about the little girl that was pushing the mother away, too. Then, for the next few weeks, the father would come in alone, anxious and unhappy. He would spend hours sitting beside Fanny's incubator, without daring to ask any questions of the medical staff.

One evening when we were having a talk, he told me how worried he was about his daughter, but also about his wife, who seemed to be getting more and more sad since she had been discharged. He was wondering whether they would be able to stay together as a couple following the birth of this child. "I don't understand what's happening," he said, "she wanted this child so much." He explained that he came to see Fanny as often as possible, so that she would not feel alone, but that he was not sure that could replace her mother's presence. He was upset by the nurses' questions: "Why doesn't your wife come to visit? Fanny needs her." He was ashamed that he could not convince his wife to come into the unit. "I've got work to do," he said, "I can't keep on coming like this. And what will happen when Fanny comes home? I'm really disappointed in my wife, everything has changed between us, I had no idea she would react like this."

During our conversations, which took place during the evenings when I stayed on at the unit, he took the decision to persuade his wife, not to come and visit her daughter, but to come and see me, to talk to me about her child and the relationship with her husband.

A week later, Fanny's mother came to see me in my consulting room. I did not suggest we should go back to the unit; on the contrary, I listened to her while she spoke about her anguish, of the distress she had found herself in and the difficulties she had had in feeling that she was a mother and a woman. She was not concerned for the baby, but she herself felt "on the edge". "Those two get on too well with each other," she said, "they don't need me." This fascination with the father–daughter couple reflected something of her own history, of course. It was a passionate oedipal story, which had been brought back to life by this premature birth.

After a number of sessions, during which she was able to put her past suffering into words, she was finally able to go back into the unit to get to know her baby, and was able to reconnect with her husband.

Ludivine

"I called her Ludivine because she's a gift from God," said the baby's father when we first met. Ludivine was a little girl born at thirty-two weeks, and weighing 1.75 kg. She had not caused any particular problems to the team, and she was developing normally.

I had met the father as soon as the baby was admitted to the service, but no one had seen the mother. She had only visited the unit once or twice, had only stayed a short time, and would not speak. The father, on the other hand, was much appreciated by the nurses. "He's marvellous," they would say, "we've never seen such a good dad. He changes nappies and gives her bottles just like a mum." He was, indeed, very present, spending whole days with the baby, singing songs to her, speaking to her lovingly, and as soon as it was possible, he would cuddle her and cover her in kisses.

When the mother was eventually referred to me, she spoke about her own history.

She had met Ludivine's father shortly beforehand, when she was already expecting Ludivine. So he was not the biological father, but had recognised her as his own before she was born.

This woman had found she was pregnant after she had been raped. She did not want to keep this baby, the very idea of which filled her with horror. She had been on the point of having a termination. A few days before this was due, she had met Ludivine's father while visiting friends, and told him the whole story. From the very first meeting, he tried to persuade her not to have an abortion. He had always dreamed of having a child. He was prepared to marry her and recognise the child as his own and bring it up, if she would agree to keep it. Completely bewildered, in financial difficulties, illegally resident in France, and unable to return to her country of origin, Ludivine's mother accepted his proposal.

"I didn't really understand what he wanted with this baby," she said, "I was really afraid that after the birth, he'd only be interested in her, and certainly not in me. I'm still afraid he'll dump me now he's got his baby."

Ludivine's mother could not invest emotionally in her baby at all, and the fact that she was premature was not the only reason. "When I knew I was going into premature labour, I hoped she would die. But if she'd died he would certainly have dumped me, and I don't know what would have become of me."

I asked this woman if she would permit me to speak about what she had said to the child's father. She seemed relieved that we would speak about it together. "I can't take care of the baby when he's all over her like that. He keeps saying that I don't know how to do it, and that I'm going to hurt her. I don't know, maybe he's right."

Ludivine's father came regularly to the sessions after that. This man also had a very difficult history, had never known his own father, and had dreamed of having a child for as long as he could remember. He spoke of his mother as an exceptional woman whom he would like to emulate. "I would like to bring up my daughter," he said, "exactly the way she brought me up." He did not want to make babies himself. On the contrary, he had often thought about adopting, but, he said, a single man these days has problems doing that. If he had adopted a child, he thought that his mother, who was still alive, would certainly have been willing to help him, but he had not dared to approach the adoption services.

He adored this girl, Ludivine, who had been sent to him from heaven. "I just want to eat her up, she's so cute; with me she'll be as happy as a little queen."

An omnipotent mother, he was completely fulfilled by the birth of this little girl, and he scarcely mentioned his wife. The only thing that worried him where she was concerned was contraception. Each day he would ask a different nurse if she could make an appointment with family planning, so that his wife would not "fall pregnant". He did not want any more children.

He said, "Ludivine won't have any rivals, she's a princess, she'll have the best of everything, she'll have everything because she's everything to me."

What is the fantasy that supports his desire? What had been played out in the bond with his mother, in the absence of his father, and his childhood identifications? What sort of place could he make for this woman who felt she had been raped over again in this obligation he had thrust upon her to become a mother? What was it in this story of rape that had signified for him, and made him decide to choose her in particular?

It would have taken a long piece of psychoanalytic work to unravel all this. But, within the framework of the neonatal resuscitation service, that kind of work is not possible, and in any case, this man was not asking to go any further with the work. All we could do was to ensure, by talking with the father and with the staff, that a place, however small, was created for the mother. The father, now less idealised by the team, who had shown himself to be more of a mother than a father, gradually made a small amount of space for something to develop between the mother and the baby. He had not been encouraged to do this at the start of the admission because the nurses had admired him too much.

Ludivine's mother was discharged from the unit, and we heard that some time after the baby herself was discharged, the mother went to see the psychiatrist I had referred her to.

"Holding" and the place of the father

As long as we as a team pay careful attention to the parents' suffering, and are available for them, they will be able to adapt to parenthood without too much difficulty. However, in some cases a period of analytic work will be necessary for them to be able to take into account whatever it is in their own history that has dealt them such a poor hand and, in the wake of this premature birth, has made it impossible for them to take up their places alongside their baby.

Sometimes it is possible for the team, by listening to the fathers, to identify the tormenting circumstances in which they find themselves trapped. Sometimes it takes very little for them to be able to fulfil the function of supporting, of "holding", as Winnicott called it; and it is a function that is all the more necessary for the mother when the birth has been so difficult. Winnicott also says that the father is the one who allows the woman to feel secure enough to be able to sustain her own "primary maternal preoccupation". This paternal function is often forgotten by the team when they think the father is "good", especially when he helps to look after the baby just like a mother. How often we have had to intervene in the unit to stop the team forcing the fathers to "play at being mum"! We realised very quickly that the team's tendency to push the father into the mother's place would not be of any help to him. Indeed, the caring staff have a habit of more or less insisting that the father should be like a mother to the baby if the actual mother is still too unwell or too anguished, and does not come to see the baby. The fathers are asked to change nappies, give bottles, and give skin-to-skin contact ("kangaroo care"). In many cases, the fathers will flee in terror, from what they experience as an anxiety-provoking feminisation. "No, he's too tiny, you'll have to wait for my wife, I don't know how to do all that! I don't even dare to touch big babies, so you can imagine how I feel about this one!"

A good father is not necessarily one who will identify with a mother. If the team makes this kind of demand, it may be taken as a sort of "feminist revenge"; and that is not much use to the baby. On the contrary, encouraging the caregivers to be sensitive to a father's capacity to be supportive to the mother while she is getting to know her baby is much more likely to have positive results in helping both parents to reorientate themselves and find a place in relation to the child.

More often than not, by modifying our attitude, we can help the father to understand what it is that the baby and the mother expect of him. Sometimes it takes a period of psychoanalytic work, if the father's history is preventing him from being anything other than a mythical and devoted mother to his child.

Fathers can of course take care of their children, but only if they do so from the place of a father, from a place that is not maternal.

Baby Sarah's father, a head chef, told me, "Babies? It's like cooking; you can't leave it all to the women. Anyway, when a man does it, it tastes different!"

It is this "different taste" that will enable the child to find himself, and from which the team should take its bearings.

Couples

While it is true that any birth means that the couple will have to readjust, a premature birth always represents a far more acute crisis. Some parents will go as far as breaking up when their child arrives suspended between life and death, and disrupts everything in their respective histories. Guilt feelings may mean accusations will be thrown at "the other", or make both partners believe that if they stay together everything will continue to go dramatically wrong. The couple will then have to reinvent itself, and find new bearings. Some will find they are more united after this testing time; others will not survive. Staying together after certain highly sophisticated forms of ART is not always straightforward, either. For some parents, the intervention of scientific technology may be experienced as intrusive; the donation of gametes, the sexual relations programmed by doctors, may disturb the ideas in the minds of the couple on questions of filiation and sexuality. Such patients need to be made of solid stuff to survive these experiences.

Desire becomes difficult to manage, and the bond between the parents may find itself in such stormy waters that shipwreck is unavoidable. In particular, it is extremely difficult to live through the death of a child together.

One woman who had given birth to a premature baby who was now in good health, told me in her session: "Sébastien is from my second marriage. Five years ago, I gave birth to a little boy from my first husband, but he was born at twenty-five weeks, and didn't survive. My husband had been very present, very loving, around the time the baby died, we had always got on really well. But it was awful for me, I couldn't be his wife any more. I tried to deal with it in every possible way, but every second I spent with him was sheer torment. He reminded me too much of my baby. I had absolutely no desire for him any more. With him, I could think of nothing else; he was kind to me, and didn't talk about it, but just his presence reminded me of the little one and it got to the point where I couldn't stand him. He was marked with the baby's death. I think I would have died too if I hadn't left him. I met another man who didn't remind me of my baby, and I found peace with him, and now I've got a baby who's alive and well."

Couples can indeed be terribly "thrown" by the dramas surrounding a birth; in order to pull through, they often need considerable support from family and friends, but also from the caring staff in the neonatal unit, who need to remain present and attentive to their needs, without taking up a position for or against one or other parent (and this is not always easy for the team), on the occasions when one parent complains about the other. The staff never really know what is playing itself out between them. The best help for the couple at times like this is to listen to them without introducing one's own feelings and prejudices.

The parents' club

Anyone arriving in our service will be struck by how vast it is. It is certainly much bigger than the old unit, where we were physically packed very close together, but at the same time felt closer in other ways. Nowadays there are many private rooms, and the parents can spend whole days in there without meeting any other parents. Similarly, the staff caring for a baby at the far end of the service do not necessarily come across the staff closer to the entrance. They will not get to meet them until a baby is discharged, when he will be given into their care. We quickly realised that it was a good idea to help parents make contact with other parents, as well as with other members of the team, even if it was just to prepare them for a change of consultant. Where the team members are concerned, it is easy for us to talk to one another because we have meetings. But we wondered if the parents might feel isolated, without there being some structure in place that would at least allow them to meet others. We wondered if it would be possible, through bringing other identifications into play, to create the possibility of other bonds being formed that might allow them to feel less isolated.

In some NICUs there are groups for parents to meet and talk. But our idea was slightly different. Our aim was not to set up a "therapeutic" group, but simply to set aside a space where they could meet each other and meet the team, even if it was just for a coffee. The psycho-motor therapist and I were therefore put in charge of making a small room available inside the unit once a week. We organised a time for the families to meet over coffee and cake, or fruit juice; it was open to all the parents who wanted to join in, and to all members of the team. It offered a break and a rest for the nursery nurses and the doctors, if they could take time out from their duties. As well as making coffee, I make introductions, welcome the parents and help them to get to know other parents, telling them in each case a little about the baby: the name, the age, the room number, and how the admission is going. So the parents are presented as Sam's (or Julien's or Sarah's) parents. When a member of the team arrives, I also say his or her name, function, and role in caring for the babies. And very soon, everyone is talking. It is much more relaxed and free than when they come to me or to one of the doctors for a consultation in a consulting room. I was also struck by the difference in the register of the things parents would say to me in a session and the discussions they would have over coffee.

Over the weeks, a core group of participants formed, and real bonds were created between the families, who would even meet up outside the service. Over coffee, the mothers would mainly talk about their delivery, how violent it was, how suddenly they had been told, "Your baby is going to be born today." They recalled how sure they had felt that something dramatic was happening: "He was too small, it was far too early, I was terrified he wasn't going to live." They find there are a lot of similarities in how these births happened, many similar emotions which they can now share with someone who has experienced something much the same. The fathers, who often come along too, tell each other how they felt, how afraid they were, the difficulties they have encountered. This kind of exchange enables the parents to feel less alone. They also talk about their baby and their difficulties in bonding with the child. Some of the babies have just been born, and are still on the critical list; others are in intensive care and others are still in the neonatal unit, coming towards the end of their admission. The parents whose babies are closer to discharge can reply to those whose baby is still in the NICU, "We know what that's like, it's really tough, but you'll get through it." They talk about their own parents, and their friends' reactions when they told them about the birth. They speak of how isolated and alone they felt, and of how friends and family simply could not understand what they were going through. "When we come to the club, we don't feel so alone," they would say, "it makes you realise that others are going through the same thing, and that they're being put to the test in the same way." The psychomotor therapist and I do not intervene much, only rephrasing a question, punctuating the way something is said, or helping a conversation along. The nature of this kind of group work requires us not to be too intrusive. Some questions of a more personal nature may be taken up in individual sessions with the parents each week. But very soon the mothers and fathers seem able to regulate things for themselves much more successfully, and do not probe too deeply into intimate matters. On the other hand, they will speak to us about problems they are having with members of the team, and this opening-up that we have facilitated has improved the quality of dialogue with the team.

Over a coffee, the mothers feel empowered to ask the nursery nurses if they have children of their own, and whether they think about the babies they are looking after in the unit on their days off. Lina's mother said to one of them, "You must be really laid back with you own baby. You know so much, you're not like me, you can't ever be worried that you'll do the wrong thing." The nursery nurse replied, "Don't you believe it! Even when you know the theory, everyone has to start from the beginning when your own baby arrives and you become a mum. I was just like you at the beginning, I didn't have much of a clue. He taught me what to do. Just trust your little son, he's a very good teacher!" This nurse told me a few days later how her relationship with this mother had changed. Up till then, she had been very cold and mistrustful. Now she would come to her and ask plenty of questions. For her own part, Mehdi's mother told one of our doctors, "It's really strange seeing you here. You don't seem like the same person. I usually don't see you very often. And anyway, I don't go looking for you. Every time you come into my son's room, I think you're going to tell me some disaster has happened." "It's funny in this service," said one of the fathers, "with the doctors, you're hoping to see them so you can find out more about how the baby's doing, but at the same time you're avoiding them because you're afraid of them. Yesterday I knew you were doing your round. But I ran away before you arrived." The doctor, who was sitting next to them while he had a coffee, was able to take up what they had said when he gave an update on the babies. He said he always told the parents any concerns the team had, and what stage they were at with regard to hypotheses and questions about how their baby was likely to develop. "Maybe you'd prefer us not to tell you anything?" "Oh, no! You're right. I trust you because I know you tell us everything. It's just that I've got to learn not to expect that you're going to announce some disaster every time. Or maybe you could say, 'Everything's fine' before you talk to me, and then I won't be so afraid." Thanks to this exchange, the following day, Mehdi's mother was able to take up the notion of the "disaster" she was expecting to be told about, and realised that the disaster in question had already happened many years before, in her own family history. It was this drama from long ago that the birth of her son had brought back to life. The doctor, for his part, was also led to question how his own anxiety influenced the way he spoke to patients. We were amazed to see how much the parents' club can set things in motion. From the starting point of this completely informal and improvised space, speech begins to circulate in a different way; the staff begin to ask themselves questions, and the parents start to feel they have the right to speak out a little more.

One morning in May 2011, Fatoumata's mother came to the club. She had given birth prematurely to twins, a boy and a girl. Two days after they were born, the little boy died in the service. Fatoumata, who was now two months old, had come through without residual problems. She was starting to be bottle fed, everything was going well, but the nurses said they found her a little sad and distant, just like her mother, who had found it hard to smile at Fatoumata or indeed at any of the team, since the death of her son. I was seeing the mother regularly, but I found her quite difficult to reach; she spoke very little, complained of nothing, and seemed resigned and absent. On that day, at the parents' club, I introduced her to the other women, telling them she was Fatoumata's and Ismaël's mother, that Ismaël had been too little and too weak, and had not been able to survive being so premature, but that his sister was doing fine now. Leslie's mother, who was sitting opposite her, suddenly burst into tears. Her husband, who was sitting beside her, tried to comfort her. Fatoumata's mother looked amazed. She said, "You shouldn't cry, it's life, that's just the way it is. There's nothing you can do." But Leslie's mother could not stop crying. In between sobs, she explained that a year before she had Leslie, who was now out of danger, she had had a little boy, who had been born even more prematurely, and had died a few days after he was born. She had never got over it, would never be able to forget him. "It's too much," she said. Leslie's father again tried to comfort her, saying that for a father, the hardest thing is not to be able to do anything to console his wife. He was at a loss, and started to cry himself. Sitting opposite them, still retaining her dignity, Fatoumata's mother wept silently. Tears poured down her cheeks. "I couldn't cry before," she said, "I thought it would bring bad luck for Fatoumata, that it would be bad for her." Leslie's mother replied, "But if you don't cry, you'll never get over it. I cried, but now I can be glad when I'm with Leslie and when I pick her up and cuddle her." Fatou's mother was certainly crying now: she cried her heart out during the following week. Thanks to this, we were able to establish a different kind of contact with her, and she was now able to allow the team, whom she had kept at a distance, to help her. Without the help of this other mother, would Fatou's mother have been able to show her distress? Would she have been able to ask us to help her? From then on, we were able to speak to her about her pain, and to Fatou about her brother. The following week, both women came to the parents' club at the appointed time. Fatou's mother seemed to be a little better.

One of the nurses also told us that Fatou seemed to be more lively and dynamic. The nurse went straight on to tell Fatou's mother what a good mood she had been in that week. The mother explained, "When my son died, they told me in the service that I mustn't cry in front of Fatou, otherwise there was a risk it would harm her, too. They said studies had been done that showed that babies pick it up if their parents are upset, and that it was very bad for their health. So I was terrified I'd kill my daughter if I cried." As for Leslie's mother, she said that she had had no idea how unhappy her husband had been when their son had died. "It's so hard to know with him," she said, "usually he doesn't say a word." This time, at the club, he had been able to speak.

The parents' club, as we can see, is very useful to the team. What people say to us at these meetings, so long as we agree to hear it, enables us radically to put into question the way we are all intervening, including the doctors. Of course we need an experienced team, but above all its members need to be prepared to reassess their procedures at any time, and be prepared to change for the better. It became clear that certain ways of speaking, which were intended to be helpful, would only add to the burden of guilt and distress which weighs down on the parents in such tragic circumstances as these. Superegoic injunctions are never of any help. And in any case, who were the team trying to protect by ordering this woman not to show her grief? Fatou? Or was it that the team members were having trouble dealing with their own feelings of failure occasioned by Ismaël's death? On the basis of what Leslie's mother had said at the meeting of the parents' club, we were able to take up this question at the next team meeting. The club is just as helpful for the team, because it means we can re-examine our day-to-day practice. The group processes that emerge help to mobilise new thinking for the team, and are reparative for the parents. By sharing their emotions, the parents feel they are understood, and no longer alone; they are in the company of others who are going through the same traumatic experience, with an attentive and supportive team, whose members help to contain their upset and their reactions that may appear strange to others, but not to them. Most traumatised parents say that they no longer recognise themselves; they have completely lost their bearings.

More recently, we decided to invite parents whose children had already been at home for some time, to come to the club. When they come for check-ups, we suggest they might like to come back to the unit with their baby to have a coffee with us, at the time when the club meets. These parents are very happy to do so. It is always a joyful moment when a former premature baby is brought in. The parents with babies still in hospital bombard the parents whose babies have pulled through with questions, and go into ecstasies over these children. "He's so lovely! Is it really possible that he was premature too?" They ask a lot of practical questions: What was it like when she came home? Did the baby sleep in their room? What did he eat? Did she cry a lot? And there are also a lot of less concrete questions: Was it easy for you to recover after the birth? Do you still think of your baby as a "former premature baby"? At what point did you stop being afraid? Do you feel you're a mother like any other? At the club meetings, parents ask questions they would never dare to ask otherwise. Supported by the group and contained by the team, which is now prepared and able to hear their fears and sometimes also their criticisms, they feel understood, recognised, and accepted. And even though this aim of setting up the club was not overtly therapeutic (it is not a talking group for the purpose of treating them), this time to pause and reflect has obvious therapeutic effects for the parents, and considerably changes the ways in which they invest emotionally both in their baby and in the unit itself. Maybe it is because the aim is not "therapeutic" that we can achieve these effects.

Meeting the brothers and sisters

On my way out of the service, I met a woman who had come to introduce her three-and-a-half-year-old eldest son to his little sister. For the time being, the introduction had to be made in the visitors' corridor. When Kevin pressed his nose to the glass, he saw this tiny little girl, plugged in to her monitor and bathed in the blue light of phototherapy. The mother was very upset, and said to me, "I asked him if he wanted to go in to get a better look at her, but he didn't seem interested." When I bent down towards the little boy to speak to him, he said to me, "Mummy said she'd shown me my little sister ... But it's not even true." He looked disappointed.

The mother interrupted: "Don't worry, she'll soon be coming home with us!"

"No, she won't," replied Kevin, visibly annoyed, "you can see perfectly well that she's not there!"

"Come on, you saw there was a baby in the incubator!"

"No, there wasn't anything, I saw a light and a doctor, that's all. You can see very well that they haven't finished making her yet!"

What was this little boy talking about? What was it he wanted to see? Was he referring to the lack in the little sister who was not made the same way as him?

I suggested he might tell me a bit more about it, so he explained: "There's lots of noise and lots of colours that get in your eyes, she's not allowed to see them." I thought he might be referring to the spectacles that hide the baby's eyes to protect them from the phototherapy lamps, so again I asked him to tell me more. He said, "It's the doctors that make the babies, but she's not allowed to look."

When a baby arrives and is suspended between life and death in intensive care, the whole family waits and suffers. While, fortunately, parents come in to the services more willingly than they used to, it is also the case that the siblings are now also allowed to visit the new babies. It has taken a long time to set up this opportunity for the brothers and sisters. First of all, it was feared that they would increase the risk of contagion. The contagious diseases of childhood are not welcome in NICUs. But once a protocol had been established, the doctors were reassured and happy to let the children come in. What was more complicated for them, however, was to manage, or at least understand, the reactions of the siblings and to evaluate the risks that the visit might present for them. These questions are still very much under discussion, because going in to one of these units is not straightforward for an adult, so how will a child react? What if the baby is very sick? Should we reply to their questions, or not? Will the child be overwhelmed? Traumatised, even? What thoughts will pass through the mind of a child on entering this place where life and death are so closely intertwined? And in any case, aren't these children too small to understand, or even to think about it?

Oh, but they do think! When they visit, they will ask endless questions about life and death, sexuality, and of course this is not easy for the caring staff. Similarly, their way of thinking may be quite unsettling for the scientists.

Initially, the medical team thought as follows: they would organise a meeting with the service psychologist to "prepare" the child, give him or her some information, and, if possible, pre-empt some of their questions, so that they would not be "shocked" by the encounter.

But in the end, it was the team that was "shocked" by the thoughts the children had when they came out! Their reactions are sometimes astonishing, because through all their innumerable questions, the child is asking above all how babies are made. And they are not simply looking for a "medical" or "scientific" explanation; that will not satisfy them. For these children, the idea of the birth of babies is linked with death, sexual difference, and castration. And the older siblings who come in to the service to see the new baby are all caught up in this problematic.

Our preoccupation with what children think is a relatively recent phenomenon in our culture. It is only since Freud that "we know what a child thinks", as he said in 1909. Before that, it seems, no one wanted to know. Nor did anyone want to imagine that a baby comes into the world experiencing autoerotic feelings, and that the care given by family and others may arouse excitations of pleasure and unpleasure. It was impossible to think that there was such a thing as infantile sexuality, or worse still, that sexuality could only ever be infantile, including that of adults. Public opinion was shaken to its core, and Freud's ideas were considered scandalous.

Children, faced with the enigma of the birth of babies, try to find out how they are made, try to make a link with what they feel of their own sexuality, with what their parents tell them, and what they are led to believe by their everyday experience. Everything becomes more complicated when they start to think that their parents may also have their own sexuality, and they never give up trying to get answers out of them, especially from their mother. It is mainly the mother who is asked questions by the children, and it is her replies that interest them most. What is at stake, in this attempt to discover how the mother's desire is orientated, is essential. It is partly what structures the subject.

A little girl of seven, whose mother had had several miscarriages, and who had just given birth to an extremely premature baby, asked us, "But why can't my Mummy make babies any more, since I was born? Do you think she doesn't know how to do it any more, or doesn't she want to? She won't tell me. What about you, do you know?"

How can anyone know something about the mother's desire? Of course, faced with this question, the adults whom the child asks find themselves at a loss.

Faced with the enigma of the mother's desire and the parents' sexuality, children seek answers that can satisfy them, while at the same time forbidding themselves to know anything about these matters. Knowledge always has a relation to desire. But desire inexorably escapes the subject. It is this very impossibility that may lead the child to engage in an infinite quest for more knowledge, which will take on a dimension of transgression, or on the contrary may inhibit the child to the point of no longer wishing to know anything about it. This is something we encounter every day, when a child is referred to us because of failure at school. Martine Menès emphasises this: "The relation to knowledge is supported by desire, and the desire for knowledge—the wish to learn—is only one manifestation. This connection remains and develops throughout life. It is what Freud called *libido*" (Menès, 2012, p. 14 [translated for this edition]).

The enigma that confronts the child is like the riddle of the sphinx. Giving an answer may in certain cases constitute a threat, or even a prohibition. In order for the spirit of research to be allowed to develop, it is also necessary that the Other to whom the child addresses himself allows the question of desire to be asked, even if it remains impossible to answer. In child analysis, we can see how fantasy reflects fantasy, how children create their own pathways based on elements that are their own, but also in response to what we can discern of the parents' fantasy. On this basis, children construct "theories", some of which are quite astonishing, but to which they cling.

Freud also observed that, however much they may appear to be fantastical, these theories are always founded in reality. "These false sexual theories," he writes, "all have one very curious characteristic. Although they go astray in a grotesque fashion, yet each one of them contains a fragment of real truth; and in this they are analogous to the attempts of adults, which are looked at as strokes of genius, at solving the problems of the universe which are too hard for human comprehension" (Freud, 1908c, p. 214). Here we discover the extraordinary, eccentric aspects of the poetic creations of childhood. This is how they respond to the questions life poses. They are never fully convinced by "ready-made" answers that we give them when they visit the unit. Our theories do not correspond at all with what they had imagined. If we insist, they become perplexed, distrustful, and feel that their research has ground to a halt. Their creative urge is blocked, and they lose the connections they have made in their thoughts and their particular analogies.

These days, however, we really do insist, and children do not lack explanations. When they ask questions, they are given answers; and even when they don't ask questions ... Sex education is now part of the school curriculum, as is general hygiene, such as how to brush your teeth. No more stork, no more gooseberry bushes. They know how babies are made, in scientific detail, but still our everyday clinical experience shows us that for all the strenuous efforts made by adults, children continue to fabricate their own sexual theories. The explanations given to them by adults and doctors seem to give them a feeling of disturbing strangeness.

The information about birth does not stop children from refusing the potty, around the age of two, in case a new baby comes out of their tummy, or to say that if the lady is very fat, it is certainly because she has eaten too much.

More often than not, explanations about ovules and spermatozoa leave children completely cold, as does information about the little brother in the incubator, the role of machines and monitors, and the doctor's prognosis. But what is it we are trying to convince them of in our insistence on reassuring them? Is it about wanting them to trust us and believe that our interventions are scientific?

Here again, the most useful thing would be to listen to what they have to say to us about the birth, without wanting to impose what we believe to be our own adult certainties on them at any price.

Octave Mannoni said that, where belief was concerned, it was the belief that the maternal phallus existed "anyway".

In *Clefs pour l'imaginaire*, he tells of a Hopi festival during which terrifying figures wearing horrible masks—the Katcina—come to the village to eat all the children. The mothers have to buy back their children with offerings of meat, and the Katcina, in exchange, give the children balls of Piki maize, coloured red, which are supposed to have been made by the Katcina monsters themselves. Talayesva, a little Hopi boy, told the following story: "Once when there was supposed to be a Katcina dance, I caught my mother cooking Piki. When I saw that it was red Piki, I was really upset. That evening, I couldn't eat, and when the Katcina gave out their presents, I didn't want any of their Piki. But it wasn't red Piki they gave me, it was yellow. So then I felt happy" (Mannoni, 1969, p. 29 [translated for this edition]).

Octave Mannoni explains: "The crisis of belief in the Katcina reproduced the structure of the crisis relating to the belief in the phallus. We can already recognise castration in the emotion that overwhelms the young Hopi boy." In Hopi culture, the truth is only revealed to the child much later, at the time of initiation. On that occasion, he will learn that behind the masks of the Katcina are hidden the fathers and uncles. But at the same moment he will learn the secret of the mystical truth into which he is now initiated.

Throughout childhood, it is the adults who sustain the child's belief. To what extent does the child's belief sustain that of the adults? It is certainly true that parents want to think that their child believes in Santa Claus. How often do we hear children saying that they really knew a long time ago that Santa Claus did not exist, but that they did not want to tell their parents in order not to hurt their feelings? The entire faith of the Hopi is founded on a primary mystification. The young men who become adults will not stop believing, but they will believe differently. Belief is no longer of the order of the imaginary, but becomes symbolised and accedes to the order of faith.

In that case, it means something has to be lost in order to be found again in a different way. It is a question of time, a necessary moment in time which adults need to take care not to bring on prematurely.

These days, we tend to rush everything. Children must know everything, understand everything, and behave like mini-adults. Later, however, they remain infantile, and are sometimes prevented from taking on their responsibilities. It is as if the children knew of the dangers of occupying an adult's place in childhood, so they resist and refuse their parents' explanations. They want to go on believing in their own theories.

If their time has not come, the parents' explanations about birth will have no effect, and the children will continue to work things out in their own normal way. In other cases, as clinical practice shows us, the adults' explanations will have a devastating effect, which will stop their thinking in its tracks and prevent them from discovering "the pleasures of thinking".

The scientific truth of the explanations given by parents sometimes stops children from "playing at thinking". "Don't be so childish," said one mother to her five-year-old son, "you know very well that babies aren't found under gooseberry bushes. I've told you a thousand times how you were born, you don't need to keep asking yourself all these questions. You even know that your little sister was born because the doctors kept her in a test-tube for a while, that's why she's still in an incubator at the hospital." But the little boy kept on making up his stories. Fortunately, children are usually quite robust; they resist scientific explanations and continue to dream, even though it may be more difficult in a world where test-tubes have taken the place of storks.

The myths offered nowadays by parents—as modernity obliges them to do—have themselves become scientific. That is where our faith now resides. Sometimes they are botanical, such as the little seed that helps make a baby grow.

I remember a little three-year-old girl who had a panic attack when she saw her father sowing grass seed on the lawn, believing that each seed would grow into a baby right there on the lawn.

But the new myths are also often linked to medicine. "Take her back to the doctor," is what children sometimes say when the mother comes home with a new baby.

According to some children these days, it is the doctors who make babies. This is a fantasy which has been prevalent among mothers, and is now supported by reality. François, aged four, told me: "My Mummy, when she wants a baby, she goes and asks the doctor. He puts one in her tummy, and when it's got bigger, he opens up her tummy to get it out." Sometimes this kind of story is still related to science fiction, and the baby comes out of the mother's tummy like a threatening alien.

Simon was five years old when we first met in the neonatal unit. His little twin brothers, who were extremely premature, had just been born. He already knew that his parents had had the help of doctors in making the babies. On this day, he had come to see them through the window of the service. From that moment on, he refused to leave his room, spending all his time creating "machines to make babies". He showed absolute respect for the technology: cardboard boxes, drawings on the boxes representing the monitors, electrodes made of sticking plaster stuck to the teddy-bears in the incubators, wool of all colours coming out of balls hitched up on the ceiling, representing the babies' different lines into the machines. Simon worked tirelessly, and no longer wanted to do anything else. He paid careful attention to the technical explanations his parents gave him about the incubators, and so had managed to reproduce the machine with extraordinary precision. However, this activity became an obsession; he appeared anxious and found it difficult to sleep at night, pestering his parents with endless questions. They become concerned, and asked me to speak with their son. Simon came straight out with what he was doing: he was going to be a "baby-maker" when he grew up; "That'll mean I can decide if I want to make them or not." As well as giving him prestige, this position of "maker" would also allow him to have control over the possible arrival of other babies in the family. But on the day we met, something else was worrying him. "Do you know what you need to put in the machine to make a baby?" When I asked him what he thought, he replied, "My parents says it's an egg from the mummy and a seed from the daddy that makes babies. But I know that's not true, I saw that it's the doctors who make the babies in the machine ... but no one knows what they use ..." Of course, that is the question. It is Simon's question, but it is also his parents' question, as it is for those who resuscitate the babies that are "miracles of science". How can they be there? How is it that they are now in this incubator? Is it right to continue to "make" them, to resuscitate them, when they are so extremely tiny and the risks of disability are so high?

Whose twins are these? Do they belong to the parents, or to the scientists? Out of whose desire were these babies born? Simon's question was exactly that. Faced with this question, adults themselves, whether they are parents or doctors, try to construct their own infantile sexual theories in order to protect themselves.

Children are specialists in asking the question of desire. They put adults to the test by rejecting their scientific answers. And what is more—as is the case for all children when faced with the discovery of their parents' sexuality, because their narcissism receives such a blow—they want to preserve an idealised image of the parents, who cannot possibly give themselves up to the sexual practices they describe, and at the same time preserve an idealised image of themselves, who cannot possibly have been born as a result of such practices. The most unbearable is the horror of the parents' jouissance. That is what is repressed in the primal scene. Time and again in adult analysis we witness just how impossible it is for this jouissance to be represented. Even years later, the parents' sexuality cannot be thought of. Freud had already observed this in *The Wolf Man*.

The scientific myth, just like the myth of the stork, allows us to set aside the primal scene, since now procreation can be separated from the sexual act, and at the same time to set aside the idea of nothingness. The storks will go and fish babies, which have existed for ever, out of lakes, and drop them on our doorsteps. Doctors give parents babies which they have constructed from the various parts, and they know how to put them together. As for those who come from another planet, they have existed for a long time, and there is no reason to suppose they would not be happy to swap their single ticket for a return. If the question of life can be answered in this way, then it enables us to keep the question of death at a distance, too. Botanical or biological information does not provide the answers children are looking for in their sophisticated research. So they cling on to mystery. That is where they seek for desire. It is a realm in which science fails, and no explanation, however sophisticated, can convince children, who persist in inventing their own solutions, constructing theories to cover up the Real with a screen.

Sexuality, whether infantile or adult, is impossible for the subject to represent. What is the relation these days between sexuality and procreation? And what impact does the intervention of a third party have on each? In a world of surrogate mothers, egg donation, the link between gestation and motherhood is also questionable. And what of filiation in the light of scientific progress? Certainly, the secret of origins is not revealed by technical explanations about sperm donation, pre-implantation diagnosis, or frozen embryos. The origin remains unattainable. It will have to be invented retroactively. Fantasies of origins, which are the child's response to the questions they ask themselves about the mystery of origins, are linked to infantile sexual theories. These questions lead us towards the Real, and the impossibility of the sexual relation. In order to confront this Real, and to protect ourselves from the horror it arouses in us, everyone produces their own theory, their own fiction, some finding a solution in the new scientific myths of biotechnology, thus making science into a modern "infantile sexual theory" for adults. And this is the theory that adults try to force upon children.

In the past, for their own good, children were kept away from the life of adults and all the questions about sexuality. Nowadays, still for their own good, and influenced by a fantasy of transparency, we speak to them about donor insemination and *in vitro* fertilisation, egg donation, test-tubes, all these shiny adornments of our "blingy" society. We think we are telling them the "truth" about their birth. But how can anyone actually imagine, when speaking to a child in this way, that she is telling him the truth about his history? No one knows in what circumstances any child has been brought into the world. They will have to make something of their past by inventing their own theories and myths. It is the elaboration of these myths that we hear in therapy. We can say nothing of the parents' desire, there is nothing we can affirm, even if our good intention might be to reassure or reinforce the patient's narcissism, as we hear spoken of today. It is a modern deception, upheld by, among other things, contraception and ART, to think that you can make a child how you want, when you want. Even medicine, speaking from a position of mastery, can tell children nothing of their parents' desire. It is this knowledge about origins which escapes the parents themselves, and nothing can close the gap. But specialists in childhood insist on foregrounding their own version of the truth, believing that it will be therapeutic. Sometimes they confuse scientific truth, historical truth, and the truth of an individual's history.

Each time we meet the brothers and sisters who come to the unit to visit a baby, they confront us with the same question. They have been carefully "prepared" by their parents, and often also by members of the team, so there is nothing left for these children to learn about the baby's hospitalisation—which absolutely does not mean that they will not hold on to their own ideas on the question. Their questions are not about the technical scheme of things. They are far less easily duped than grown-ups, and are not particularly impressed by scientific truths; their questions concern the history of the newborn, as well as their own, in a quite different way. It is important that we listen to these questions at this point, so that we can help them to grasp what is going on for them during this first encounter with the new baby.

These days, parents believe they can transmit everything necessary to their children on the basis of scientific knowledge. They do not understand why the child refuses to believe what they say, and is so resistant to explanations. But there is a huge discrepancy between what is said and what the child wants to hear. That is what is lacking, and is never conveyed by explanations. Desire is not of the order of what can be spoken. It is indeed something obscure: "For psychoanalysis not everything is language; at the same time, this lack in language, which is imaginarised and represented in various ways, is fundamental. If speech has a function, there is no organ that is adequate for it; this is the very meaning of castration" (Vanier, 2003 [translated for this edition]).

There is a radical lack of knowledge about sexuality. The science of medicine cannot fill this lack, and it is this which for us (analysts) touches on the Real. The subject is constituted on the basis of this lack in knowledge. That is precisely what myths attempt to capture. Is it possible that we will be able to create some sort of myth with medicine in our modern world? Will the modality of this discourse allow children to engage in the same work of research and elaboration as storks and fairy tales?

While historical truth and scientific truth are both important, it is still vital that they are spoken about without crushing this obscure navel of discourse, this impossibility around which myths are articulated. How can we speak to children and still leave open to them this field of enquiry which should be theirs, without stopping them thinking about their own history, without allowing them a place for mystery? But it is precisely this obscure point that adults want to ignore; these children's questions are just too upsetting!

Today's explanations, while comforting for adults with their faith in science, appear to fulfil the same function as the stork used to.

Is it not still a way of giving children an answer in order to stop them thinking? It is as if we were saying to them, "Take that and be quiet, accept what has been said, stop asking yourself questions, and stop asking us." Our wish to transmit the supposed truth is what risks annulling their questions.

Making children be quiet (or wanting to do so by "preparing" them for the visit) is a way of silencing the question of desire, which is precisely what is at stake in infantile sexual theories. Some children will be left deadened, or be made ill, by the impossibility of seeking and learning. It is important to recognise the incestuous basis of desire. It means that in each case, each human being has to extract something from the knowledge that is prohibited; man is confronted by his own limits, by the fundamental prohibition which structures him. In order to know nothing about it, it is necessary to stop children from speaking and to avoid hearing what they have to say to us. As far as this is concerned, we may think that the revelations and the explanations which seem indispensable to us make us adults no different from those who were Freud's contemporaries. We know what children think, as we have already said. We know it very well, but all the same, do we really want to know what children are thinking about, any more than people did before Freud?

In sessions with children who are going to visit the service, as well as after they have been, it is a question not of giving explanations, but rather of giving them time to speak about the new baby, and to listen to the questions they are asking themselves. After a visit to the service, they can talk about how they found the baby, and what they think about all that. There is always a great deal to learn from children. It is they who teach us.

We ask them if they would like to say how they had imagined the baby, would they like to draw him? How do they think about the baby and their parents, who are caught up in the anguish of this long and difficult birth? What do they think will happen when they take the baby home? Their comments always have a measure of pertinence. In some cases, they will only talk about these things in a session.

One five-year-old girl told me, as she was leaving the unit, "I thought babies were supposed to be beautiful, but this one's really ugly, that's why Mummy's crying. Now I understand, she's not sad, she's angry because Daddy won't go and buy her another one." Of course it was pointless to explain to this little girl that you cannot buy babies. Quite obviously, that was not the question she was asking. On the contrary, she had a better understanding than most in pinpointing the mother's rancour at being deprived of the father's "phallic gift"; clearly that was the question that interested her. A few days later, the mother told me: "She was very happy when she came out. She's never played with dolls before, but she was pestering her father to buy her a really beautiful one."

In some difficult cases, children will be brought to visit the baby when he is undergoing palliative care. I remember a little girl called Estelle, who was eight years old, and when she heard that her little brother was not going to survive, she insisted on being allowed to go to see him. This baby was the fourth in the family. Two other little brothers had been born between Estelle and him, and both of them had been extremely premature; both had died a few days after birth. The head of service, who was concerned about the possible effects of this visit, asked me to see her before she went in.

On the occasion of our session, she explained to me, "Two times I had little brothers, but both times they died before I got to know them, it was like I had never had them, and my parents never talk about them. I want to see this one so I can tell him he's got a big sister, I want to be sure he really exists."

Above all in this session, she asked questions about motherhood and femininity. She was a daughter from a first marriage, and her father had custody of her. She spoke of her stepmother in absolute terms: "I want her to be my real mother," she said, "it's not fair that she can't have babies. My mother is always having babies, but she says she doesn't want them. I can't understand how that's possible. But I'm not sure if I'm like my mother or my stepmother. I think I love babies ... But I don't know, I've never really seen one." The question, as always, was quite different and far more delicate that expected. In this case, to give "technical" explanations on the hospitalisation of the baby and his state of health would not have been sufficient. This child needed to be listened to differently so that she could articulate her questions, and so that some analytic work could be suggested.

All these children ask questions that go far beyond the baby and his stay in hospital. Some talk about their own birth on these occasions, wondering if it was like that for them, too. Some of them say they do not think the baby will be able to come home with them, and that they would like to meet him, to be sure that he really exists. Some speak of death, even if the baby is not receiving palliative care. For many of these children, guilt will be at the forefront, possibly echoing the way the parents are feeling, or possibly being their own guilt, because they are not entirely ignorant of the ambivalence surrounding the arrival of this new intruder into the family. Because there is always an element of "ferocity" at work, they are wondering if they might also be partly responsible for what is now happening to the baby. They ask themselves a host of questions about the parents: Why are they so sad at the moment? Is it only the baby that counts for them? The children want to know if they, the older ones, still mean something to them. "If it was me in hospital, how would my parents react?" asked Rémy. They wonder what it takes to make a baby live or die; they even question their parents' capacity to care for a baby, since he has not been taken home. A little girl of seven, who had been premature herself, asked me if, one day, she would be able to be a mother herself, or if, like her mother, she would always have babies that were "not finished".[7]

Bearing in mind the common danger of repetition, and the efficacy of "sorcery", both of which are at work in these histories, we can well imagine that these meetings with the brothers and sisters allow us to do some work that is of the order of prevention. By listening to them and allowing them to speak, without imposing a "right way" of thinking that attempts to be positive, rational, and reassuring, we can help them to construct their own theories and face the Real of this birth, enabling them to symbolise it.

Preparing to take the baby home

When the baby is discharged from hospital, the parents' anxiety becomes apparent. The mother is often worried that she will not be able to manage looking after her baby on her own. Each discharge needs to be prepared for in its own way. The approach may vary considerably from case to case, and the style may change from one baby to the next. We have to think about each baby's history "blow by blow", because each family has its own singularity. No baby will react quite like another to an admission to a NICU, and each parent (depending on the individual's history) will have a new way of experiencing this painful time. That is why particular attention is given to the preparation for discharge. Some women seem to be panic-stricken at the point when it is time for the baby to go home. "How am I going to manage?" they will often say. "I won't have the monitors any more, so I won't be able to know if he's all right. He's still so fragile. I won't know what to do without you."

In this case, we felt it was important to take time to prepare for the discharge, taking time to give the mother back her confidence, particularly in her capacity to be "good" for her baby. It is the neonatal nurses who are most active around such mothers, who surround them at bath times, nappy changes, and interactions with the baby. If the discharge is not sufficiently well prepared for, the bond which has been established between the mothers and the team is sometimes hard to loosen. The nurses have also been replacement mothers to those women who are afraid to find themselves brutally alone again.

At the point of discharge, if the parents request it, contacts are made with outpatient departments between our team and theirs. In France, mothers and babies are seen in the *Centre de protection maternelle et infantile* (PMI); in the *Unité acceuil mères-enfants* (UAME), an outpatient perinatal psychiatric service, which is part of the District Service of Paediatric psychiatry; or in the *Centre médico-psychologique* (CMP), an outpatient therapy centre. Thanks to the local network organised by Seine-Saint-Denis-West, notably by Dr. Rotten and Dr. Decroix, contacts are facilitated, and the families are better followed up after discharge. Once a week, a nursery nurse from the PMI comes to the unit to meet the mothers and to offer them a home visit a few days after they take the baby home with them, and before their appointment at the PMI.

In the service, an experimental "accompanied discharge" has been tried out, where the baby and the family are seen at home by one of our nursery nurses. Nearly all families request this service; and the visits can be repeated if they wish. In fact, many of them do so, because they feel reassured by the presence of a nurse who already knows their baby, and who can speak with them about everyday matters, feeding, or possible health problems. Often she will be asked questions about the baby's psychological development. She pays close attention to all the difficulties the parents might encounter with the child. This "home nursery nurse" also takes part in team meetings at the unit, and works in close collaboration with the other nurses, the psychomotor therapist, and myself.

Prior to discharge, we have a room available where the mother can stay in hospital with her baby for a few days.

The mother-and-baby room

During the last days in hospital, the mothers can, if they wish, stay full-time with their baby in the same sort of conditions they would have been in if they had been in the maternity unit, if the baby had been born at term, without machines, without the permanent presence of a nursery nurse, but being able to call on us at any moment. The fathers can also spend the whole day with the mother and baby, just as they can in the maternity unit. The mothers talk of this phase as a "rebirth", a privileged moment when they feel they are emerging from a nightmare. "My baby is alive. I'm here with him and it's me who is looking after him. I never thought, two months ago, that it would be possible one day," said Mattéo's mother. This period in hospital, according to the mothers, puts them into a setting where they can have a sense of a normal delivery.

The consultation

For some time now, I have offered neonatal consultations to children born prematurely who were treated in our service; it is usually the parents who make the request. Sometimes, however, it is the doctors who suggest making an appointment, when the parents bring the child for a check-up and complain of psychological difficulties. This possibility of having an appointment "retroactively" is a rich learning experience, because it allows us, with hindsight, to realise what was going on for the parents and for the baby at the time of the hospitalisation. If there is a demand for psychoanalytic treatment, I refer the parents to paediatric psychology liaison, or to the *centre medico-psycho-pédagogique* (CMPP), an outpatient therapy centre for children.

Thanks to these consultations, we can now come closer to working with what happens to those children who were born prematurely.

We are still developing this aspect of our service, but we can already say that being a "former premature baby" is never straightforward. Although after a certain age, the doctors no longer speak in terms of "age-adjustment", the parents do not find it so easy to forget this "correction". It is as if their child, even at the age of ten or twelve years, were still in danger, still just as fragile, still giving cause for concern. For them, the "former" remains real and present.

Notes

1. A superb illustration of this was the production of *Médée* by M. -A. Charpentier, directed by P. Audi, at the Champs-Élysees Theatre in 2012.
2. This is a technical term [in French], which indicates that the baby is hooked up to machines; it should be expunged from medical vocabulary as soon as possible!
3. One woman said to me in a session, "My mother, my daughter and me, we're all alike, we're exactly the same as each other, like those Russian dolls." But when the Russian dolls are all put together, they demonstrate the perpetual state of pregnancy in which these women find themselves stuck. There is only one who can enclose all the others. How can we deal with this in analytic treatment?
4. This paragraph contains passages previously published in an article in Vanier, C., 2010, p. 37.
5. These days it is presented by E. Tronick, and can be seen on the internet, as can many other experiments cited in this book.
6. The governmental research department MIRE (Mission, Recherche Expérimentation) was created by the French Ministry of Health in 1982 to set up and support research projects in the domain of health, solidarity, and social protection.
7. We frequently find out, when speaking with parents in the service, that there have been other premature births in the sibling group.

CHAPTER THREE

Babies who "walk the tightrope"

Babies made by science

Ève was still a very small patient, just a little "egg", when she became the "object" of a biologist who specialised in procreation using IVF. "The biologist involved in procreation," says Jacques Testart, "does not have a passion for babies. His object is the egg, and even if he gets to know a particular one, he is hardly going to fall in love with any one of these rudimentary beings, without colour or flavour." Several months later, when Ève was born prematurely, the NICU team were looking after her. Ten years earlier, the delivery would have been classified as a stillbirth. Now she was in intensive care, looked after by doctors who, with the back-up of sophisticated machinery and up-to-the-minute technology, were struggling to keep her alive.

While parents dream of a marvellous baby, biologists dream of "beautiful, regular embryos which over time increase the number of their blastomeres." Neonatal teams dream of a good PCO2,[1] or of managing to avoid or cure hyaline membrane disease[2] or enterocolitis.[3] For their part, the new breed of psychologists, these other scientists of the new world, dream of good "adaptation" between the mother and baby, of a bond that can be sustained, of successful "attunement". The "cure" can be measured, filmed, and scientifically validated.

Psychoanalysts are less prone to have dreams of this type. They prefer to interpret them. However, psychoanalysts are no strangers to the modern world, because it would be impossible for them to work, as Lacan reminds us in "The function and field of speech and language in psychoanalysis", without knowing what is going on in the world in which the subject who comes to analysis is developing. "Let whoever cannot meet at its horizon the subjectivity of his time give [the practice of psychoanalysis] up then. For how could he who knows nothing of the dialectic that engages him in a symbolic movement with so many lives possibly make his being the axis of those lives? Let him be well acquainted with the whorl into which his era draws him in the ongoing enterprise of Babel, and let him be aware of his function as an interpreter in the strife of languages" (Lacan, 2005, p. 264).

How should we understand our role of interpreter in today's world?

The mother, who arrived in the service just as the doctors were gathered around Ève's incubator, was able to say only one thing, shyly backing into a corner of the ward: "Just pretend I'm not here." It is true that from the very beginning of this story, that is precisely what everyone had done. The baby, who had been conceived outside her body, had continued to grow without her, outside her body. All that was asked of her was that she should not disturb the doctors at their work. "When I come into the unit, and someone asks me, 'Are you Ève's mum?', I'm completely thrown for a moment, I never know what to say." This sense of being thrown came up again when the mother was encouraged to speak about her daughter. She knew nothing about the baby. It was a sort of reverse delivery, in which the mother was the baby and the baby, the mother. It seemed that there was a disturbance of filiation. "I've got nothing to say about her, nothing at all," was this mother's refrain. How indeed could a mother suppose a subject in this baby and turn her attention in the baby's direction, when the child had been almost entirely the object of science? As we recall, Winnicott said that a baby does not exist. Lacan emphasised that: "Communication as such is not what is primordial, because at the origin, [the baby] has got nothing to communicate for the reason that all the instruments of communication lie on the other side, in the field of the Other, and it is from the Other that [the baby] stands to receive them" (Lacan, 2014a, p. 272).

The subject is in the Other. We have already seen how the entire team in our service works on the basis of a "supposition of the subject" so that the child is not just the object of medical attention. By making the human egg a "desired object", or a newborn baby the "object of care", scientists set aside the question of the subject, while at the same time pushing further and further the limits of the means at their disposal to satisfy those whom they now call "service users".

It is with this new set of circumstances that psychoanalysts now have to work and certainly, unless we are to become completely obsolete, we have to consider how we can adapt our tools. We have to be creative, and not lament the passing of the good old days. And anyway, were they really all that good?

Doctors are now also asking themselves questions. They realise more and more that unusual methods of conception are catalysts for fantasies, and they see, if in a rather confused way, that there are risks which go beyond the medical ones. Statistics show that very often, children who have been saved by medicine suffer from illnesses which the doctors cannot cure. In spite of technological refinements, scientific progress, computers, statistics, and all our current knowledge, fantasy can still block the path to recovery. For example, when it is a question of curing infertility by all possible means, what is actually being cured? What will the consequences be?

The media get hold of the most sensational cases, and sometimes distort the truth of them. Thus, for example, we learn of a mother who was surrogate for her daughter and son-in-law; of a grandfather who donated sperm to inseminate his daughter-in-law; of a grandmother who chose a surrogate mother to give her the child of her son who had been dead for years. Or a sixty-two-year-old woman who made a baby with her brother, deceiving the American doctors about the identity of the latter, so that the baby "wouldn't go out of the family". When "service users" read these articles, it sets off their imagination. In France, however, assisted births are subject to very strict regulation, and "all forms of manipulation aimed at transgressing the prohibition of consanguinity" are forbidden, as Élisabeth Roudinesco (2002) reminds us. While such practices are enshrined in law, they have become the substrate for fantasies, because they give the illusion that everything is possible, feeding an Imaginary register in which doctors are invested with omnipotence. Again, this is not intended as an attack on the advances in science and technology we all benefit from; but all progress has its drawbacks, and this considerable mutation in civilisation is destroying meaning. What is at stake now is to maintain a structure that puts into question the place of the subject, in order to resist and challenge other arrangements which purport to give meaning, but which are not without their dangers. That is why the place of the psychoanalyst in medicine is so important.

Babies, as we have seen, do not always respond in the same way to the same type of intervention. It is precisely this impossibility of gene-ralisation that gives rise to subjectivity. As Lacan said, "Our science is transmitted only by articulating what is particular in the situation" (Lacan, 2005, p. 528). What discourse is animating this individual baby's body, which will react differently to a particular treatment? The work of the psychoanalyst is to recognise the power of the signifier in and on the body, the impact of speech, and to grasp its implications. In order to have some chance of transmitting this principle, it seems to me that an analyst should introduce into medicine the notion of the "not-all", which makes generalisation impossible. If analysts want to introduce the logic of the "not-all", then there is no comfortable way of taking up a position of mastery which, in fantasy, would guarantee their power, and would be nothing more than a mirror image of the position of the doctors. "Mirrors," said Cocteau, "would do well to reflect a little before they show us our images." It is not a question of opposing one form of absolute knowledge to another. A wish to impose the "psychoanalytic whole" in a medical service is never anything but a resistance to psy-choanalysis itself. The Real eludes us. Death is always present: it is not just part of life elsewhere, it is the basis of life itself. We have to accept the limits of the Real, but also those of the signifier. "This baby," said one doctor, "will survive if she was born under a lucky star." Analysts have no more power over what the stars presage than doctors do. An analyst may, however, just about manage to spot the good or bad fairy leaning over the cradle. It is only by giving up the position of mastery that a dialogue can begin between medicine and psychoanalysis, and the only shared ground will be what remains impossible to explain. A psychoanalyst in a medical service will need to listen with a different ear to what is going on for any given subject, whether patient or doctor. This type of listening will allow the cards to be dealt anew, and may sometimes enable doctors to think differently about how they act.

Medically assisted procreation raises the question of desire, of course, and that of filiation. But it is a desire that does not speak of desire. It is treated as if it were something deliberate; you want a coveted object, an object you do not have. The child is prescribed by the doctors to cure a sick desire. But how can unconscious desire be understood, when a child has been "demanded" by doctors or parents, and ultimately produced in a way that can almost be described as industrial? This cold desire which is spoken of in this context makes us think of the coldness of the stainless steel work surfaces in the laboratory where babies are made, to frozen embryos, as well as new infantile sexual theories created by children, of course, but also by scientists who only ask to be allowed to believe in them.

Where do babies come from these days, and where do parents come from? That question has come to mean something different in the last few years. In our time, when sexuality and procreation can be dissociated from one another, the new technologies present the problem of the family in a different light. We need a new definition of family. Nowadays, a child can have two fathers or two mothers. It is even possible to have three mothers; for example, one who donates the egg, one who bears the child, and one who brings the child up. There may even be a fourth if the family is reconfigured, and another mother looks after the child. There may also be several fathers. Rather than taking a rigid, moralising stance, we need to think differently about what a family is. What is a mother, what is a father? Far beyond biological inheritance, which does not give us an adequate answer, we need to put the question differently. As Paola Mieli (1999) points out, even more than in the past, children nowadays have to construct themselves within a "web of desires", a network, a fabric woven of different desires. What about the desire of the woman who donates the egg, or the one who bears the child, or the one who brings him up? Their reasons are not always either economic or altruistic, and whatever they may say, we know that their explanations are never sufficient.

One woman explained how she had come to agree to be the surrogate mother of her daughter's triplets. She had become pregnant by her son-in-law in order to do this. But honour was saved, because obviously she had not made love with him. But had she made babies with her daughter? Or had the daughter given babies to her mother? This remains a mystery. The fact remains that they will have to explain to the children that their grandmother carried them in her tummy, that daddy gave the little seed, and that they came out of the same tummy as mummy did. According to the doctors, the grandmother's tummy was the perfect solution, because you could not find a uterus any closer to being the mother's itself!

In September 2012 in Stockholm, a medical team carried out uterus transplants. Two patients each received their own mother's uterus. According to the journal article, the choice was determined for the doctors because of the "theoretical advantage" of a graft taken from a parent.[4] Professor Mats Bränneströme, who oversaw the operations, explained that the grafted uteruses "had proved that they functioned, that they were capable of carrying a child". But what about the effects on the recipients of these transplants of having to carry a child in their own mother's womb? Nobody asked the question, probably because this new advance in science was simply so fascinating.

The passion for having the same thing, the similar thing, the lack of differentiation, is what calls the shots. Everything is the same. It seems we even want to get round the difference between the sexes, the very presence of alterity. This leads to a confusion of generations, a misunderstanding about desire, and a threat of incest. Never mind; if sexuality can be set aside, everything will be fine. Well, more or less …

Goethe showed how it is possible to destroy as well as to create when Faust created a strange being in his laboratory from all sorts of bits and pieces. The creature was made in a glass vessel. One morning, the creature turned to Wagner, Faust's assistant, called him over and said to him, "Come, come, press me tenderly to your heart, but not too hard. Be careful. Not too hard, be careful not to break the glass." Maybe we should take this as a warning not to go too far.

But science continues to make advances. There is no going back. We must not forget that sometimes the tiniest babies are resuscitated without suffering disability, and that following the most complicated assisted medical conceptions, there are babies who turn out to be fine. What makes the difference between the success and failure of any given case? For psychoanalysts, the difference is located in the field of desire, which needs to be watched over but not ousted, and in the field of speech, which needs to be listened to. This applies both to the parents and to the children, who are the ones who bring us back into line: "Watch out, don't break the glass!" We need to keep their point of view in mind. It is the lost object, according to Freud, which constitutes desire and which supports the fantasy. Freud said: "In cases where the wish-fulfilment is unrecognizable, where it has been disguised, there must have existed some inclination to put up a defence against the wish; and owing to this defence the wish was unable to express itself except in a distorted shape" (Freud, 1900a, p. 140). Everything leads us to believe that it is through attempting to spot this distortion of desire that we may be able to avoid bringing deformed human beings into the world—deformed, but in a different way: broken, because there was a desire to make them too well, and in the process they were crushed by our haste and our clumsiness.

The place of the child in our society

In our time, the world of childhood seems to both disturb and fascinate adults. Children certainly have a very particular place for us. They are desired, expected, valued; they have become more and more precious. For parents, their child is not just a person, as we like to think nowadays. No, a child is also a fantasy, an object of jouissance, a mirror in a world which is becoming ever more narcissistic. A child can be a "must-have" in order for the parents to succeed in life, a supreme object in our consumer society. We may think, as Alain Vanier does, that the child seems to be the last refuge of the "messianic promise", in a world in which adults no longer expect anything good to happen.

While there are now such things as the "rights of the child", the "right to have a child" seems to be very present in the adult camp. It is true that advances in science, contraception, and medically assisted conception have certainly changed the deal and put the child in a different place. In some countries, you can even buy one of these precious things from a sperm bank, or even have it borne by another woman. In our world of "bling", there are even catalogues you can choose a baby from. And of course, it is a condition that the baby will be delivered on time and in perfect condition; it has to be "satisfactory". However the family is configured, be it a "traditional" one, or a single parent, or a homosexual couple, families most often put the child at the centre of their lives. In earlier times, having children was almost a secondary consideration, the logical consequence of the life of a couple, an inevitable consequence that some would rather have avoided. I recall one woman from that era who told me, "As far as children go, I'd rather start a hundred than bring a single one into the world!"

These days, in this incredible era when it is possible to separate sexuality and procreation, it is sometimes the "bringing into the world", the "having", that becomes the most important thing. It is true that we often observe that the child makes the couple, rather than the other way round. While Françoise Dolto kept repeating that a child should be kept at the periphery of a couple, today he is at the centre of the couple, and is often the only reason for there to be a couple in the first place. Everything revolves around him, and he partakes of this "right to happiness" that is so much trumpeted nowadays. The family circle has become the place where the child is literally surrounded, and the happiness of the parents is sometimes transformed into a nightmare when the child does everything in his power to prevent the parents from taking advantage of him.

It is understandable, then, that the premature arrival of a baby would be a source of great anguish for the parents, delivering an insurmountable narcissistic blow. This minuscule baby, who has even more of the status of "His Majesty" than ever before, dramatically invalidates the parents. Caught between a fantasy of omnipotence and the incredibly powerful image that research has given of the prowess of the modern baby, they can only be terribly disappointed by this birth, which they experience as a disaster. Can this sick baby ever live up to their expectations?

The behavioural abilities of newborns

Many studies have been carried out over many years on the behavioural abilities of newborns. While this is a field of research that differs from our own, it seems impossible to me that any psychoanalyst working with babies would not be interested in this work, and want to become familiar with it.

Newborns look at the faces that peer into the cradle, already recognise the smell of their mother, can distinguish her voice, react to being touched and to the presence of those around them. The baby's sensory receptors and paths of conductivity are formed very early on (in the seventh week of gestation), and then the various systems—smell, taste, hearing, and sight—come into being. In the course of the sixth month of gestation, they all become operational. The growth of neurones is at its peak at the end of pregnancy. At the moment of birth, the synapses between the neurones increase dramatically.

Nowadays the newborn baby is looked upon by scientists as some kind of high-performance computer, capable of making infinite numbers of connections and links. After birth, these synaptic connections organise themselves, and the death of the neurones begins (de Boysson-Bardies, 2001).

The organisation of the human brain depends on the use the baby makes of his experiences, in conjunction with whatever the outside world contributes to the process.

A child's genetic potential, which is present at birth, will be "fashioned" by what the baby lives through, and by the responses received from the entourage from the moment of birth.

The recent discoveries of researchers have surprised the scientific community, and yet long before this, before these experiments, observations, and collections of data, babies were already considered to have immense, and sometimes disconcerting, knowledge at their disposal. An angel was supposed to lean over babies at birth, sealing their lips with one finger, a way of telling them to remain silent, and leaving the mark of the philtrum, which they would keep for the rest of their lives.

In some African tribes designated as "primitive", newborns are still considered venerable, containing the soul of an ancestor and, therefore, an infinite knowledge. In the Western world, with the birth of the natural sciences, babies were relegated to the rank of "empty vessel". Babies had everything to learn; they were deaf, blind, incapable of recognising anything, of making correlations, incapable of the slightest discrimination. English empiricism, more particularly, promulgated an image of the newborn child as being utterly incompetent.

However, from around 1980, scientists decided to study newborns in depth; many experiments were carried out.

From then on, a baby became a super-mechanism with a brain that was, if anything, more complex and better developed than those of the scientists given the job of studying it! It was shown that babies are neither blind nor deaf. Indeed, although they are myopic and somewhat astigmatic, they can see clearly if objects are shown at a distance of twenty to thirty centimetres. A baby's close-up vision at birth is as good as an adult's (Adams, 1987).

Experiments were also carried out on premature babies born at thirty-four and thirty-seven weeks. Whether a baby is premature or not, close-up vision is excellent. It is interesting to note that none of these experiments points out that the babies' ability to accommodate visually allows them to see the mother's face clearly when they are breastfeeding or being bottle-fed, if they are held in the crook of the mother's arm. The distance between the baby's face and the mother's is just right for them to be able to look at her without any problem.

As babies grow, the myopia diminishes, and at around one year, because the fovea (the central area of the retina) has matured, they will have the same quality of vision as an adult.

Thus it is always the case that the mother's face can be seen from birth. After forty-eight hours of life, babies placed at 30 centimetres from a wall in which there are two windows, will stare at the one where the mother's face appears, even if the face of another woman with the same colour hair, same hairstyle, and same shaped face appears at the other window. Of course, perfume is sprayed on the wall so that the babies cannot recognise their mother's smell. The two women are required to remain silent and maintain the most neutral and fixed expression possible. So after a few feeds, babies are already "marked" by their mother's face (Field, Cohen, Garcia, & Greenberg, 1984). Even before birth it is certain that babies are already marked; but in this case, in some innate, "genetic" way without any connection to experience, the human face makes its mark. Just after birth, babies (who, according to protocol, have been prevented from seeing any faces on the labour ward) spontaneously turn towards pictures of human faces (which are shown at a distance of thirty centimetres). They do not show any interest in misshapen faces or drawings showing a blank oval. It seems babies are predestined to recognise the image of their fellow creatures (Goren, Sarty, & Wu, 1975). They are born human. This recognition is innate, just as is the bodily schema that, according to Jacques Mehler, is not just the fruit of experience. "Newborns do not need to learn what the human face is; on the contrary, everything happens as if they already knew in advance; they seem to be born with a schema which corresponds to the prototype of their fellow creatures" (Mehler & Dupoux, 1995, p. 153 [translated for this edition]). Other experiments have shown that this applies to the human body as well as the face.

"At birth, human beings already have a schema of the body, which allows not only the control of their own body, but also the recognition of their fellow creatures. The representation they make for themselves is at least partly innate. Therefore it is not necessary for us to assimilate the form of the face and body of our fellow creatures through a kind of learning. Our inheritance has programmed us in advance" (ibid, p. 156). Françoise Dolto (1984) also presupposed the "innateness" of the bodily schema, but spoke of it in terms of the unconscious image of the body as being a symbolic incarnation of the desiring subject, and she showed that one can be aware of the existence of one's hands without being able to use them. One can also be convinced that one has two feet and still put them both into the same shoe. There is a difference between "genetic" knowledge of the existence of the body, and the body we represent to ourselves and that we inhabit as desiring beings. This body is an eroticised body which will develop meaning in relation to the other. Without this dimension of desire, all its genetic potential will suffer from arrested development.

Where hearing is concerned, babies are also highly developed; they can pick up auditory information and organise it in much the same way as an adult (Werner & Bargones, 1993). They can hear even before birth, from the sixth month of gestation—the mother's voice, the father's voice, and intra- and extra-uterine sounds (Granier-Deferre, 1994).

From the moment of birth, the technique of "non-nutritive sucking", thanks to a bottle connected to a computer, enables us to observe just how much attention the newborn gives to the external world. The rhythm and power of sucking give the researcher an indication of the level of interest aroused in the baby by various stimuli. We also know that babies can not only recognise differences in sounds and intonation, but that they can also request, by changing the rhythm of sucking, one stimulus rather than another. What a little "zapper", changing channels all the time! Babies can keep watching their favourite programmes: for example, the poem the mother recited during the last months of pregnancy, even if it is another woman reciting the same poem. Do they understand the words? The meaning of the words? Or is it just the rhythm they recognise, or the intonation? The question of meaning still remains an enigma, and has not been scientifically proven.

With regard to the sense of smell, we know that human newborns react to a wide variety of olfactory stimuli. One-day-old babies recognise a smell. If it has been around their cradle since birth, they will turn towards this familiar smell in the days that follow and fall peacefully asleep (Balogh & Porter, 1986).

Two-day-old newborns will choose the smell of their mother's amniotic fluid, based on information acquired *in utero* (Schaal, 1995).

At the age of three or four days, a baby will systematically turn towards the scarf his mother has been wearing rather than that of another woman. The sense of smell is very important for babies, and we still do not know the full extent of what comes into play in this subtle exchange of smells given off by the mother's and the baby's bodies.

Babies also recognise differences in taste. "When infants only a few weeks old are given either a spoonful of sweet liquid or a spoonful of bitter liquid, they react with gestures that are already quite typical: they part their lips and perform little rhythmic lickings in the case of the sweet liquid, and they close their mouths, pull down the corners, and blink their eyes in the case of the bitter liquid" (de Boysson-Bardies, 2001, p. 73).

Regarding the sense of touch, tactile sensitivity is already present during the foetal stage. Proprioception is possible from the moment of birth, and gives babies the means to recognise their environment before the maturation of central or peripheral receptors. Response to stimulation can be observed from the very earliest weeks of foetal life (Humphrey, 1964). All the cutaneous receptors are present. Tactile sensitivity is present in newborn babies: they will respond, according to some researchers, to questions they are asked about the texture or shape (rectangle, square, triangle) of an object if it is placed in their hands. Babies will recognise (using the non-nutritive sucking method) an object that is presented visually if the sense of touch (a teat that is smooth or rough) is associated with the visual presentation. So there we have it—nowadays, babies have become clever again, and able to feel emotions, thanks to scientific research.

But babies' abilities go beyond the realm of cognition. They also have abilities in the domain of emotions and feelings, according to Colwin Trevarthen, who wrote at the conclusion of his numerous experiments in the delivery room: "A newborn may imitate expressions of an adult's motives and emotions within minutes of birth. [...] A happy baby enjoys 'showing off' how clever he or she is, and receiving due praise from the sympathy of the adult's response. [...] The pleasure we feel in being successful in what we do, and the shame or sadness we feel if we fail to come up to other's expectations have their origins in the motives of very young children to understand the world in the company of the people they know best" (Trevarthen, 2004, p. 4, 8). This goes far beyond abilities in the "cognitive" domain. However premature babies are, they can very quickly enter into communication with the world around them, as long as it is peopled by those who try to decode what the babies are trying to say.

Nora

Nora weighed in at 820 grams, and was born at twenty-seven weeks; the hours following her admission to the service were particularly fraught with anxiety and demanded a great deal of attention. This minuscule baby mobilised the team and, as is always the case with babies born so prematurely, the prognosis had to be reconsidered hour by hour. Would she live? Would her brain survive the brutal change of environment? Would she ever be able to breathe on her own?

The mother told me later than one of the midwives had said at the moment when the baby was delivered, "Don't hold out any hope, she's too small, she's definitely going to die." And yet, in spite of her apparent fragility, Nora battled against death with astounding vigour.

One day, I told Françoise Dolto of my amazement when I am confronted with these babies who already seem to have a different way of coming into the world and who, even though they are suffering from the same sorts of difficulties, may either let themselves die or will fight from the moment of birth with the most astonishing life-force. She replied, "This force comes to them well before birth, from the beginning of pregnancy; maybe it's the force of the parents' desire at the moment of conception; in any case, the desire to live or die is always linked to the subject's history, possibly going back several generations." Nora's mother and father were deeply impressed when they first visited her. However could such a tiny baby survive? "We'd better not get too attached to her just yet, it would be too hard for us if she didn't survive." And after this first visit, they did not return at visiting time for several weeks.

When Nora's mother came to see me, she told me how worried she had been. This baby frightened her. She was already the mother of a little boy who had also been extremely premature, but on top of that, he suffered from DiGeorge syndrome[5] and club feet, which meant he spent a great deal of time in hospital or rehabilitation. The mother told me of the difficulties she was having with her son, and how she did not want to find herself having similar problems with her daughter. We tried in vain to explain to her that Nora was not suffering from any illness other than extreme prematurity; the mother, exhausted by the difficulties she was encountering, could only keep saying that she hoped Nora would die as soon as possible.

Of course, the information given by doctors is always as close to the truth as possible, but parents only understand what they are capable of understanding. The parents reinterpret the doctors' words through the distorting prisms of fantasy and beliefs. This is the version that analysts allow them to speak about in their sessions. It is also for the teams, in their own way, to fulfil the role of mediator between parents and children.

Nora's mother obviously did not want to relive with her daughter what she had been through with her son. But, as she asked me during one of her sessions, what can you do when you are cursed?

Before she herself was born, her mother had given birth to a disabled boy and to a little girl who died a few weeks after birth. She was the third baby, viable and in good health. But in an identification with her own mother, she had convinced herself that history was bound to repeat itself. It was her particular way of being a mother. "In our family, you have to pay with your first two children, and after that, it's OK," she said. Where did this belief come from? What was it based on? She herself had no idea. At this point, the team was still having to manage with the absence of Nora's mother after several weeks.

The baby, who was now suffering from bronchodysplasia,[6] had to remain in the service for eight months. She continued to be intubated and ventilated, and could not manage without her machine.

Nora rapidly started to pose problems other than mere medical ones. She soon became very demanding with the nurses, insisting on their presence but then pushing them away when they came to speak to her.

Indeed, following a period of great passivity during her first month in hospital, Nora made the team feel that she was furious, that she was rebelling against something. "She's moody, she's bossy," said one of the junior doctors one day, "we mustn't let her get away with it."

Babies' "moods"

The moodiness of these newborn babies is never moodiness in the sense that adults understand it. If such tiny babies have no way of letting others know that something is wrong, the only solution is to cry. If no one appears to understand, then they will cry louder and louder; and if no one tries to respond to them by saying something, the crying will turn to panic.

This was what was happening to Nora, and the time I spent around her enabled me to understand better what her "moods" were about. In the absence of her parents, we have seen that the team gave a little more attention than usual to this child. Nora, who had attracted the particular attention of the whole unit during the first month of her life, because she was in such a serious state, and because she was all alone, seemed to have decided that nobody was going to be allowed to forget that she was there. When she was about three months old, she started to show the most terrible anger; she would struggle and wriggle, trying to pull out the various lines that connected her to the machines, and when all else failed, would begin to choke. Because she was suffering from bronchopulmonary dysplasia, she would be overcome by terrifying spasms. She would turn blue and stop breathing. All the alarms would go off, and the team would rush to her cradle. It was not long before the nurses began to dread these spectacular spasms. "This time, I really thought she was going to die in my arms," each nurse would say in turn. Nora was ensuring that a terrible threat hung over those who were caring for her. At each intervention, every time her lungs were aspirated, there was a high risk of the child's state becoming even more serious.

One day, a nurse told me that every time there was a new admission to the service, in other words, each time the team was mobilised, preparing for an emergency, Nora would set off her alarms. "She senses that we're busy somewhere else, so she calls us back to her," she said.

In just a few months, this minuscule, fragile little girl had succeeded in making an impression as quite a character in the service! It took a number of liaison meetings to enable this baby to be thought about in a different way by those who were looking after her. Each time I walked through the unit, I would talk to Nora about the disorder she was throwing us all into, and I kept on telling her how worried her parents were about her, and how her mother was terrified that her history was repeating itself. I would stay close to her cot, with my hand on her back or on her tummy, and I spoke to her about her rage, about the machines she didn't want any more to do with, but that she needed to put up with for a little longer so that she would be able to find out how to breathe all on her own, to play, and eventually to move around. Her eyes never left mine, and I kept talking of the difficult things she was going through, how strong she had been since she was born, and how she was showing us what we thought was an amazing desire to live. And if her anger was going to help her to live, well, then, we would accept her anger, too.

Little by little, the team grew to accept her particular way of expressing herself. Rather than reassuring Nora, and telling her "everything's fine", the staff changed the way they spoke to her, to the point of showing their approval: "You're right to be angry, we haven't got much time to give you, and your life isn't very pleasant."

Gradually Nora's tantrums and spasms became less frequent. The nurses decided to put on some music in her room, the doctors allowed a few toys to be placed around her cot, and Nora's life was to some extent humanised.

There is no doubt that the difference was made by the team finding a way of engaging with her other than simply reassuring her. It is not sufficient merely to speak to children—it is important to tell them the truth about the reality of the suffering and abandonment they are experiencing. It is not always easy for the staff to speak these words, but they are far more effective than sweet words of consolation, which may, instead of appeasing a child, increase the level of anger at not being listened to.

But Nora had been in such grave danger, the threat of her dying had weighed so heavily on the team, that even now they still could not bear to hear her crying "for no reason", as they put it, and began to bear her a grudge for all the terrifying times they had been through with her.

Babies and language

Babies are "spoken" before they learn to speak. Even before they can speak, they live in a "bath of language". They are spoken of before, during, and after they are born. Later they will acquire language through a process which seems to be genetically programmed. But they will not be able to speak unless they understand how to speak. It is easy to observe how interested babies are in speech. When they are spoken to, even when they are only a few hours old, they are alert and attentive, and very often they open their mouths wide as if to swallow the voice that is above them: "he drinks in our words like mother's milk", as the expression goes. It is certain that all babies, even the most premature ones, are thirsty for words. They are predisposed to deal with sounds. All at once, they will know how to differentiate ambient noises from words which carry meaning. Nowadays the "innate knowledge" that children have of speech can be demonstrated experimentally.

When babies are only a few hours old, they can recognise and show preference for their own mother's voice, which they will have heard *in utero*, over those of other women (Casper & Fifer, 1980, p. 1174, 1176). Babies can pick out their own language, and will lose the capacity to learn other languages over time. They are capable of amazement and curiosity about all the phenomena they encounter in the first few days of life. They are particularly interested in different voices, tonality, indeed everything which, in communication with the other, constitutes a call or sign. Catherine Dolto (2001 [translated for this edition]) reminds us of the importance the parents' voices have even *in utero*: "The inflections of this voice (the mother's) count for the baby. The father's voice, and those of the future brothers and sisters, are also very important ... Thanks to the father's voice, which moves away and then gets closer again, which comes from all directions, the child develops a sense of space beyond the maternal bosom. If the father speaks often to the child, and the mother enjoys that, the child will always move towards the side where this familiar and pleasant voice is when the father speaks, even if he is not addressing the child directly." She speaks of foetuses as perpetually seeking communication; they are, she says, "joyfully expectant, always on the look-out for the presence of the other" (Dolto, 1995, (translated for this edition]).

Marie-Claire Busnel (1993) also showed, through her rigorous experiments, how sensitive babies are, even during the foetal stage, to the voice and to the affects imparted by language. M. Masakowski, in his medical thesis at the University of New York in 1996, demonstrated that children are sensitive to affects. At two days old, the children's reactions were recorded and it was observed that they were different depending on whether the mother spoke to them in a sad, happy, or angry way. On the other hand, babies do not react if they are played the same words spoken by the mother through a tape recorder, in reverse. The researchers wondered: do babies understand the meaning of words? Or is it the way in which they are spoken? Myriam Szejer emphasised: "Babies not only react much more to a familiar story or piece of music than to those they do not know; they also show to an even greater extent that what is being spoken has an emotional content for them or for the mother" (Szejer, 1997 [translated for this edition]).

Twenty years earlier, Françoise Dolto had already tried to get us to understand how sensitive babies are to what is said to them, and how reactive they are to their mothers' different emotional states. We listened, but did we really understand?

"Motherese"

Babies do not speak, but the adults who surround them lean over their cradles. The mothers, the grandmothers, the witches and fairies, are either cross or captivated. They may cast spells or make wishes which may be self-fulfilling prophecies. The ways in which these adults speak to babies is quite particular; their voices change, the intonation and rhythm are different from normal. Some people find this way of speaking rather grotesque. "I found my mother completely ridiculous when she spoke to my baby, but I realise, now I've taken him home, that I'm also a bit 'gaga' around him," one mother told me. Researchers have turned their attention to this speciality of mothers, too. They have concluded that it is almost a different language, a dialect which they have called "motherese", the language spoken in the land of mums. The researchers analysed and made graphs of melodic shapes which are long, broad and gentle; an amplified prosodic rhythm, with high-pitched modulations, and strong and modulated intonation. These characteristics are found during the first days of life, when mothers speak to their babies, but never when they speak to other adults (Fernald & Simon, 1984). So it certainly is a separate language, destined exclusively for babies. It is the English-speaking countries that introduced the term "motherese", designating it a magic charm which attracts babies to those who speak it. There are some who believe that it is the babies who bring on this way of speaking in a voice that is higher, more melodious and exaggerated, just as they bring on lactation. In any case, babies like this language, and very soon show that they prefer a woman who speaks "motherese" to them, even if she does so in a language that is foreign to them, and if she is not their mother. It seems that it matters very little what is actually said. It is not the words that attract babies' attention, but rather the intonation of the person who is speaking at that moment. What do we think of the results of these studies? What we do know is that babies are very interested in the world around them, right from the start. They can already imitate adults, be interested in them, and they really do seem to seek contact. We can also observe these phenomena in extremely premature babies at the moment of birth, during the few minutes before they are sedated and connected up to their machines. They all seem to be waiting for a response, a reaction, something to tell them about the effect of their arrival on the adults who surround them.

Since the 1970s it has been known that babies can tell the difference between languages. Their capacity for acoustic discrimination appears very early on. By recording variations in non-nutritive sucking rhythms, it is possible to observe that they speed up when a baby hears a new sound. The baby is also capable of choosing one sound rather than another, by accelerating the rhythm of sucking (De Casper & Spence, 1986). French babies can distinguish, for example, between French and

Russian, from the age of four days; not only that, but they can also show that they prefer French (Mehler et al., 1988). Between two women who talk to them, they will choose the one who speaks "motherese". These experiments also show that in proto-conversations (the conversation that happens before an actual conversation), mothers speak to their babies and leave gaps for the babies to "speak". This kind of speaking is called "turntalking" (Ferreira, 1995), and occurs immediately after birth, as soon as the baby produces any sound. As soon as the baby gives a sign, the mother translates: "What's that, my little one, are you hungry?" She is waiting for a reply. At that moment, the baby vocal-ises, or makes a sign. But the mother "speaks" the reply when she per-ceives two different sounds, which she then interprets straight away as a phrase. She will say to the baby, "Yes, Mummy, I'm hungry." The mother speaks for the baby. Just two different sounds, and she assumes it is a reply she has given the baby time to make. It is a "translation" she has made, which in some sense makes the baby an interlocutor. Here again we find the notion of the "supposition of a subject". Between four and six weeks, according to the researchers, there are more and more "proto-conversations", and babies becomes more and more active in taking turns. The musicality of the vocalisations seems to mean more to the babies than the words (Malloch, 1999). Marie-Christine Laznik, who has worked intensively on motherese, tells us: "The voice, its musical-ity, is a fundamental tool of expression for babies. It is in the interstices of musical rhythm and proto-conversations, in this playful interchange, that babies construct themselves within this bond, which we can call the primordial Other; the musicality in these proto-conversations will allow for the sharing of intersubjective experiences" (Laznik, 2010 [translated for this edition]).

The baby and the voice

Working with tiny newborns, we too have been able to establish just how eager babies seem to be for speech addressed to them—eager to hear our voices. They reply to us with their expressions, and above all with their mouths. Freud wrote: "The first organ to emerge as an erotogenic zone and to make libidinal demands on the mind is, from the time of birth onwards, the mouth. To begin with, all psychi-cal activity is concentrated on providing satisfaction for the needs of that zone. Primarily, of course, this satisfaction serves the purpose of self-preservation by means of nourishment; but physiology should not be confused with psychology. The baby's obstinate persistence in sucking gives evidence at an early stage of a need for satisfaction which, though it originates from and is instigated by the taking of nourishment, nevertheless strives to obtain pleasure independently of nourishment and for that reason may and should be termed sexual" (Freud, 1940a, pp. 152–153). Hearing the voice, and responding with movements of the mouth, is linked with orality. For babies, it is a "pleasure of the mouth". Certainly, when we speak to babies, they open their mouths wide as if to drink in our words, and wave their arms and legs, showing that they are interested and excited. They seem happy to hear our voices, and do not seek silence. It is true that foetal life is noisy, and babies are always reassured by what they already know. We now know that sounds travel through amniotic fluid, and may sometimes be muffled, but can also be amplified or distorted. This is the case with the sounds of the mother's body transmitted to the foetus *in utero*—heartbeats, intestinal gurgling, but also the cavernous voice of the mother which can be heard. Other sounds arrive from outside: the father's more serious voice, the voices of brothers and sisters, music and all sorts of other sounds coming from the environment.[7]

At the moment of birth, when babies give their first cry, the one which reassures the mother but has no meaning for the baby, signification is given to the cry by the entourage. The baby is definitely alive. In the minutes that follow, as soon as the baby shows himself, the mother, thanks to her primary maternal preoccupation, will try to guess what the baby is trying to say to her. The cry will quickly be transformed into, "He's hungry". Once this initial interpretation has been made, nothing will ever be the same again for the baby. The cry will have been transformed into a demand. From then on, because the object is irremediably lost, a network of interactions is put in place. The first response, that of the mother's voice, "You're hungry, my little one," introduces the question of jouissance for the baby. Babies can make their mothers understand something about them, and jouissance can be located. A mother (in her primary maternal preoccupation, which entails the supposition of the subject), supposes what the baby is demanding and tells him that she can satisfy the demand. "You're crying because you're hungry." The mother's voice takes on the value of jouissance; the baby can be understood, and the mother is delighted that she can understand. While awaiting this response, the baby will demand to be loved and understood, and this demand will accompany him throughout life. Verlaine certainly knew something about this in the *Poems under Saturn*:

> Oft do I dream this strange and penetrating dream:
> An unknown woman, whom I love, who loves me well,
> Who does not every time quite change, nor yet quite dwell
> The same,—and loves me well, and knows me as I am.
>
> For she knows me! My heart, clear as a crystal beam
> To her alone, ceases to be inscrutable
> To her alone, and she alone knows to dispel
> My grief, cooling my brow with her tears' gentle stream.
>
> Is she of favour dark or fair?—I do not know.
> Her name? All I remember is that it doth flow
> Softly, as do the names of them we loved and lost.
>
> Her eyes are like the statues',—mild and grave and wide;
> And for her voice she has as if it were the ghost
> Of other voices,—well-loved voices that have died.
>
> (Verlaine, 1895)

If babies open their mouths, it does not simply indicate a wish to satisfy their hunger, but also signifies that they want to be understood and included; and that they want to communicate, as the voice becomes an object of the drive, an object *a*, as Lacan called it. "The mouth that opens in the register of the drive—it is not the food that satisfies it [...] That is why, in analytic experience, the oral drive is encountered at the final term, in a situation when it does no more than order the menu" (Lacan, 1998, p. 167). The drive, he tells us, is not satisfied by its object. No need can succeed in satisfying the drive, the voice being the object of the invocatory drive for Lacan (ibid.). As we have seen, newborns are interested in the speech addressed to them in motherese, with its particular intonation and its different prosodic peaks. Babies are seduced, just as Ulysses was, by the song of the sirens. And it seems that babies seek above all to set in motion the arrival of signs of the other's jouissance, which the usage of motherese also confirms. As Hervé Bentata puts it, "Listen to a mother speaking to her baby. She speaks in a singing tone, slowly, emphasising each word. The 'song' of her voice is full of prosodic peaks. These prosodic peaks of 'motherese' can also be found in the cry for milk, in exclamations of surprise or extreme admiration. The mother draws the baby in with her song, in order to attach him or her to herself. As for the baby, he or she falls madly in love with the mother. And yet her way of speaking slowly and word by word is like a dotted line; you only have to follow them along in order to cut them out; and this prepares the baby for the cut of the signifier, and at the same time for his or her detachment from the mother" (Bentata, 2011 [translated for this edition]). It is this subtle blend of attachment and detachment which will allow babies to construct themselves. If a baby is not on the look-out for these signs, then it does not bode well as far as later development is concerned (Laznik, 1996). Marie-Christine Laznik maintains that this constitutes one of the early signs of autism in the PREAUT protocol.[8]

Freud had identified three moments in the constitution of the drives: a time when babies seek an object of satisfaction, a time when they take a part of their own body as an object of satisfaction, and a third time when they make themselves the object of the satisfaction of the drives for the Other. Babies find their bearings with regard to jouissance in the mother's voice—the invocatory drive—and in her look—the scopic drive. Marie-Christine Laznik shows that in autism, babies do not make themselves the object of the satisfaction of the Other's drives; they do not look at the Other, and above all, do not seek to be looked at by the Other. So it seems that the third moment of the drive fails. The development of the scopic drive and the invocatory drive is stalled.

We have often described the long hours spent alongside these extremely premature babies in order to try to "seek them out", to try to establish contact, to try to encourage them to enter into communication with us or with their nursery nurses. This is certainly the area in which we find similarities between the work carried out with autistic children, the ones we see every day, and the work with these very premature babies. Obviously there are certain types of exchanges between mother and baby which are not easy in a NICU. It is very hard for these mothers to transform their baby's cry into a call. Geneviève Haag, speaking of autism, also underlines the importance of enabling the child to feel understood: "The aim is to communicate the maximum understanding to autistic subjects, because that is one of the environmental factors that facilitate the construction of their ability to contain themselves bodily and emotionally" (Haag, 2005 [translated for this edition]).

Melissa

I remember Melissa, born by caesarean section at twenty-nine weeks and weighing 850 grams. It took her mother a long time to recover from the operation. The doctors had been very clear: "Your baby is suffering from retarded intra-uterine growth. She is not safe in your womb." She did not want to come and see her baby. "I prefer to think she hasn't been born, that none of that actually happened." This woman had not wanted to come in to the service to see her baby, but she had come to an appointment the doctor had made for her, and that is the occasion on which I saw her. Once the wound from the caesarean started to hurt less, she spoke about another source of hurt—her own childhood. She spoke about her mother's violence, and her own fear that she would never be able to love her baby. Faced with this mother who was in difficulties, the team took on the task of looking after the baby, without pressing the mother to come in and take care of the little girl. "I'm too afraid," she said, "I'm afraid for Melissa and I'm afraid for myself. I just think the nightmare of her being born never really happened." It took a very long time for her to come and meet her baby. One day, finally, standing by the incubator in the service, she turned towards me and said, "Oh, I think she's crying because she's hungry. Now I know she's there and she's calling me." Finally she could hear her daughter's cry as a call; up to that point, it had been the team who fulfilled that function for Melissa. Once she had overcome this obstacle, Melissa's mother still needed to begin to authorise herself to find pleasure in being near her daughter. She needed to listen to her, to learn to decode what the baby was trying to say to her, so that eventually the third moment of the drive could be put in place. Then Melissa was able to make a move towards her mother, looking for signs other than those of the anguish and suffering that had been unleashed by her extreme prematurity and fragility at birth. It was only her mother's voice that could constitute an invocatory drive, finally giving the child a taste for survival and being resuscitated. Resuscitating, being resuscitated, getting oneself resuscitated … This is another important landmark in what has become our work in neonatology today.

What premature babies teach us

A while ago, as I was talking to a baby in the service, I heard a nurse telling an African mother about the latest discoveries regarding the capabilities of newborns.

"Talk to him," she said, "he recognises your voice, it's been proved, he recognises your smell. Put your hands in the incubator, he'll recognise you: the experiments are conclusive, it's been shown scientifically."

The woman listened without saying anything; she appeared docile and smiled at the nurse. A few minutes later I found her at the entry/ exit vestibule, leaving after visiting her baby. She was getting dressed to go. I said to her jokingly, "So now you know all about the latest scientific discoveries!" She smiled at me and said, "I don't know why the scientists make such a fuss about demonstrating things that our grandmothers have always known! Of course my son understands everything, it's obvious!"

Winnicott observed how obvious these things are to mothers, saying, "Mothers must be expected to see more than is there, and scientists must be expected to see nothing unless it is first proved" (2009, p. 32).

This vision of things is given to them when primary maternal pre-occupation is possible. It is, he says, "an amazing capacity for identification with the baby [...] in a way that no machine can imitate, and no teaching can reach."

This woman was right to point out that this knowledge about babies is transmitted as long as thing have gone well between mother and daughter. It is a knowledge linked to a mother's libidinal investment in her child. For these mothers, there is no need for scientific research—they think their child is marvellous anyway. Freud explains the reason for this by defining the place the child occupies for those who have created him: "The child shall have a better time than his parents; he shall not be subject to the necessities which they have recognized as paramount in life. Illness, death, renunciation of enjoyment, restrictions on his own will, shall not touch him; the laws of nature and of society shall be abrogated in his favour; he shall once more really be the centre and core of creation—'His Majesty the Baby' [...] Parental love, which is so moving and at bottom so childish, is nothing but the parents' narcissism born again" (Freud, 1914c, p. 90).

It is this narcissism that will be severely put to the test when the parents of a premature baby discover this tiny body at the bottom of an incubator, kept alive by all the lines going in to this strange machine. The laws of nature will not have come to a standstill for this one.

Some parents will ask the doctors, "Is he in pain?" While the experiments carried out on newborns run the risk of turning them into human potential to be exploited, and can sometimes look like abuse of the child or the foetus, at least they have the merit of making the doctors pay attention to this question.

We now know that babies born prematurely are not beings without feeling, nor are they so immature that the sensory system cannot enable them to be aware of and feel the world around them. And this makes it much more complicated for the medical services treating them.

It is no longer possible to imagine that newborns do not suffer. Nowadays we even believe that they suffer more at this stage: they are hypersensitive, because their neuro-biochemistry is so immature that systems to inhibit pain have yet to be put in place. This means that doctors have to find analgesics and new methods of anaesthesia which are suitable for the low birth weight and the fragility of these babies.

How much easier it was, some years ago, when newborns were treated without anaesthesia, because it was believed that they were completely insensitive to pain.

Of course, in that case it was the discourse of the doctors and not of the mothers.

Physiological and neurosensory development are, as we now know, connected with the baby's psychological development.

From the moment these discoveries were known about, intensive care services could no longer have a clear conscience. What questions now had to be asked? What about the risks of babies suffering, or being under- or over-stimulated? Should the parents be allowed to spend longer periods in the service? Should music be played to the babies, should they be massaged, moved into different positions, given water beds; should there be protocols for non-nutritional sucking, in order to study the babies' reactions?

By the way, none of this very rigorous research addressed the question of whether those caring for the babies might just speak directly to the babies.

For the time being, the only thing that counted was sensory stimulation of premature babies, as if they were beyond language.

The idea was to reproduce the intra-uterine milieu for the babies, that is to say, act as if they were still unborn, so that the incubator would replace the mother's womb as nearly as possible. Recordings of the mother's heartbeat and of her voice through water were made and played to the babies, in order to reproduce the sounds a baby was familiar with as closely as possible. It was only the sound of the voice that counted, not the actual words spoken by the mother. It is interesting to note that in this case, the fantasy of the scientists is the same as that of the mothers: to do everything as if the babies were not yet born. But surely this involves a disavowal, because these children certainly have come into the world, and are no longer in their mother's womb. The reasons for the babies' arrival are multiple, but one cannot act as if nothing has happened. These babies are certainly there, and are without doubt more vulnerable than those born at full term.

In this situation, the role of the psychoanalyst will be to "suppose the baby as subject", to enable the separation to have actually taken place, rather than doing everything possible to pretend it never happened.

This precocious experience determines how a system functions, and, as we now know, can even determine the anatomy of a system (Changeux & Dachin, 1974).

It is a heavy responsibility to take care of an extremely premature baby. These babies are hypersensitive to painful stimuli, and have no means of putting in place a system to reduce the excitation. They are suspended between life and death like tightrope-walkers who may lose their balance at any given moment. We certainly cannot help them by pretending they have not been born, and putting everything in place to support this pretence. Our prevention operates at a different level.

"Extremely premature babies who have been in intensive care, who are absolutely without any system to reduce the impact of excitation or to contain tactile sensations, without external protection, and are submitted to overstimulations to which they are hypersensitive, are highly likely to suffer neuropsychical sequelae ... The confirmation of the existence of these sequelae and their nature is not yet within the scope of our practice" (Granboulan, 1995 [translated for this edition]).

Medical teams are certainly concerned about the iatrogenic risks of intensive care, and question the impact of their interventions on the subsequent development of newborns. In NICUs, the jury is still out on the question of "overstimulation" versus "under-stimulation". But the problem does not seem to be of this order. For us, it is a question of the quality of the stimulations rather than of their quantity. Of course, the interventions of intensive care are indispensable, and babies in intensive care are always going to be overstimulated, but at the same time they are most often deprived of the type of stimulation that would "call the subject into being". And beyond the interventions that ensure comfort and well-being, this latter type of stimulation is absolutely necessary.

Perhaps it is to help reduce anxiety that the idea of "pretending" the baby has not been born, "pretending" that all is well, has arisen: to reduce anxiety, or perhaps simply because it is easier.

In order to make sure the well-being of the babies is catered for, psychologists have gone into NICUs and "observed" the newborns and reassured the staff. But what is there to see? Tiny beings, devoid of flesh, stuck in the bottom of incubators, bristling with monitors and tubes, with expressions that screw up their features into a face that looks more like that of a dying old person than a newborn. Beyond the rather challenging nature of the scene, what is there to observe? Can we actually see that these babies can feel things in their bodies? Can we witness, day after day, the desire to live gradually disintegrating in them?

What is happening for a child in this situation will never be visible to an observer. And yet it is precisely here that we should be focusing our research.

As for the team, what reassurance can we offer to them? Letting them have a sense of having done everything possible, while taking into account the future psychological development of the babies? The illusion that by observing the babies, we will be able to prevent problems from developing?

In a NICU, the babies are constantly being observed—and mercifully, because this vigilance is vital for their survival. The doctors keep an eye on their skin colour, their reactivity, their ECG, their EEG. At the slightest sign of any complication, they will intervene, and in most cases are in a position to save the baby's life.

It is therefore understandable that they more easily accept the collaboration of psychologists, who, like them, observe the babies. Psychologists are more easily accepted in the service, because they are more reassuring.

We, however, think that however premature newborns may be, while of course they need the doctors to observe them to ensure their very survival, it is also possible to try to make contact with them; there is a need for someone to be looking "elsewhere" rather than just at the screens of the monitors, and to encounter them on a different level.

All human beings have a need for communication. Extreme immaturity does not preclude a desire on the part of the tiny being to be heard by others.

"All infants, programmed to initiate contact with their environment (Brazelton, Tronick, Adamson, Als, & Wise, 1975), need responses to their attempts to communicate if they are to thrive" (Freud, W. E., 1989, p. 263).

Premature babies are often so sick that they find communication very difficult. It is therefore up to the team to make an effort to decode the smallest of their appeals in order to try to respond to them. It is no longer a question of observing from outside, but of accepting being connected with the child, of intervening, of allowing oneself to be taken by surprise, and of offering the child something more than the neutral researcher's camera lens.

If no one intervenes in response to the babies, they run a significant risk of falling into depressive states, as Spitz described in 1945 (Spitz, 1993), which may lead to anaclitic depression and hospitalism.

In France, Jenny Aubry (2003) reported as early as 1946 on the disastrous effects of precocious separation from mothers and lack of maternal care; she demonstrated in a way that was very subversive for its time that these abandoned children could come to suffer from severe psychical problems. She was a pioneer, and paved the way for several generations of child psychoanalysts.

A few years later, Bernard Golse (2010) developed the idea that babies can become depressed even if they are neither hospitalised nor separated from their parents. He created the concept of "depressive emotion". This emotion was linked to a "co-phenomenon" which would appear in relation to the other and as a function of this relation. It would not necessarily be a question of the loss of an object, and there would not even necessarily be an object, since it might not have been emotionally invested (Lebovici, 1960). But in the absence of language, the affect would become an essential element in the process of communication, as Daniel Stern (1985) has also shown. Faced with a mother who is absent or depressed, even if she is physically present, babies may become depressed in their turn, as we have seen in the "still face" experiment. Where this situation is not merely experimental, it also evokes the "dead mother" which Green (1984, pp. 49–59) speaks of. For example, a mother who is grieving or very depressed cannot respond to her child. Her thoughts are entirely elsewhere, she is overcome with depression, and cannot show herself to be reactive and alive for her baby. From the affective and emotional point of view, she will be "as if dead", she will be absent for the baby. In order to grow, the baby needs the Other. This is what, in their own way, the authors of attachment theory were trying to demonstrate. The fundamental idea is as follows: in order to experience normal social and emotional development, young children need to develop a relationship of attachment to at least one "caregiver", a person who cares for them in a coherent and continuous way. This theory is formulated in the works of John Bowlby (1969). More recently, Peter Fonagy (2001) attempted to make an epistemological connection between psychoanalysis and attachment theory. Even if these are in fact two bodies of differing doctrines, it is interesting for us to know them both, and to try to see how the many works available to us on the subject of babies can help us to progress.

If we take clinical experience as our guide, even the tiniest babies will be waiting for the Other. They will be awaiting a response according to what they already know how to decode; they were already getting their bearings while they were in their mother's womb. The babies had already been thought about by their mother. Again, we can think of Winnicott's "primary maternal preoccupation", this particular state which allows the mother to put herself in her child's place, to identify with him, and to invest emotionally in the baby even before birth, but also after birth, through the care she gives. The mother, Winnicott writes, is "able to meet the basic needs of the infant in a way that no machine can imitate, and no teaching can reach [...] the prototype of all infant care is holding [...] An infant who is held well enough is quite a different thing from one who has not been held well enough" (Winnicott, 2009, p. 33).

How can a mother experience this primary maternal preoccupation when her baby is in hospital? And what sort of holding and handling will the baby experience? If the mother finds she cannot do it, how can we enable the team to do it in her place?

Winnicott explains: "Paediatricians on the whole are people who are able to identify with the infant and to hold an infant, and perhaps it is this capacity to identify that draws people to paediatrics" (ibid.).

Whether holding comes from the mother or from someone else who is looking after the child, if it is insufficient the baby will retain a lifelong trace of this *primitive agony*, this fear of collapse. Babies "exist" in so far as they are taken care of. "Babies are human from the beginning [...] If someone is there (one could say) to collect experiences, to collate them, to feel and to distinguish between feelings, to be apprehensive at the appropriate moment and to begin to organise defences against mental pain, then I would say the infant *is*" (ibid., p. 35).

In order to invest emotionally in themselves, newborns have to be invested in emotionally by the Other; they cannot create the experience of existing all by themselves. Contrary to what we so often hear these days, a baby is not yet anyone, but will become someone when he is addressed as such. But it is important that everyone believes this, because the person who takes care of the baby needs to transmit to him not only the idea that he exists, but also that he will continue to exist, and of what he will become. It is the project of desiring on behalf of the baby that will mean that he can live, and which initiates the child into what Françoise Dolto called "towards-becoming in the endowment of his or her sex."

The existence of a child is indissolubly linked to the presence of the Other, whether it is the mother or the team looking after him, acting as a container for him. As Daniel Stern has shown, in normal circumstances, the parents are obliged to imagine the whole world for their newborn baby at every moment of the day or night (Stern, 1992).

In order for babies to "be", they need to be enveloped in multiple networks of "attention" to them. There needs to be a certain type of communication, a certain way of touching them, replying to them, addressing them as one human being to another, being inhabited by affects, thoughts, and desires. It is this address to the other, caught up in language, and beyond words, which seem to us to be decisive for the child. And it seems less essential to know whether or not the child actually understands the meaning of the words. But words are all we have as a tool to address these babies, to transmit our emotions and affects, and to enable them to understand that they exist and that they are here with us. The voice and the intonation are the essential elements. If we envelop these children as we talk to them, if we touch them and are touched by them in turn, if we suppose "something of a subject" in each of them, then they will be able to construct themselves in this process of exchange.

It has often been observed that if you speak to a baby in a "fake", artificial way, while you are thinking about something else, and without really putting your heart into what you are saying, but saying something because you feel you should—which is current practice in many medical services—the child will remain deaf to those words, which although coming from the other, do not sound like true speech.

In the absence of words truly addressed to the baby, there is a real risk of collapse. A machine, however sophisticated, will never be in a position to "suppose something of a subject" in a baby, as we will see later in Anna's case. It also seems to me that it is this ability truly to address the baby that is at the heart of Winnicott's "primary maternal preoccupation."

So the newborn with absolutely no knowledge, Aristotle's *tabula rasa*, has been replaced by the baby born with abilities, capable of entering into a relationship, of recognising his mother-tongue, and the voice of the mother or father. Newborns are always extremely hungry for words. The idea of addressing oneself to a newborn has not come from the work of those undertaking infant observation, who by definition are not allowed to intervene, so that they do not falsify the experiment.

In order to live, one needs to be inscribed in speech, and this speech is different for each individual according to his or her history. The speech has to be truthful. There is no point in telling babies they have not yet been born. There is no point in denying their suffering, or the painful interventions that they must surely experience as so much maltreatment.

Nor is there any point in denying their own aggressivity, nor that of the adults who surround them. These babies, tiny as they are, seem to be extremely sensitive to the truth or otherwise of what is said around them and about them. It is as if the recognition of the drama they are living through gives them the courage to overcome their difficulties.

We are a long way from the saccharine discourse that sometimes surrounds the most dramatic births. Who, after all, is being protected by smoothing things over to such an extent?

When I started working in a neonatal resuscitation service, I still had everything to discover, everything to learn from the mothers and babies, and from the doctors—how they resuscitated babies, what was customary for them, what they were afraid of. I was like an ethnologist in an unknown land. My only compass was my experience as an analyst, and all I had brought with me was what I had learned from Freud, Lacan, and a few others. At the time, I was in supervision with Françoise Dolto, who taught me a great deal about the day-to-day clinic with such tiny babies. At the time, she was the only analyst in the École freudienne who thought it was possible to be a "resuscitating analyst", as she called it, and certainly she was the only one who was convinced that it was possible to work with babies who weighed 500 grams! Later on, I also went to Ginette Raimbault for supervision, to find out how she worked with doctors. Maud Mannoni helped me to think about the problems posed by the institution.

I learned a great deal from the writings of Winnicott and from his work with newborns. A considerable part of his thinking was devoted to babies. He studied how they feel, what they try to do, while at the same time studying their entourage, their environment. For Winnicott, when a birth is traumatic (which, unlike Rank, he did not believe was always the case), it can result in serious illnesses, and psychoses in particular. According to him, a birth trauma can give rise to a congenital state of paranoia which is not, however, genetic. What could be more traumatic for babies and their entourage than premature birth?

And yet, in a 1945 paper, "Primitive emotional development", Winnicott wrote: "There is also this question: how early do important things happen? For instance, does the unborn child have to be considered? And if so, at what age after conception does psychology come in? I would answer that if there is an important stage at five to six months there is also an important stage round about birth. My reason for saying this is the great differences that can be noticed if the baby is pre-mature or post-mature. I suggest that at the end of nine months' gestation an infant becomes ripe for emotional development, and that if an infant is post-mature he has reached this stage in the womb and one is therefore forced to consider his feelings before and during birth. On the other hand a premature infant is not experiencing much that is vital till he has reached the age at which he should have been born, that is to say some weeks after birth. At any rate," Winnicott stresses "this forms a basis for discussion" (1945, p. 138). So is it the case that premature babies feel nothing until they reach term? Nor does Winnicott speak of what might happen to the mother–baby bond in the case of prematurity. Later on, he would even say that the best thing for a premature baby is his incubator.

"Psychology is a gradual extension of physiology. There is no need for quarrelling over the date of this change. It could be variable according to events. However, the birthdate could be taken as a time when big changes occur in this field, so that the premature infant may be far better off psychologically in an incubator, whereas a postmature infant would not thrive in one but would need human arms and body contact" (Winnicott, 2009, p. 32).

Although Winnicott had initially been a paediatrician, this idea still seems surprising coming from him, and it is a type of affirmation very similar to those made by doctors whom I worked with fifteen years ago; it was a question above all of ensuring survival. And yet there seem to be a number of contradictions in this way of thinking. It seems out of step with the rest of Winnicott's work, in which he gives great importance to the delivery and the first moments of life outside the womb; but there are also contradictions within the paragraph itself. How indeed can we speak of the importance of the fifth and sixth months of pregnancy (the age at which the majority of the babies in NICUs are born) and of the baby's "feelings" before and during birth while claiming that the premature baby feels nothing vital before full term? Clinical experience with babies has shown me quite clearly that the contrary is true. Their reactivity, their astonishing presence, and their insatiable thirst for the other have forced me to keep on posing more and more questions. It was through reading this article while working with the babies themselves, that I reopened this discussion that Winnicott had started in the mid-1940s.

For an analyst entering the world of a NICU, it is impossible not to notice the effect of words on the babies' bodies, and the effects of what the babies hear, of their presence, and the transference effects on the parents and on the doctors. How is a baby's psychical world constructed? How are we to understand the fact that, of two babies born with the same birth weight at the same number of weeks, given the same care, one will survive and the other will die?

And if a baby does not die, how can we account for the current statistics, which show a very high incidence of psychosis, autism, and hyperactivity in those children born extremely prematurely, even if they do not have neurological sequelae? In 1969, Jean Bergès described a syndrome found in children who had been born prematurely (Bergès, Lezine, Harrisson, & Boisselier, 1969), involving psychomotor difficulties, poor spatial recognition, and disturbances of body image, which led to learning difficulties and problems in individuation. Later on, many authors we have already referred to would focus on the difficulties in establishing the mother–baby bond.

Although his opinions differ from ours, I came to realise how precious Winnicott's work is for all babies, whether premature or not, when I started to work on these questions again, to think about babies, and to establish just how much else there is, beyond mere attunement, between the mother and the baby.

The statistical findings regarding extremely premature babies do not go back very far. Between twenty-two and twenty-five weeks, mortality is terribly high, as are the risks of serious sequelae. After twenty-five weeks, there is a sudden change, as there is now a fifty per cent chance of survival, and a fifty per cent risk of disability. While the most common sequelae are pulmonary and neurological, there are others in another register: autism, psychosis, psychomotor retardation, learning difficulties, and hyperactivity. Each further week of gestation sees a reduction in neurological and psychomotor risks; however, those of autism, psychosis, and hyperactivity remain just as high.

What happens to the baby during resuscitation? What traces will remain of this period of death at the beginning of life? When older children and young adults come for analysis, they teach us how persistent these traces can be: their desire, their fantasy, and their very life force are all marked by it. Winnicott explained that at birth, it is not a question of memory as such, but of mnemic traces. Doctors are well aware of these risks.

Winnicott offered a notion which might at first sight appear reassuring for neonatal teams: "A baby does not exist," he said. But the relief does not last long once you explain what Winnicott actually meant. A baby does not exist, but the mother–baby couple does; and the centre of gravity of the human being can be found in what is shaped by this couple, in a one-to-one relation that certainly evokes the transitional space. So on the basis of this knowledge, if we are to resuscitate babies and give them a chance of "being", the service needs to take care of the mother as well; and this makes the work of resuscitation far more complicated.

Babies are subjected to experiences they do not understand, but which are laid down in their memory. In the womb, from as early as the fourth month of pregnancy, they receive a gamut of sensory information, and then again at the time of delivery and during the first days of life. The more premature babies are, the more difficult it will doubtless be for them to decode the information. It is impossible to believe that babies will not receive some sort of information about the fact of their prematurity; nor, surely, can we believe that it is right to pretend babies have not been born until they are full term. It is no longer a question of a foetus, but of a baby. Winnicott clarifies this: babies, who do not exist if they are alone, are constructed, we may say, by means of the response from the mother or the person who looks after them to the various pains and discomforts that their body causes them, and which have no meaning at all for them. According to the responses they receive, a feeling of security or insecurity will gradually be established. In order for babies to construct themselves, their mothers need to adapt to their bodily needs.

Winnicott speaks of this capacity of mothers to adapt as an "illness", a benign illness they suffer from if everything is going well, when they themselves feel sufficiently reassured and supported. They are then able to give the baby the sense of existing. In order for security to be established, the extreme fragility of premature babies requires even more presence and even more appropriate responses; and women who become mothers prematurely are most often thwarted in their ability to respond in this way.

Even when a baby is born at full term, if the baby's need for reassurance is not taken into account, or if the mother's response is absent or too incoherent, the baby will sink into terrible despair. According to Winnicott, the baby's experience can be described by such words as: "going to pieces; falling for ever; dying and dying and dying; losing all vestige of hope of the renewal of contacts" (2009, p. 67).

As the baby grows, he will carry the memory of this lived catastrophe, the trace of this threat of annihilation.

Winnicott shows us how distressed babies are when they are not being carried, when the mother's "holding" has been made impossible. Holding and handling are indispensable to the completion of the baby. Winnicott says that "the inherited potential of an infant cannot become an infant unless linked to maternal care" (Winnicott, 1965). For Winnicott, holding involves not just the way the mother carries the baby physically and psychically, but also the function of the father, who "carries" the mother by taking care of her environment, that is to say, the life of the father, mother and baby together. Winnicott (ibid.) insists on this father–mother–baby triangle, and it cannot but evoke another triangle, the one we find in the work of Lacan. Rather than there being an absence of risk for the baby in the incubator, there is actually a significant risk: there is virtually no handling (mothers are only allowed to carry out a few interventions for the baby's well-being), and holding is very problematic because of the circumstances of the baby's birth.

The mother feels distant from her child, the caregivers have taken her place, and as for the father—he is unable to give her any reassurance since the doctors cannot say anything, and so he finds himself unable to support her. How can we avoid the baby sensing this "primitive agony" that Winnicott speaks of?

Physical pain linked to psychical pain is further aggravated by the interventions necessary during resuscitation. How can we give babies the responses they are expecting?

Some of these babies withdraw, and do not communicate. Others, if they survive, become hyperactive, and sometimes hyper-mature. In an attempt to protect the mother, they look after her by being hyper-demanding, and communicating a great deal if she has difficulty in communicating. But they may also try to be very good in order to reassure her and reinforce her narcissism, or they may keep falling ill, sending out an appeal via their physical symptoms which will attract attention, so that they and their mother will be taken care of; in this way they can look after her by proxy.

Certainly, the mothers of these babies who are suspended between life and death are very fragile. They may come to resent their babies. And on top of prematurity, we can add the seventeen reasons Winnicott gave for a mother to hate her baby:

A. The baby is not her own (mental) conception.
B. The baby is not the one of childhood play, father's child, brother's child, etc.
C. The baby is not magically produced.
D. The baby is a danger to her body in pregnancy and at birth.
E. The baby is an interference with her private life, a challenge to preoccupation.
F. To a greater or lesser extent a mother feels that her own mother demands a baby, so that her baby is produced to placate her mother.
G. The baby hurts her nipples even by suckling, which is at first a chewing activity.
H. He is ruthless, treats her as scum, an unpaid servant, a slave.
I. She has to love him, excretions and all, at any rate at the beginning, till he has doubts about himself.
J. He tries to hurt her, periodically bites her, all in love.
K. He shows disillusionment about her.

L. His excited love is cupboard love, so that having got what he wants he throws her away like orange peel.

M. The baby at first must dominate, he must be protected from coincidences, life must unfold at the baby's rate and all this needs his mother's continuous and detailed study. For instance, she must not be anxious when holding him, etc.

N. At first he does not know at all what she does or what she sacrifices for him. Especially he cannot allow for her hate.

O. He is suspicious, refuses her good food, and makes her doubt herself, but eats well with his aunt.

P. After an awful morning with him she goes out, and he smiles at a stranger, who says: "Isn't he sweet!"

Q. If she fails him at the start she knows he will pay her out for ever.

R. He excites her but frustrates—she mustn't eat him or trade in sex with him. (Winnicott, 1949, pp. 72–73)

Anne and Anna

On this particular morning, as I arrived in the service, I recognised the atmosphere of extreme emergency. We know it well; it weighs heavily on us, and has a flavour of extreme tension and great calm at the same time. There is never any sense of panic, and no one hurries. The more precious the minutes are, the more the team seems to be plunged into timelessness.

Two little girls had been born an hour apart, and their given names, Anne and Anna, were almost identical, as were the circumstances of their birth.

Anne was born at twenty-six-and-a-half weeks, and weighed 850 grams. Anna weighed 820 grams, having been born at twenty-seven weeks. While the team were bent over the incubators, inserting catheters and lines for monitoring and ventilation, the two mothers were waiting in their rooms in the maternity unit for the doctors' verdicts.

Anne's mother, Lila, had been admitted to the maternity unit three days before the baby was delivered, because of the risk of premature labour. The obstetricians had tried everything to delay the onset, but they did not succeed, and Anne was born after a trouble-free labour. Lila, still somewhat unsteady on her feet, nevertheless came to see her daughter in the evening after she was delivered. She stood by the incubator, overwhelmed by the machinery, the many electrical cables, the sounds of the monitor and the wheezing of the oxygen; she listened to the nurse's explanations, refused to touch her baby, and said through her tears, "She's too small, she won't survive".

She did not come to see her daughter the following day, and only came to the service at the end of the day after that, when she had an appointment with me. I saw her in my office. She started the session by saying that she did not dare ask me how Anne was doing. Was she dead? Wouldn't it be better if she died, anyway? And even if she didn't die, there would surely be consequences because of the resuscitation? She could think of nothing but the death of her daughter. "The sooner she dies, the better; I mustn't let myself get attached to her."

Of course, in the service, as soon as she had started to speak like this, she had been told to be quiet. "And yet," she said, "this baby I was carrying was my only joy, my only hope; it was she who kept me alive."

Lila, originally from Algeria, had been in France for two years, and lived with her sister and brother-in-law, having fled from her family whom she said had been too strict. Not long after she arrived in France, she fell passionately in love with a man who was handsome, rich, and intelligent. On the day she proudly announced her pregnancy to him, her Prince Charming told her he was married and had children. Her fairy tale turned into a nightmare. He asked her to have an abortion, but she categorically refused. He decided they should split up, and Lila started to look for work to help her sister financially. "It was tough," she said, "but my baby and me, we wanted to get through it on our own. I wanted to fight for her."

I pointed out to her that now her little girl was battling with death, no doubt with all the strength she had given her during the time she was carrying her in her womb. Lila seemed to come out of her daze, and said, "I would go and see her, but the doctors seem so pessimistic, I daren't tell her to keep on fighting."

"What would you like to say to her?"

"I'd like to tell her not to give up, that she's strong and that she'll pull through."

"What is it that's stopping you?"

"I just feel it's not my place, it's for the specialists to be there, and that I don't know, but they do."

I told Lila that that she was the only one who really knew where her place was, and what she wanted to say to her daughter. She could allow herself, whatever the diagnosis was, to listen differently from the doctors, and to speak to her baby with a different voice. There was no need for her to think like them.

When she left my office, she went straight in to the service. When I went in through the entry vestibule two hours later, I noticed her sitting beside her baby's incubator. I slightly opened the lid of the incubator and said, "Like that, she'll be able to hear you," and left them alone, engrossed in their conversation. Lila spoke to Anne until the service closed, and then from then on, would be there every day, speaking to her tirelessly.

Not long after this, the baby weighed only 780 grams. And Lila was beginning to make life very difficult for the caregivers.

Very often Lila would ask to see me, but some days the head nurse would also call me back, more for the team than for Lila, when they could no longer stand her shouting, her tears, and her aggressivity. What they found most difficult was when her aggressivity was turned on her daughter: "You'd think she wanted her to die; but does she love her, that mother?"

The team never stopped asking these questions. At the same time, Anne seemed less and less present, as if she was withdrawing into her pain. She no longer sought our presence, and did not respond to our concern.

The caregivers, who realised she was fading away, put the blame on the mother. For a neonatal resuscitation team, the only way of loving is to want the baby to live at any price. When the parents "don't go down that road", when their anguish leads them to doubt, when they think ahead to the grief they will probably have to go through, it leads the doctors and nurses to experience them as "bad".

Babies also seem to be the conduit for various tensions between parents and care-givers, and we have established that their state of health can be seriously affected by this. It is essential that guilt and hate, as well as love, can be spoken about and recognised; if this can happen, then mutual trust can be restored.

By speaking with Lila and working with the nurses, by watching Anne for the slightest signs of suffering or the most fragile attempts at communication, and showing that it was possible to respond to her in our turn, the dialogue could begin again between Lila, Anne, and the team.

And now Lila was being looked after in some way, as well as Anne.

"This mother is sucking us dry," said one of the care-givers one day, "it's like her baby with the perfusions." Anne, for her part, was doing better and better. No one could help being interested in her and respecting her. But when the doctors decided to take her off the respirator, new difficulties arose, and her heart rate began to slow down.

As soon as Anne would fall into too deep a sleep, the monitor would start bleeping, until there was only a flat line on the screen. Anne soon realised that if she fell asleep, she was putting her life at risk; and now she would cling on to our fingers for hours on end, battling with sleep. The simple fact of being beside her and speaking to her, without any intervention to resuscitate her, would increase her heart rate and stabilise her PCO2.[9] Anne always managed to ensure someone was by her side. A junior doctor said to me one day, "It's strange, you could almost say she's replaced the oxygen with the words she insists we speak to her."

It seems that it was thanks to our words that Anne could bear to lose a part of herself. This machine, which rhythmically raised her thorax, covered her head and kept her alive, had up till now been a part of her body. By tearing it away from her, we were depriving her of sensations which had allowed her to construct herself. When the machine was taken away, she doubtless felt a sense of panic. When we explained to her that she might be suffering from this hole where her mouth was, and that she must certainly be frightened, we could imagine that an initial element of loss was being constituted for her. The hole could now exist differently, since our words, without filling it again, were able to constitute it. While the rhythm of the sound of our voices did not have the regularity of the sound of the machine, it did at least carry the desire for Anne to live.

During this period, the mother fell apart again. "She can't take any more, let her die. She can't live, it's best if she dies." But as she left, she whispered in Anne's ear, "Hang in there tonight, I'll be back tomorrow."

After more sessions with the mother, and a reduction in the episodes and severity of bradycardia, calm was restored both for the team and for Lila, who said one day to the head nurse, "My daughter and I owe our lives to you." At Lila's request, Anne's father came into the service. After that, he would come regularly to talk to Anne. He said she had given him the strength to stop running away, the strength to tackle what he called the error of his ways. Their history could finally be put into words.

When Anne was discharged from the service at the age of one hundred and forty days, she was accompanied by her mother and her father. She then came for check-ups given by the doctors in the service until she was four years old. She always seemed happy to come back, and would smile at the nurses she recognised each time she came. She was a cheerful little girl, and in perfect health. There was a very precise entry in the file on the occasion of her final visit. She no longer recognised anyone, and refused to go to the nurses in uniform when they held out their arms to her.

At this point, she had truly left us; she was now focussed entirely on her parents, and we could consider that our work with her was finished.

Alongside Anne, a little girl called Anna had been growing in the service. Born weighing 820 grams at twenty-seven weeks, she presented more or less the same developmental picture as Anne, and did not pose any particular problems. Her lowest weight was recorded as 760 grams, and just like Anne, she was intubated, ventilated, and perfused. Their development was very similar; their history was not.

Her mother, Lise, had been admitted to the maternity unit as an emergency, following a serious haemorrhage. She had already gone into labour; there was no question of trying anything at all to delay the birth, and Anna was born after a one-and-a-half-hour labour, without other complications.

Anna's mother had come in to our reception the day after the birth and asked to see the doctor responsible for the baby's admission. After she had spoken to him, she went in to see her daughter; but both the doctor and the nurses had been astonished by this mum's lack of reaction.

Doing as she was told, she had touched the baby. Being a well-brought-up woman, she had thanked the doctor for all he was doing, but did not ask a single question about her daughter.

The first session with me was strange. After I had explained to Lise how the unit worked, and spoken to her at length about her baby, she remained silent, as if it had nothing to do with her. She sat with an air of resignation; she appeared calm, and said she had no questions for me. When I asked her if she was worried, she replied, "We'll see, she's not very strong, you never know what's going to happen." Then she stood up and left my office without asking me any questions, just as she had left the doctor the previous day.

During another appointment with her, I commented again, "It's funny, you talk about this baby as if she's not yours."

"Yes," she replied, "it's true, I can't really take her on. I've just been discharged from the maternity unit, and I've got a lot to do at home. Anyway, I don't think I'm going to be able to come any more. Will you mind?"

When I had explained to her that we were not there to make any sort of judgements about her behaviour, but simply to help her and her daughter to understand each other better and get to know each other, she told me the following story. Lise had been married for four years. She already had two daughters, one of three years and one of nine months. She was still breast-feeding the little one, and had not thought it was possible to become pregnant before the baby was weaned. It was only when her GP sent her for a scan after she had complained that her stomach simply would not go flat again, that she discovered that she was four months pregnant with another little girl. Because it was too late for a legal abortion, she decided, with her husband's concurrence, to go to an "angel maker". It was in her panic about the bleeding triggered by this procedure that she had been admitted to hospital, where she had not expected to give birth to a live baby. When she told the story of this delivery, she also spoke of another—her own birth. Her mother was fifteen when Lise arrived, and she was convinced that she, too, had been born following an attempted late abortion. She did not know who her father was, and her mother, who was now dead, had taken the secret with her to her grave. But Lise was convinced she was the product of incest. Everything about her mother's behaviour had led her to believe this was the truth.

During the next few weeks, Anna had some feeding problems.

Lise would come to see her, but never stayer longer than ten minutes. Unlike Lila, she never said she wanted her daughter to die. She withdrew, and did not speak to anyone.

I noticed at this point that it was becoming more and more difficult to speak to Anna. When I was near her, I realised that she scarcely responded to my presence. She was still on a ventilator, and spent hours at a time staring fixedly somewhere to her left, possibly at a reflection on the connector for the ventilator. It became more and more difficult to attract her attention.

Some babies on ventilators will stare at a particular place on the machine which they seem to become attached to, in the way people who have been shipwrecked will cling to a lifebuoy. These babies in suspense are doubtless trying to get a grip on themselves, to find something to bring them back to life, by clinging to a point in the world outside, perhaps fighting against the fragmentation caused by pain and panic. The type of work we can do with these babies is similar to our work with autistic children. What is this defect in the mechanism of the drives? These newborns teach us how this mechanism, which is not of course mechanical, in that it is not attached to a machine, may fail to be instated. Spending many hours alongside these babies, speaking to them, and speaking about their history, about the treatment they are undergoing, about their parents, sometimes allows them to come back towards the world. Words, and more words: a "music of words", written with a "pen of words", which will allow them to construct themselves, by giving them the content they lack.

But what is it in these words that they understand? Do they grasp the meaning? Or is it rather the intention, or the affect?

We leave these sessions exhausted, feeling empty, in a state not unlike the one we find ourselves in at the end of certain sessions with autistic children. What is the part of ourselves that they take away with them?

It is only once contact has been established, and the baby is back among us, that we can begin to decode each signal given as an attempt at communication. The essence of our work from then on is to allow the parents, and the mother in particular, to allow themselves to recognise the calls of the child for themselves, and to respond in their own way.

It was impossible to carry out any of this work with Lise. When Anna was around fifty days old, the doctors thought that she, like Anne, was capable of breathing on her own.

At this time, the mother would only come in once a week. So the machine was stopped when she was not there. But Anna was unable to breathe on her own, and at each attempt she had to be reconnected. One morning when I arrived in the service, they finally told me that Anna had at last been weaned!

A solution had been found: she could manage without oxygen, so long as she could still hear the sound of the machine beside her. So now Anna was connected to the sound of the machine, just as Anne had been connected to our presence, our speech, and the words her mother spoke. But what different music! The music of a machine could not suppose something of a subject for Anna. While the machine had become the only possibility of identification for her, as we often see in autistic children, there was nothing that could be the bearer of her desire. We may wonder whether this impossibility of desire refers us back to the mother's refusal to desire this child.

Or—and this seems more likely—does it refer us to the mother's own childhood, in which the impossibility of inscribing her history had left both desire and filiation in a state of dereliction, and had meant that the trauma of this birth was impossible to inscribe?

I then proposed to the team that we should meet up to put into question this supposed "miracle cure" brought about by the machine.

Following this meeting, the highly motivated team spent even more time around Anna's incubator, making sure she was never alone; but they failed again in the work with the mother.

"We never worry about taking her away from her mum and putting her back in her incubator, if we are called to work somewhere else, because mum never says anything," said the nursing auxiliaries.

When I tried to explain to the team that Anna was going to lose the company of her mother, and that it was vital not to allow our zeal to annul the bond with the family, they could not hear it. It would take many more years, and many more meetings would have to take place before there was real co-operation between the caregivers (who were still quite mistrustful) and myself. Anna was over-invested and the mother too side-lined for my warnings to be heeded, and the team's transference to this baby could not be modified. It was difficult to put the transference into question at first. On the other hand, before Anna was discharged, the head nurse, who was worried, registered her concern with the PMI (*Protection maternelle et infantile*). At that time, this was the protocol that was routinely in place for problematic cases, in order to resolve any difficulties.

Anna was one hundred and twenty days old when she was taken home. Her mother came alone to collect her. At that time, we had started to set up a kind of rite of passage for the time of discharge; we had decided, in a series of meetings, that each of the nurses would find the time to come and say goodbye to the baby, and that the doctor would see the parents for the last time. These were to be symbolic landmarks which would allow the baby and the family not to blank out this transition, but to use it as the basis for constructing and integrating the baby's history.

But on this occasion, the mother refused. She didn't have time, it wasn't possible, any more than it had been possible to have a rite of passage at the moment of admission. Lise was in a hurry, her two daughters were waiting for her. A junior doctor pointed out to me, just before the discharge, that Lise never said "my three daughters", but only ever "my two daughters". What sort of place did that leave for this third one?

The final medical report, completed before Anna was discharged, stipulated that, as had been the case for Anne, the child was in perfect health, with no apparent sequelae following resuscitation:

- scan and EEG normal
- bloods and digestive values normal
- respiration normal
- hearing and eye tests perfect.

The clinical examination was satisfactory; Anna was a lively and vigorous little girl.

As had been the case with Anne, the neonatal unit could be satisfied that the job had been well done.

Ten days later, an ambulance brought Anna's body back to the hospital; she had died suddenly in the night. The post-mortem confirmed that it had indeed been an unexplained sudden infant death.

Babies and machines

Once babies are hooked up to machines, it is difficult for them not to stay alive, yet they do manage to "do some silly things", as the doctors say. They may become desaturated, there may be bradycardia.[10] But it is difficult to escape their vigilance, and the machine will restart again immediately. In our service it is rare for babies to die against medical advice.

The machine never dies, and never slips out of the room. But if the drive is activated by the echoing of speech in the body, how can we set the circuit of the drives in motion for these babies? In this environment, the body's structuring by the drive is indeed problematic. What happens to the child's body of jouissance in the conditions inside an incubator? The babies are attached to and completely dependent on the machines for their survival. The body's orifices are deprived of their functions.

The umbilicus remains perforated by the catheter. The nose is used not only for breathing but also for feeding: not air but milk is delivered via a line through the nostril. Meanwhile, the mouth is intubated and can no longer be used for feeding. These babies cannot make sounds. Later on, they may be subject to a tracheotomy. The body's orifices are diverted from their usual functions. The babies have holes made in them, and fluid sucked out of them. Oral satisfaction is disrupted. The babies never feel hungry because they are continually fed. The bodily envelope no longer guarantees the separation between interior and exterior. Liquids and gases are collected, measured, analysed. The babies' entire bodies are made transparent by radiograms and echograms, and their only integrity is through the inscriptions of graphs and luminous numbers on a machine which collects together everything that is known about them. It is hard not to think of the epistemo-somatic gap that Lacan spoke of in his 1966 paper at the Collège de medicine (2003): the gap between this "much-fêted" body, photographed in its entirety, calibrated, drawn up in diagrams, susceptible in every way to conditioning; and the body of jouissance, this "body made for jouissance". The body of jouissance is totally excluded from this epistemo-somatic relation.

During resuscitation, it is the machine which administers the correct dosage of oxygen, which feeds the babies without interruption, continuously, without making them wait, without fail.

The machine provides everything, but responds to nothing. This begs the question of the initiation of the circuits of the drives. In a NICU, babies do not know any lack, and their cries are not transformed into an appeal by the Other, who can be of help, who can bring help from the outside (Freud, 1950, p. 317). We have often observed that if no one addresses the babies during their first days of life, they will withdraw, and will stop seeking contact and communication; they will absent themselves. But the function of the voice, mixed with the sounds of the machines, can change this situation, unless the person who addresses the babies is actually identified with the machine.

It is not easy to work with mothers in a NICU, and initially their visits are often sporadic. The babies need the Other right away, and the Other is often constituted by the caregivers in the service. But resuscitations have become more and more difficult, and the associated risks have become ever greater, as the number of weeks of gestation has gone down. Thus, since smaller and smaller newborns are being resuscitated, the caregivers are also at risk of failure; just like the parents they hesitate to make an emotional investment in the babies because they are afraid that a few weeks down the line they will have to decide to withdraw all but palliative care. Babies in a NICU, as we have seen, can often give rise to more anguish than pleasure. These days, we run the risk of having to face the following situation: first, resuscitating, but keeping some distance to monitor developments over a few weeks; both resuscitating and not resuscitating; resuscitating, while protecting ourselves from having too much faith in the process. If the team withdraws emotionally, in the expectation that there will be uncertainties, if the mothers are invalidated in just the same way that the caregivers are, only for different reasons, then the babies remain in a void, as the difficulties they encounter in later years will testify. What becomes of them if they do not have an Other for whom they can make themselves an object? If they do not encounter the words of the Other because the parents are prevented from speaking to them, or the caregivers do not speak to them in a meaningful way, they will not be able to become inscribed in the signifying chain, in other words, as Lacan points out, in the symbolic world which is specific to human beings. Having to do without the signifiers of the Other means encountering a loss—a real loss and a symbolic lack, which is the first form in which castration appears. Without an encounter with the Other, the trauma of premature babies left to their machines could well be the traumatisation that is now represented by the impossibility of being traumatised by the encounter. The encounter with the desire of the Other, in other words, with the lack in the Other, constitutes a traumatisation which is indispensable in the constitution of the human subject.

If there is no Other for the babies to make themselves an object for, then they will identify with the world that surrounds them, and to which they can give absolutely no meaning—a pure Real. Winnicott gave us some idea of how babies feel, alone in their incubators. Cut off from their mothers, having lost all sign of her—her voice, her warmth, her smells, her rhythms, the sounds of her body—they cannot but be affected in their relation to the continuum of life. They begin to confuse themselves with the absolute Other, if no one comes to mediate between them. The machine becomes part of their body. What is more, in order for ventilation to be effective, these babies must not struggle against the machine with their own attempts at breathing. They have to become part of the machine, lose themselves in it. They cannot have a sense of existing, only of the machine existing for them in a closed system. When this happens, we can no longer attract their attention, they will not look at us. They become fascinated by the machine, and fall in love with it. It is the machine that gives them oxygen, feeds them without interruption or discontinuity, without making them wait. This is the moment when the question of the initiation of the circuit of the drives is posed. In a NICU, the babies know no lack. Babies on ventilators cannot call out. On the other hand, they can cry silently. But their tears are not detected by the machine; no sense can be made of them. They cannot unleash any emotion. The machine makes a noise, but it sees nothing, feels nothing, says nothing. It records numbers and graphs, but it understands nothing. Unlike the mother, it is never overwhelmed. And yet it is to this machine that the babies find themselves attached, both literally and metaphorically.

Whatever happens, the machine provides oxygen, nourishment, and the medication necessary for survival—whatever happens, without interruption, without cutting out, without delay, without making the babies wait; there is no rhythm in the lives of these babies, no discontinuity; there is no day or night; they are never hungry; they live outside time. With these machines, there is no time lag. It makes it difficult to historicise what is happening. The machine goes on feeding and oxygenating without saying anything and without making the babies wait. The machine itself does not expect anything. The only rhythm that can be counted on is the rhythm of the delivery of treatment, and treatment which is often painful. Pain is regarded as an extra element in the circuit of the drives; so how does that work for these babies? The regular rhythms for them are the ministrations of the nurses, the doctors' visits, the aspirations, the collection of samples, everything programmed at precise intervals, and doubtless they play an important role in finding a way to instil a sense of rhythm. It is in this rhythm that there is a place for a cut, for the presence and absence of the caregiver who mediates between the babies and their machines. What happens at these times is essential for the babies. It is then that the drives can enter into the equation for these babies, because in spite of all the denials of those who surround them, they have already been born, and they are already alive. Where will they find the strength to go on surviving? Certainly not in the machines, although they are indispensable. The caregivers will need to set aside their own infallibility, and agree to behave differently from the machines; they will need to be flexible enough to take part in the game of the supposition of subjectivity in the babies; and they, like the mothers, need to be able to reach the point where it is acceptable to do what is normal and leave the room. It is not easy for them, and sometimes it is painful, given that they have been trained to believe that medicine never "walks away". What is needed is the presence of the Other. There cannot be a register of the drive without the Other's demand, and there can be no satisfaction unless there is the question of the Other's jouissance. And this Other, laying down the armour of scientific immunity, needs to bear witness to something of her own jouissance in the presence of the babies, about whether they eat or breathe; and the Other needs also to show that she has limitations, and is concerned about the babies.

In the imagination of the parents, the machines that replace them are often threatening mother-figures, who suspect the mothers of not having done their work properly. The imaginary is unleashed, and the symbolic bearings are lost.

Colette Misrahi recalls in a paper on the family: "The machinery functions very well these days in hospital services where, in an atmosphere that is positively science fiction, premature babies, who are in mortal danger, grow and struggle. If they decide to live, they will babble, speak and walk 'like the others'. The symbolic can also function through a machine built by humans, for humans" (Misrahi, 1982 [translated for this edition]).

These machines, indeed, are the tools of the doctors' desire on behalf of the babies. They enable them not to die, "if they decide to live", as she explains. This is the desire that is at stake, this is what we need to pay attention to. Two babies, with the same weight, and born at the same term, attached to the same machines: one will die, and the other will live. That was the case with Anne and Anna. As we have seen, in order for the machine to function, it not only needs to work properly, but it also needs to be an integral part of the world of the babies and their parents. They need to take on a "human" meaning. That is why it is essential that parents take part in the care of their babies while they are in hospital.

"In some resuscitation services," wrote Françoise Loux, "they prefer to keep the parents away from this spectacle, which is certainly challenging. For me, it would have been far worse not to see Valentin. That would have left my imagination to run riot about the grief I would suffer, and the machines would have become devouring creatures.

I managed to get to know them [...] so in some way we became part of the care-giving team" (Loux, 1991, p. 56).

The machine should be at the service of those others who are around the babies, an intermediary between them and the babies. It should never be the babies' only "referent", for otherwise, if they are left in the void, the babies will exist without truly existing. Will they actually have the status of being, or will they be "machine bodies", alive, but without life?

In conclusion, I would like to quote Winnicott again, to give a different slant to this question, both for the teams and for the parents: let us not forget, he said, that the baby is a "potential individual", which to us looks "all the time like a human baby" (Winnicott, 1975, pp. 98–99). This affirmation, which is so subversive in a medical service, needs all our unceasing efforts—we must not rest until we can resuscitate it.

The birth of the subject

What are the likely psychical consequences of a stay in a high-tech medical unit, for these babies who are remarkably well cared for by specialists in neonatal resuscitation, surrounded by extremely attentive teams who have been trained in developmental care? How will these babies make the transition from being the object of medical care and science to the status of human subject? Because while looking after the well-being of the babies, and welcoming the parents, and reducing post-traumatic stress, are all of the greatest importance, it quickly became clear to us that this is not enough.

In order for babies to be born into the status of human subject, there has to be a supposition of subjectivity in them, as we have emphasised throughout this book. It is this "supposition of subjectivity" that supports the entire orientation of our work in neonatology. The subject is in the Other, whether this is constituted by the parents, the doctors, the nurses, or any of the other people who look into the incubator.

What is more, we have to consider that these babies have actually been born. This is not altogether straightforward in a NICU, where the prevailing fantasy seems to be to try to keep the babies in the same situation they were used to *in utero*. Everything seems to be done to make sure that the pregnancy continues in the incubator, waiting for the babies to reach maturity, and to breathe on their own, take nourishment themselves, and communicate.[11] The fantasy prevalent among doctors and teams reflects that of the mothers: "I can't believe I've been delivered, I can still feel him moving around in my belly." We have given a number of examples of this. The mother has still not separated from her baby, and that is why we have been able to demonstrate how difficult it has been for her to symbolise the birth.

Thus, where the baby is concerned, the psychoanalyst's role is to enable the subject-baby to come into being. As Colette Soler put it, it is a question of "mediating the operation of the signifier": "When the baby who comes to analysis is what I have called an 'object-baby', it is up to the analyst to mediate the operation of the signifier, that is to say, to produce what has not yet happened, and what can be called various things: cutting, separation, negativisation, the hole. In other words, to engender a subject-effect where there was none, which will have the scope of a defence against the Real" (Soler, 1994 [translated for this edition]).

Initially, the neonatology service must play the role of third party that will enable this separation. The service also needs to acknowledge that the baby has been born and allow something to have been lost. It is only on the basis of this loss that the subject can be constructed. That is what is at stake in order for subjectivity to be born; it is the opposite of making sure that absolutely nothing is lacking, either for the mother or the baby. At the heart of the subject is the void left by this necessary loss. The loss is necessary so that the subject can emerge from the Other.

This is because the subject, as we understand it, is neither the person nor the individual. It is a certain position in relation to speech and discourse that will allow it to emerge. While it is spoken about before it can speak, its anticipated articulation in the discourse of the Other prepares the pathway for its emergence when it begins to speak. This is where the "supposition of the subject" comes in, as we understand it to be a necessary moment in anticipation of its coming into being.

Where the parents are concerned, we now know that it is not sufficient to help them get used to the consequences of the traumatic birth, nor for them to have skin-to-skin contact with the baby, nor to let them help with caregiving, nor to educate them to behave correctly. It is more a question of allowing them to come to terms with the loss themselves, as well as with the importance of their own role (which is not just changing nappies or doing small things to make the baby comfortable). It is about allowing them to think, to find the words to speak about what the violence of the birth means for them in terms of their own history, and helping them to find out how, on the basis of what has happened, they can find a way to bond with their baby.

As far as the team is concerned, it is also a question of giving up the idea of omnipotence in order to become truly effective, and accepting the notion of presenting themselves as lacking subjects to help these babies, who ask for nothing more than to be communicated with, in however small a way. This is how psychical resuscitation will be possible, and the babies will have a chance of being born as human subjects.

Notes

1. Evaluation of carbon dioxide level in the blood.
2. An illness specific to newborns, occurring at birth and causing respiratory distress.
3. An acute intestinal infection which may occur during the premature baby's stay in hospital.
4. "De mères en filles: une équipe suédoise réalise deux transplantations d'utérus", *Journal international de medicine*, 19 September 2012. See also the BBC report "Mother-to-daughter womb transplant 'success' in Sweden", 18 September 2012.
5. A genetically determined condition associated with cardiac problems, anomalies of the palate, poor regulation of calcium, disturbance of the immune system, and learning difficulties.
6. Respiratory sequelae of hyaline membrane disease in premature babies, which require oxygen therapy beyond the twenty-eighth day of life and/or the thirty-sixth week since the last menstrual period.
7. We can now see why plunging babies into an artificial and completely soundless universe, as may sometimes be the case in a NICU, would cause them anguish.
8. The research protocol developed by the French PREAUT team (Prevention of Autism) offers a range of tools to identify early disturbances in communication that may be predictive of a serious developmental disturbance.
9. Oxygenation measured by a cutaneous monitor.
10. Lowering of heart rate.
11. Again we recall D. W. Winnicott's claim that premature babies would feel nothing until they had reached the age at which they were due to be born, and that up to that point, the best thing for them was the incubator.

CHAPTER FOUR

Working with the team

The neonatal unit team

The team of personnel working in a NICU is rather like the crew of a ship. Each individual fulfils a very precise function, from the captain to the lowest ranking sailor; they all depend on one another in order to ensure that the ship sails well. The individual members need to share a common philosophy, a common purpose, so that in spite of poor weather, or moments of discouragement or uncertainty, they can keep heading for their destination. In a NICU, the ship will pass through many storms.

A nurse said to me one day, "It's a bit like living in wartime, we have to battle on all fronts." It is a constant struggle against death—which cannot be countenanced for a newborn—against the risks of taking one's eye off the ball, which could result in disastrous errors, against one's own anxiety, and sometimes against the parents, who seem to come just to "get in the way", or to make the team's work even more difficult. Sometimes it may even happen that there will be open or barely concealed strife within the team, when certain decisions seem incomprehensible.

Why is resuscitation being continued when all it is doing is making the baby suffer unnecessarily? Why is one intervention decided on rather than another that might be more comfortable for the newborn?

The decision-makers have to keep explaining why they have decided to intervene in a particular way, so that the team continues to trust in them, and the whole ship's crew feels safe. But safety in a NICU can only ever be a relative thing. In spite of all the progress made in recent years, science does not have the answer to everything. Even if decisions are taken unanimously by all the doctors on the team, even if their wisdom, their knowledge, and their will to cure cannot be doubted, it is doubt that constantly dogs them. Nursery nurses, auxiliaries, or nurses are not alone in suffering this anguish. It haunts the doctors, too, and brings with it the risk of depression or aggressivity; they, more than the others, are constantly faced with their own limitations, and for each doctor in his or her own way, with the problematic of grief.

While there is no shortage of difficulties, it is these very difficulties that prove that the team is still alive. It is the struggle for life that quite consciously serves as a compass; unconsciously, the question is complicated by the death drive, which is working silently in each individual. This unseen force sometimes brings about crises which are not always easy to resolve. The majority of doctors working in NICUs are former paediatricians who have been drawn to neonatology by a passion for high-tech medicine, by whatever is represented for them by the idea of being closer to life and death, by a taste for pushing themselves further and further in an environment where the smallest of decisions or interventions, in a matter of seconds, can enable a life to be saved. Nothing is known in advance; each baby is different and presents an enigma for the doctor that forces him or her to question everything over again.

We can only admire the seriousness and the responsible attitude that each one of these doctors brings to his or her work. Nonetheless, psychoanalysts will discern other unconscious motivations in this choice of career. Might someone choose paediatrics through an identification with the child one never stops trying to heal? Might it be in order to restore the mother's imaginary baby in order to give this marvellous baby back to her in good health, this baby she must not be deprived of? Or could it be in order to save the little brother or sister one might have wished to strangle with one's own hands in his or her crib, when overwhelmed by the ferocious *invidia* that is usual in childhood?

While this debate might be of some theoretical interest, I do not personally believe that it is particularly useful in an analyst's work in a NICU. It is not the analysis of the doctors' unconscious motivations that will enable the doctors to take the best possible care of the babies they are responsible for; that is not the role of the analyst.

The main aim of the work, for us as well as for the doctors, is the "resuscitation" of the babies, so we need to work with the doctors and not against them. What sort of analyst would boast, in some kind of fantasy of omnipotence, that she could speak the absolute truth about a doctor's unconscious, and that she was therefore in the position magically to resolve all the problems in a team? If we were to act in this way, we would certainly prevent the doctors from working at all. That is far from being our aim. What we want to do is to enable them to speak about the difficulties they are encountering, and to consider a different approach to the babies and their families. We hope that they can join us in questioning the team's transferences and their individual reactions to each baby's specific history. That would be a far more fruitful position for us to take. It is often difficult for caregivers to realise what the babies and their families are going through, because they are in such a very different position.

Alice

Alice's history teaches us this in an exemplary fashion, because this young woman had been a nurse in our unit for two years. She knew the whole team, and had good memories of those two years of work, until her own baby was transferred to our service after she gave birth prematurely. She told us of the terrible feeling of strangeness that overwhelmed her. She had completely forgotten how to care for a newborn, and did not dare to look after her son, but rather waited for authorisation from the nurses; and although she came to see him every day, she told me that when he was discharged a month after the delivery, she had the feeling she did not know him at all. He was a stranger, and she was at a loss. She told me that she had stayed at home for five days and nights, holding the baby in her arms, before she realised that the nightmare was over, and they could finally bond with each other. Alice told me jokingly, "Really, I think things would have gone better in the service if I could have put my white coat back on ... I'd have been better off if he hadn't been my baby, if I'd just been his nursery nurse. It's really not the same thing, being a mum. Everything confuses us, we're terrified of everything, we ask idiotic questions even if we know exactly what the answers are; we just forget everything we knew!"

A few weeks later, Julien's mother, who had never been a nurse, said, "When I leave the service, I'm going to buy a white coat so that my son thinks I'm a doctor and will feel reassured."

But isn't it rather the mother who is reassured by the white coat, who feels the need to slip into someone else's skin, that of the person who knows how to give life, and appears to be sure of what she is doing? Alice was surprised that she felt very aggressive towards her former nursing colleagues on some days. "I resented them looking after my son in my place. I had no idea that a NICU could have that effect on a mother. I was awful to the team!"

Sometimes the parents' violence can emerge among the caregivers in the service. Some mothers unleash aggressivity in the caregivers, as they project on to the hospital the image of a monstrous place inhabited by demonic creatures who are taking pleasure in kidnapping and tormenting their babies.

But in such cases, the team needs to realise that this is projection, that the mother is desperately trying to distance herself from the awful reality, and to see herself as "good".

It is during the period of separation that the mothers, with the help of the team, should be able to develop a sense of motherhood. Often these mothers will go through significant psychical changes, which will eventually enable them to start to build a relationship with their baby.

Babies and their caregivers

In some NICUs, the auxiliaries are also called "baby-whisperers"; their mission, in addition to their normal caregiving, is to "enchant" the babies. They get to know them very well, they often manage to express what the babies are feeling, what they want, and they find it easier to speak of their character or their habits than the doctors do. They will immediately pick up the rhythm of the babies' breathing, an insistent look, a wish to withdraw or avoid contact. When the babies are having their nappies changed or being washed, they can sometimes be playful, and they like to take the time to speak to the babies. They will give a longer bath to a baby who seems to be enjoying it; or a quicker one to another who appears anxious. This complicity that they know how to create with the babies is extremely valuable. The head of service told me he pays a great deal of attention to their comments, for instance if they say that a baby is not drinking properly, or is too quiet. This kind of sensitivity is very important, and is complementary to the medical examination of the babies. Over the years, we have come to appreciate the capacity they have to bring the service to life. The state of mind of the caregivers is important for the babies too.

As Brazelton put it, "We have to acknowledge that infants are exquisitely sensitive to their caregivers' moods, and that this is translated into their own behaviour. [...] the effects of the still-face experiment [leave] little doubt about this" (Brazelton & Cramer, 1991, p. 142).

The "still face" experiment, which we have discussed earlier, is very well-known in the field of experimentation concerning neonates. Brazelton was the first to study the effects of the mothers' facial expressions on their babies. If babies in hospital are surrounded by impassive faces for a significant part of each day, they will not be able to go out into the world and develop normally.

It is important to note that the psychological development of many babies who are in hospital for a long time after birth is perfectly fine. There is no systematic risk of pathological development associated with the pain and difficulties of hospitalisation. Nor should we fall in to the trap of thinking that all babies who suffer in this way will be left with organic sequelae or be marked for life. It will all depend on their experience during their stay in the unit.

The operative factor will be the meaning that this time in hospital will take on for the child. The biological disturbance the babies are prone to will not necessarily entail a symbolic disturbance (Raimbault, 1982). What will they retain from this time in the NICU? Holes in their bodies? Emotional deprivation? What about the destiny of the drives? It is all right to make holes in their bodies, provided we do not make holes in the symbolic. As long as there have not been any "gaping voids" in their history, as long as their signifying bearings have been respected, there will not be a disaster. It seems there are two essential elements:

1. The team should take its bearings from the same desire to encounter the baby as a human subject. This desire should never be forgotten, because otherwise, as Freud made clear, the child can easily be caught up in the adults' perversion, and being already predisposed at this early stage to become an "erotic plaything" (Freud, 1912d, p. 180), could become an object of science and of sadism. The function of the team should be to enable the babies to live autonomously, without

ever thinking of them as anything other than human subjects. That is what will enable the babies to give meaning to their hospitalisation. The coherence of the team will avoid the risks of "gaping voids".

2. On the other hand, it is vital that the parents can be included in speaking about the rupture that has marked their history. This period of time can be used to try to deal the cards differently. The work involves both the analyst and the team. It is important that the parents have a good "reception", and that differences and individual rhythms are respected. The babies will be constituted, and their fantasies constructed, on the basis of the internal worlds of the parents and the caregivers.

Fortunately, the caregivers are living beings. They enter wholeheartedly into communicating with their little patients. They know that babies need to be cuddled and carried, and that it is not just silence and rest that they need, but exchanges, melody, sounds, voices. While some noises are best avoided so as not to overstimulate the babies (as is quite rightly prescribed in NIDCAP), other sounds, such as the voices of the caregivers, should not be silenced on the pretext of the risk of giving "excessive" stimulation. We should not confuse the sounds that disturb the babies with those that help them to live.

The melody of words, which Peter Fonagy (1983) speaks of, the rhythm of the voices of the mothers and the baby-whisperers which are addressed to the babies with this special intonation known as motherese, are necessary to newborns, and are of far greater interest to them than the normal tone of voice of one adult addressing another. It is not just that they love the melody of the words; they also need it as much as the oxygen delivered by the ventilator, or the milk delivered through the gastric tube.

In her introduction to *Clinique du reel*, Guite Guérin (1982, p. 9) reminds us of King Frederick II, in the thirteenth century, who set up his own nursery. In order to discover what language babies would speak spontaneously, the original language of human beings, he took forty babies away from their families. The women who looked after them were told to feed and wash them, but they were forbidden to speak to them, cuddle them, or address them. They were not allowed to speak to each other, either, so the children would never hear any melody, any sound of a human voice. Frederic hoped that the children would start to speak naturally at the appropriate age, and would reveal the secret of original language. But not only did none of the children ever speak, they all died before the age of eight. So let us not transform our services into Frederic II-style nurseries on the pretext of avoiding overstimulation!

The way we speak and listen to babies is mediated by the attention we give to their bodies and to the emotions they arouse in us. Nurses are very careful to try to decode the babies' cries and to make them as comfortable as possible. They are attentive to noises that might upset them, or smells they might find unpleasant. They are even concerned about the taste of the medication they give to them. They try, by "putting themselves in the babies' place", to understand what annoys them or what might contribute to their well-being. Their position in the incubator, the way they twitch when we make a noise nearby, their reactions, the faces they pull, their looks, everything has a meaning. One year, they even noticed that one of the cleaning products smelt different from usual, and that it had upset the babies, who were already accustomed to the morning cleaning ritual. They know that babies who are crying can be comforted by a change of position, and gain relief from not always being restrained and stretched out on their backs. Once the babies are clinically well enough, the caregivers will do all they can to make sure they are as comfortable as possible. But they are also well aware that babies need to hear human voices and have truthful words addressed to them.

This type of attention involves taking up a position other than that of observer. It involves being "caught up" in a relationship with the babies, and accepting that there is an interaction, an exchange. In order to be containing, one has to give something of oneself: that is what seems to us to be most essential in the bond between caregivers and babies.

All the babies' expressions, all the manifestations of their bodies, need to be picked up on; their emotions need to be recognised and transformed into words by the caregiver, who will have understood the meaning of the babies' cries, and will enable them to start to feel alive, not only because their bodies have been resuscitated, but because they have started to exist, and then their ability to think can begin to develop.

Ward rounds

In the service, ward rounds take place several times a day. The doctors and nurses pause by each incubator, collating all the latest information on the babies, evaluating how they are developing, and discussing possible changes in their treatment, or asking for tests to be carried out.

There is a "change-over" from one duty doctor to the next, as well as the file containing the scrupulously noted details of treatment and all the developmental parameters. Given the workload in the service, however, although these ward rounds are carried out extremely precisely and meticulously, they are of necessity quite brief, and do not leave time to address the babies themselves or to speak about them other than in technical terms. So we suggested that the team should make another visit during the day, going from incubator to incubator, talking to the babies and speaking with them. Gradually, the members of the team who were "intrigued" by this notion started to join us in ever-increasing numbers on this different kind of ward round. We would also speak among ourselves and with the babies about their histories, their families, and their particular ways of being with the team and dealing with the experience of being in hospital, which were different in each case.

In addition, we set up a weekly ward round in which everyone, from the head of service to the auxiliaries, would be asked to speak about possibilities and constraints from their point of view. At these meetings we would speak about the babies, the problems they were giving the caregivers, their history, their reactions, however tiny, which might give us some clue as to how we could understand them and respond to them better. We would try together to speak "from the babies' point of view". All these children are fighting for their lives, in a new environment for which they are unprepared emotionally and psychologically. There are as many possible responses to this situation as there are babies. And this is what makes life extremely difficult for the caregivers: while taking into account all the care and treatment that is indispensable for the babies' survival, they also need to take account of their suffering, what they are trying to tell us, the language that is most often mediated by their bodies, and which we have to understand in a way that is of course medical, but also as a plea addressed to the other, which requires a response that is not merely mechanical.

For example, it is not easy to have to aspirate[1] babies, which is extremely unpleasant for them, while at the same time having to take into account their discomfort and distress. This extra attention we expect from nurses puts them in a very difficult situation; it causes great anxiety and adds significantly to their workload. In order to be able to be attuned to premature babies, the caregivers need at the very least to suffer from the illness[2] that Winnicott called "primary maternal preoccupation", without, however, allowing this identification to make them carry out the necessary intervention in a hesitant way, which would only make the babies even more uncomfortable. The caregivers, who speak to the babies in terms that are not technical ones—the latter can sometimes be used as a defence—find themselves speaking about themselves, their own reactions, their children, or their childhoods. Although their listening for difficulties should be attentive and benevolent, they are never under any circumstances authorised to make "wild" interpretations. Sometimes there are liaison meetings with the maternity unit of our hospital. Midwives, nurses, and psychologists come and speak to us about the babies and their families. In our capacity as analysts, we are not in a position to evaluate or make judgements about what they say, or about the way the caregivers react; but we are all in the same boat, and we try to work alongside them in seeking new ideas, new openings which might help us all to understand the babies better and to respond to them in a more fruitful way. One child might have been upset in the last few days and unable to stop crying; another may be looking away from us, seeming to want to get away from our presence; another may be struggling against the machine which is keeping him alive, or against the care we have to lavish on him. We always try to find a reason why. Maybe we are paying too little attention to one baby, and giving too much stimulation to another. Perhaps there were some difficulties last time the parents visited.

Why is this particular baby arousing aggression in the service, or sympathy, or dislike? The caregivers always try to understand which mechanisms of projection and which conflicts within the service, or with the parents, might mean that the babies run the risk of paying the price. In these liaison meetings, we work on papers by psychoanalysts, cognitive therapists, neurologists, and linguists who write about the current understanding of babies' abilities. The paper can function as a third party; it is not a question of "fake" knowledge, but rather of allowing a different light to be cast on these cases, making us question these histories we are living through in different ways, because they are different for each baby. For example, a paper such as Sylvia Ferreira's (1998), which we mentioned earlier, on "turn-talking", enabled us to look at things differently, even though it was presented as an experiment. She describes the very subtle moment, between ten and sixteen weeks, when mothers will address their babies and respect their right to have a turn at talking: they speak, and leave the babies time to reply. What the mothers say is influenced by the way the babies respond.

There are many aspects to this exchange: looks, facial expressions, tone of voice. The language of visual signs is important, as if what interests the babies is also what can be "seen" in language.

According to this experiment, the babies' cognitive organisation will later depend on how much respect has been paid to "turn-talking". This privileged moment initiates something in the development of speech, and certainly in the emergence of the subject. What matters is that the person who speaks knows that they need to wait. It is in this waiting that something about separation can be situated. This first moment is what Colwyn Trevarthern called "the protoconversation" (Trevarthen & Marwick, 1986), as mentioned earlier. Everything happens as if the mothers, by giving them a turn to speak, were questioning their babies: "Do you desire my desire?" It is not so much the fact that the mothers speak, but that the desire of the one can be articulated with the desire of the other, which seems to us to be important in order to allow the children to find a way of communicating. So it is not sufficient to talk to babies—you also have to leave them time to reply. But do we always respect this? It is not useful to flood babies with words for the sake of it, as a recording device might do; we also need to give meaning to the words, and accept interruptions and phrasing. It takes two to speak, based on the acceptance of being separate from the other. Trevarthen has shown scientifically that babies at twenty minutes old want nothing more than to communicate with the other. They are already co-ordinated. Their hands express their emotions. Sensory exchange is vital for them, and Trevarthen calls this demand for communication "the motive"—the babies' drive to want to communicate.

Here again, it is surprising when we note that the types of research that are in fashion nowadays confirm the intuitions of psychoanalysts who have been working with babies for twenty years. Many years before, as we have already mentioned, Françoise Dolto was the first to try to convince us of what was so obvious to her. Was it because her message was not supported by graphs, graphics, or computers, that it was so hard for it to be heard?

During ward rounds and liaison meetings, the theme that recurs most often is that of separation. The problematic of grief is constantly present in teams like these. The babies are almost always in danger of death, at least during the first few days after their admission to the service.

When they recover, in some cases after many weeks in the service, they go home with their parents. The team has to grieve for its role as the good and omnipotent mother who has given life to these babies. That is the price that has to be paid so that a place can be made in the service for the actual mothers. It is not easy to go beyond this fantasy, and in every meeting we have to find a new way to deal with this question.

Baby X

Some babies are born under the sign of the "X"—meaning that they are given three first names and passed on to child social services, or else to an adoption agency. If they are premature, they will remain with us until they are out of danger, then will go to a nursery or a nanny, awaiting the day when they can be taken into an adoptive family. For the time being, however, they are nobody's baby. The team's emotional investment in these cases is rather different. Who has not, at one time or another, had the fantasy of taking one of these abandoned babies home with her? At these moments, the vocation of good mother appears in all its glory. These babies are more often taken out of their incubators and cuddled; their departure is more painful as a consequence. They will be imbued with positive qualities—he was so calm, she was so affectionate, they were livelier than the others. Things unfold as if the absence of the birth mother at visiting times allows these babies to be invested very differently.

One of the projects which came out of a series of ward rounds and liaison meetings was that an album would be made up for each of these babies, with photos from the time of birth to the point of discharge from the unit. The albums tell the story of their time with us, their medical development, but also their habits, their likes and dislikes. Photos are taken of the babies in the arms of their favourite nurses. The albums are given to the babies, and accompany them to their adoptive homes (this is now normal practice in most maternity units and NICUs, in any case of a Baby X).

It took a great deal of work to reach the point where a common agreement was made to refer in the album to the birth parents and the woman who had "given up" the baby.

All the caregivers would write a few words on the final page to say goodbye to the baby. "Think of us from time to time", "You will always be in our hearts", "You were the loveliest baby in the world". These few dedications show how deeply the teams invest emotionally in these babies; these albums act as an intermediary between the caregivers and the babies, and are equally important for all concerned.

In all cases of a Baby X, it was now possible to express this investment. It was later decided in another meeting that we would make up albums for other babies who stayed in the service for a long time, so that they too could take away something of the team with them—something they had been taking with them anyway, but now it could be symbolised by words.

Marie: the little girl who did not like fairy tales

Marie was born on a winter's morning to a young woman aged nineteen. She was full term and healthy, but had to be admitted to the service because of a sudden fever, on her second day of life.

Her mother had come to the hospital to give birth as a "Mrs. X". She had managed to hide the pregnancy from her family. The social worker at the maternity unit, who had put the file together, had as usual explained to her that she had two months in which to change her mind. But Marie's mother explained that she would not be changing her mind. She did not want to give the baby a name. She did not want to know what sex the baby was, and above all was anxious that her parents, with whom she was living, should not know anything about what had happened. Everything was done as she wished. The baby was not put into her arms when she was born; Marie was taken into the nursery without any contact with her birth mother. Mrs. X had told us that she had had a one-night stand with Marie's father, he did not know she was pregnant, and she had never seen him again since.

For the first two days, the baby had no problems. Then suddenly and brutally, she started to vomit the milk she was fed, and refused to drink any more. She was transferred to our service when she had lost twelve per cent of her birth weight. What is more, she was less reactive than she had been at birth, and her face seemed to express a profound sadness.

For a few days, the doctors paid a great deal of attention to her case, but then it became clear that she was not ill. She was letting herself die gradually, without anyone being able to offer a diagnosis of the cause of her symptoms.

My first attempt to establish contact with Marie was completely fruitless. She was a lovely baby, eight days old, but already she was looking away, avoiding contact, throwing her head backwards, and stiffening when anyone tried to pick her up. This baby seemed to be suffering terribly, and yet the fever had gone, and the doctors were convinced that it was not her body that was causing her to suffer. But she had to stay in the service because she was refusing her bottles.

I asked to be informed about what had happened in the maternity unit during the first two days of her life. They told me that nothing had happened—nothing unusual in cases of a Baby X.

Our task is always the same—we speak to the babies about their biological mothers and their biological fathers, and explain that they can't take care of them, but that some other parents will come and look after them. We speak to them in the most positive terms possible, saying that they'll have a lovely life, that they will be happy thanks to their birth mother, who has agreed to give them to parents who will be able to look after them.

We had done all this according to the book, but in Marie's case, this version of reality did not suit her; she had withdrawn from the world, avoiding contact with others to the extent of refusing her bottles.

My first meeting with Marie was difficult. It crossed my mind that she was suffering from an indigestion of words, that she did not want to hear this fairy tale story. It seemed to me that she was vomiting up all the reasonable and anodyne explanations that told her of nothing but maternal love and glorious days to come. When I picked Marie up, she was a little ball of shrieking fury, and I was quite sure she was expecting another kind of discourse.

Every time I came to see her, I decided to speak to her about the violence of the separation, and the horror and suffering she had experienced at being so harshly rejected. I spoke to her about the mother who did not want her, of her mother's voice she had heard while she was in the womb, and then had been lost for her, about the rhythms of her mother's body that she would never find again.

Little by little, day by day, Marie began to relax. She would now look at me, and rest a while in the nurses' arms, who just wanted to coddle her. She could now decide whether to live or die, but if she wanted what we could offer her, we would be there for her, because we do not live in a world where abandoned children are left alone.

What did Marie understand in my discourse? The meaning of the words, the intonation of the voice? The affect? Or was it the physical contact that I always establish with a baby I am talking to? I have no idea how to answer these questions, but in any case, day by day, she settled down, started to feed normally and accepted the mothering interventions of the nurses.

There were some more difficult moments, for example when the nanny who was to take care of her for two months before her adoption arrived in the service. Again, the team explained to her that this was not her biological mother and that it was perhaps quite normal that she didn't want to accept her from day one, and then everything seemed to settle down again.

When she was discharged from the service, taking with her the album that, as usual, told the story of her trajectory through the unit, she also took away her own mystery, and left the team feeling amazed and puzzled as to what had been going on for her in her encounter with us.

The team and the parents

During the ward rounds, the caregivers also talk about the parents. At present, in adult ICUs, the visiting hours are regulated far more than in NICUs. Only babies can benefit from the presence of the parents throughout the day. This difference is entirely due to the efforts of specialists in resuscitation in NICUs. What could be more difficult than trying to work under the close observation of the mother and father? What is more complicated than taking decisions that are sometimes urgent, and require rather harsh interventions, while trying for better or worse to reply to the thousand questions the parents are asking? Working in their presence poses plenty of questions in itself, even when the situation is not dramatic. But if the doctors accept this additional difficulty, it is because they know that the parents can help their babies' recovery, just as the babies can help them to survive the painful trials of separation.

Romana Negri[3] has spoken of the constant sense of paranoia that hovers over a NICU. Obviously it is amplified by anxiety, very real risks, and the fear of making the smallest error, but also the sense of being constantly scrutinised by the parents (Negri, 1994). While it is true that parents, caught up in their anxiety about their babies' hospitalisation, are sometimes aggressive towards members of the team, the caregivers for their part quite often find it difficult to step back a little and understand the parents' attitude, which is sometimes frankly difficult to tolerate. All sorts of projections are made on to members of the team, sometimes as superheroes who are the only ones capable of deciding matters of life and death, or sometimes as monsters who come between mothers and their babies without the slightest shred of pity. The team needs to be able to assess whether, as in most cases, it is a question of defence mechanisms, attempts at projection, ways of keeping a distance, by means of which the mother can desperately seek to see herself as "good".

In other cases, as we can see from all the clinical cases we have cited, the words of a nurse can be absolutely essential for a mother. They often say that they prefer to speak to the nurses rather than the doctors, as Françoise Loux has confirmed: "I've always preferred talking to the nurses ... What is the point of seeking out the doctors, tormenting them by forbidding them to speak about the future or say the word 'death'? ... The nurses helped me to feel at home in the hospital, where my child's daily life unfolded in an atmosphere of love and warmth. Their loving kindness managed to mask the neon lights, the noise of the machines, and the whiteness" (Loux, 1991, p. 60).

The nurses reassure the mothers, give them permission to visit their babies, and allow for more "light-hearted" conversations and a measure of complicity. Often the mothers prefer to speak to the nurses rather than the service psychologists, with whom they feel more inhibited and judged, and who do not have any physical, body-to-body contact with the babies. They want to speak about their own babies, not about themselves, at least at the beginning.

In our ward rounds, we enable the team, when speaking about the parents, not only to recognise the mechanism of transference they are caught up in, but also to cast a different light on their own transference to the parents. Speaking about the babies' histories and the family signifiers into which the babies have been born, allows all members of staff the chance to escape a little from the idea of the "norm" that is so present in the services where mothers and babies are treated, and which in itself can cause a great deal of harm. A "good mother" and a "good father" have to have just the right attitude: they have to be present, understanding, and ask questions, but not too many. They must not be afraid of their babies, must agree to touch them, change them, speak to them, visit at times that are convenient, and, preferably, show their gratitude for what is being done for them.

Working with the caregivers enables them to realise that good mothers may refuse to come into the service if they believe, for example, that they may harm their babies by going near them; or that good fathers may refuse to change nappies, or may become aggressive with doctors who have not had time to answer one of their questions.

In ward rounds, it is important that caregivers realise the scope of their responsibility, not only towards the babies but also towards the parents. What are the parameters the team uses, for example, to define good or bad parents? Because it brings them face-to-face with their own childhoods, these parameters are by definition subjective, laden with prejudices, marked with traces of their own histories, and trapped in repression.

It takes a great deal of effort to enable babies to leave the unit with parents who have actually remained their own; it entails a huge additional workload, and requires all sorts of involvement at a deeply personal level.

It seems essential to me that the team should not become identified with "good parents", just as they should not be caught up in the myth of the happy birth in which babies and parents are one. On the contrary, the principal role of the caregivers should be to act as a third party. During the phase of separation, the mothers should be developing their sense of motherhood, and the team has a fundamental role in this work. The team really has to "hand over" to the mothers, otherwise they will be stuck with the feeling of strangeness they so often express: "He won't recognise me when we get home, and I won't recognise him, either, because it won't be me who's been looking after him."

If all goes well, and if it is possible to avoid normalising or psychologising morality, we can give mothers time to get to know their babies; this will enable them to go through a significant psychological change while the baby is in hospital, and allow them to build up their maternal feelings, which do not arise automatically, in spite of ancestral beliefs which are very hard to change.

The team has to accept absolutely that mothers and fathers may not feel drawn to their babies.

"If that's what her life's going to be like," said Sabrina's mother, "it's really not worth it, it's better if she dies." Faced with sick babies, the mothers, whose desire may already have withered away, can no longer recognise themselves as mothers, and cannot recognise the babies as their own. Getting away from their babies is the only means left to them to demonstrate that they actually have a maternal instinct. At such times, it is vital that the mothers are understood and supported by the caregivers in the service. These mothers know something, and it has to be accepted. It is the old preconceived ideas that must be dealt with and turned on their heads in the ward rounds. The caregivers need to be encouraged to accept the role of protectors between the parents and the babies, without being obliged to force themselves to concoct some fantasy about the love of the parents.

There is never a good reason to "force" the relationship between mothers and their babies. We all have our prejudices, and it is not always easy to go beyond them. But it is at the heart of the work we have to do in the ward rounds and liaison meetings.

Jade

Jade's mother had just given birth prematurely at the hospital. The little girl was gorgeous; she was born at twenty-nine weeks and weighed 1.15 kilos.

This woman had been living in the psychiatric hospital for several years, where she had been diagnosed with schizophrenia, and another patient in the hospital had fathered the child.

At first, the baby did not cause the team any particular problems: it was a straightforward premature birth, without pulmonary distress, and without any complications whatsoever.

When she first visited, Jade's mother was calm, smiling, and extremely friendly with the nurses. She was gazing absently into the distance, and hardly looked at Jade at all; she went off to get dressed in the changing rooms while Jade's nurse was explaining how the incubator worked, as is usual on a parent's first visit. She agreed to come in to my office for the first appointment, which is given routinely when a baby is admitted to the service. There was no mention of Jade. She spoke about her life in the hospital; she wanted to go back as soon as possible, she said, now her stomach was flat again. She also spoke to me about her mother, and complained, in a very heartfelt and pained way, that she had never visited her once since she had been in hospital. We spoke together about this hurt, which could not be soothed by any neuroleptic. She said she could remember nothing of her childhood, and then touched her belly and said, "Right, I'm cured now, I want to go back to the hospital."

The maternity services had agreed with the psychiatric hospital that the delivery should take place under general anaesthetic. The fact that Jade was premature had meant she could not remain with her mother.

I wondered whether this woman realised she had given birth. In any case, it was about her own mother and her lack of visits that she spoke to me on the occasion of her first visit to her daughter.

The psychiatric hospital contacted the NICU in order to set up regular visits, so that she could come and see Jade accompanied by psychiatric nurses. They told us that the whole psychiatric team had high hopes of this baby making a big difference to her mother.

This woman had been maltreated in the past and, following a period of neglect and abandonment by her own mother which some neighbours reported, she had been taken into care.

The psychiatric team's hope was that this baby could cure that devastating mother–daughter relationship, as if Jade might suddenly found herself in a position to stop her mother being schizophrenic.

The young woman came to see her baby regularly, but did not want to touch her. One day I found myself standing next to her, and watched how she panicked when a nurse took Jade out of her incubator and put her into the woman's arms. At my request, we did not insist that there should be any physical contact between them. But each time she visited, we tried to speak to them both, and to speak specifically about their suffering. Jade's mother liked it when we talked to her baby. One day, she turned to me and said, "What should I say to her? When my mother comes to see me in hospital, will she speak to me?"

Jade left the service and was cared for by a nanny. But the psychiatric service, still wanting to maintain the contact at any price, organised a first visit for the mother to see her baby in the new setting. She had considerable support from the psychiatric nurses, and this visit went very well, far better than the visits to our service. The baby had been held by her mother, and she had even managed to give her a bottle. A second visit was organised for the following week by the ever-enthusiastic team from the psychiatric hospital, encouraged by what they considered to be the success of the first visit, but on the very morning of that proposed visit, Jade's mother killed herself by throwing herself from the highest window in the hospital.

The dramatic story of Jade caused a considerable stir in the NICU team. Without doubt it enabled us to understand a little better how difficult a mother, whether schizophrenic or not, may find it to encounter her own baby, or truly to take the baby on following the drama of birth.

A mother's history may prevent her from creating a bond with her child without the risk of death. Perhaps we can think that Jade's mother's abandonment of her, which dramatically repeated the abandonment she had experienced herself, was the only means she had to save her daughter. Once again, it would have been better to have listened to her, rather than thinking it was possible to re-educate her, for her own good, by "adapting" her to her daughter.

In a NICU, death is by definition a difficult subject to broach. We found out just how difficult it is when our head of service suggested we should organise some team meetings to speak about "palliative care".

Palliative care

Progress in neonatal medicine, and particularly in the field of prematurity, has been quite spectacular in recent years. Thanks to considerable technical advances, neonatology has really been able to reinvent itself, and specialists in the field have been able to rethink their practice. Whatever the discipline, rethinking a particular way of functioning is always a sign of good health. It has been possible to resuscitate babies at lower and lower birth weights (the limits of viability are fixed by the WHO at twenty-two weeks and 500 grams), and this has meant that doctors now have to make ever more difficult decisions. This new power to save lives means that teams are faced with ethical questions. It has always been the case that neonatal medicine has been torn between the desire to resuscitate, to save babies at any price, and the fear of pushing it too far, and risking creating disabled children through their excessive therapeutic zeal. In earlier days, the decision to withdraw life-support was taken clandestinely, and the parents, who were simply told that their baby's condition had worsened, would only arrive at the service after the baby had died, and the baby's body had most often already been transferred to the mortuary. The very idea of death was thus kept away from the team as a whole. Once the doctor had decided to end a baby's life by withdrawing life support, doctor and team needed to move on to something else, to remain committed to the project of life and of resuscitation.

Nowadays in France, the Kouchner Law of 2002, concerning the patient's right to information, and the Leonetti Law of 2005, concerning the patient's rights at the end of life, have made this practice impossible, because they stress the prohibition of "intentionally causing death".

Saving a baby "at any price" is thus brought back into question, and "excessive therapeutic zeal", nowadays qualified as "unreasonable obstinacy", is no longer authorised. Since these laws have been ratified, NICUs have been obliged to set up palliative care protocols, to replace medically induced death, which is now illegal.

In France article L 1110–10 of the Public Health Code defines palliative care as follows: "Active and continuing care, practised by an interdisciplinary team in an institution or at home, with the aim of relieving pain, reducing physical suffering, and safeguarding the dignity of the sick person, and supporting his or her entourage." But while palliative care is easier to think about and set up in the case of adult patients at the end of their lives, it remains poorly defined and far more difficult to organise for patients who are the beginning of their lives, whether on a labour ward or in a NICU. While we know that in giving life to a child, we also give them death (since all living beings are mortal), we still try to distance ourselves from the idea of death, to "repress" this eventuality, where the birth of a baby is concerned. Whereas death may be an acceptable idea in relation to adults, and even wished for in the case of an incurable illness, it remains extremely difficult to entertain the idea where newborn babies are concerned, however poor their state of health.

In France palliative care has become obligatory by law, but because it is still not very clearly defined for the beginning of life, the services concerned have had to invent ways of administering care and putting it in place. The exact manner in which such care should be given has not exactly been a "turnkey project" for us; and we continue to have to be creative in each case, with each different family.

In order for the teams to be able to work out how they would provide palliative care in their own way, we had to facilitate a real change of heart throughout the service, because in any case there was little appetite for this process at first. Faced with the prospect of having to wait for babies to die, the team is no longer in a position to "heal", and so may feel completely useless.

And yet what happens at the end of life can be very important for babies and their families. It is not just a case of prolonging the lives of babies who should have died at birth; it is about facilitating a real encounter between the parents and their babies.

Liu

This was the case for Liu, a little Chinese girl who died in our service more than ten years ago, at the time when palliative care was not yet on the horizon, and we did not have to deal with that type of problem. Liu was born at full term with a serious cardiac malformation which had not been detected before she was born; and in order to ensure her survival, she would have needed a heart transplant. We had alerted all the services in France as well as services abroad, to try to find a compatible donor, and we were waiting. During this time, her condition gradually deteriorated, in spite of life-support machines and treatment. The tension in the service grew as each day went by, and we had to accept that if we did not receive a response from one of the organisations we had contacted, we would have no alternative but to accompany this baby to her death.

This time, it was impossible to dodge or run away from the problem; the team knew, as did the parents, and we had to face up to this impending death without being able to avoid it. There was no question of turning off life-support machines, since at any moment an email could arrive telling us that a donor had been found. It was the first time the team had found itself in the position of having to look after a dying baby and her parents. While doing all we could to keep Liu alive for as long as possible, we also had to ensure that she was as comfortable as possible, and allow her to remain in human contact. But there was not just the baby; there was also the team to consider, and this baby demanded a great deal of them. She wanted a particular type of presence and attention; she never "let us alone", as the nursery nurses put it, and would never settle unless one of us was by her side speaking to her. We also had to deal with the parents' desolation, as they watched her get worse day by day; but it was not just theirs. Very soon, we realised we also had to deal with our own desolation, because we had become very attached to this little girl. We also had to manage our difficulties with facing death, and our own limits. We had to invent a new way of being with this baby and her parents, finding words to speak, understanding our own reactions, recognising what this encounter was bringing up for us, and what it was reactivating. We had many more meetings than usual at this time, bringing together more and more of the caregivers.

When Liu died, exhausted, at the age of three months, and without the hoped-for message having arrived on our computer screen to tell us that a donor had been found, there was a very strong sense of loss and grief in the service. The parents, with whom we had shared the last three months of this little girl's life, had asked to stay with us right to the end. The sense of trust which had grown between us was so strong that they often came to visit us in the months after Liu died. They said they were very grateful for everything we had done for her. They said how touched they had been that we had devoted so much time to them, and most of all by the sadness we had shown when she died. "This little girl," they said, "began to count for us because she counted for you. Your presence made her really exist. Thanks to you, we have been able to integrate her into our history, and into our life. If you hadn't been there, she would never have had that place for us." For these parents, in fact, Liu, who had appeared to be stillborn, had never really been born at all. It was only through the support they received from the team that they were able to accept that she existed, and that three months of life is, after all, a life. She had lived, so she could also die, and they could go through a process of mourning. For us, the story of those three months we spent with Liu had an important place in the changes that took place in our team afterwards, not only at the time of her death, but also in our day-to-day ways of working together. Sometimes, by finding deep inside ourselves the resources to accompany a child towards death, we may learn how better to accompany the others towards life.

We realised that the situation with this baby had forced us, without deliberate intention, to set up a project on palliative care. Liu had made us see that, whatever the circumstances, we can always be present for babies in ways that go beyond administering care, and this does not mean that it interferes with the effectiveness of our work. It is not a question of sentimentality or excessive empathy (it is important to take care not to identify with the parents), but rather of an ethos, that is to say, the place and the welcome we can offer to any little human being, whatever the circumstances of his birth and his chance of survival.

To try to think about palliative care is to accept a different type of caregiving, but it still remains "care". It is a project that involves care but does not aim to cure—and that is not easy for a team to countenance. This type of work makes us face death and whatever that brings up for each one of us. There is no more mastery, there are no more definitive protocols. Doubt and uncertainty, even if only about how much longer the baby will live, can throw the whole team into disarray. The team may have a shared sense of guilt about having resuscitated the baby in the first place, and then having prolonged the agony. This sense of guilt, added to that of the parents, certainly complicates the situation.

It is a time of uncertainty, and all we can do is submit to it. Sometimes palliative care can go on for a very long time. By definition, death is not within our grasp; it is precisely the point at which all our certainties evaporate. At this uncertain time, it is no longer a question of healing, but of offering a welcoming environment, comfort, and quality of life and connections. It is a time which can allow the parents, as in the case of little Liu, to inscribe their child in the family and collective discourse, a time of coming together in which the baby, whose existence has been recognised and respected by the team, can find a place in the family history. The connection of the parents to their baby can be mediated by the quality of their connections with the caregivers; and this in turn will depend on the level of trust and support that we have been able to build up with the parents, from the moment the baby is admitted into the service. In order for them to become "partners" in the caregiving, they have to trust us, and to realise that when faced with their concerns or their grief, we do not "psychopathologise" their attitudes. And most important of all: from the very beginning, the team needs to keep them involved in all discussions. While there is an obligation nowadays to inform parents about medical decisions, it is also important that discussions can take place within the team, and that "truthful speech" should apply for us within the team as it does with the parents. In other words, in spite of the heavy workload we already have, we should find time to meet more often and talk about the babies and what will happen to them. The important thing is to build up a "common project" for each baby. And here again, it is up to us as members of the team to trust and support one another.

It is not easy to make the decision to move to palliative care. It is the doctors who have to weigh up for each patient whether it is reasonable or unreasonable to continue resuscitation. Once the decision has been taken, the first step is not to obtain the parents' consent, but to speak with them to find out what they think. The doctor gives information, the parents give their opinion, and ultimately, the doctor has to make the decision. Asking the parents for their opinion is not without its difficulties, and this partnership is sometimes extremely fragile. The parents' response will have a bearing on their participation, or not, in palliative care, and their involvement in our task, which ultimately is no more than trying to give some meaning to a child's life, however short. There may be diverging points of view, even within the couple, one of the parents being for and the other against; there may be other family members who are against it, and put pressure on them, even if both parents are prepared to accept our project. We will then have to take the time to see them again and again, possibly speaking to other family members, perhaps suggesting they ask for a second opinion from another doctor in another team. But ultimately, the doctor in our service will take the decision, and it is important that the parents realise this, so that they do not feel too guilty. They are never asked to decide whether their child, who is clearly at risk of disability, should live or die. They are informed and asked to say what they think of our decision to move to palliative care, in so far as we believe it would be unreasonable to continue with active life-support. Would they like to participate with the team in the new type of care we are going to start for their baby? Would they wish to accompany their child along the way to death? Is it important for them to be with the child, or would it be too difficult for them? The parents' different positions need to be respected by the caregivers, and not judged. The team needs to understand that it may not be possible for certain parents to become involved in this process. And for some, it may not only be impossible, but also prejudicial; it will depend on the history, case by case, and will have nothing to do with the "quality" of the parents. This is why the protocol has to be reconsidered each time it is invoked.

Sometimes this takes a considerable time, and the doctor will need to see the parents several times before they are able to make a decision. It will also be necessary to speak to the team, so that they are not prevented by their own prejudices from hearing the parents' decision. Here again, each parent is different, and there is no question of forcing their decision making in any way. It is an important element of our work to respect the parents' customs and traditions, which are often unfamiliar to us. Above all, during this very special phase of care, it is necessary to recognise the impact the baby's death is likely to have in terms of their own history, both on the parents and the wider family, especially any brothers and sisters, who will need to be included in discussions about the baby. The birth and death of a baby affect the whole family. The future and the psychological stability of this whole family is at stake in the way we care for the baby and his entourage. Even if the parents accept the transition to palliative care, they may or may not agree to participate in it, or they may wish to participate in so far as they are able. We need to give up our prejudices and our certainties, and stop thinking that we know better than they do what is good for them. We have to accept that we can learn from the parents.

These days, when a close relative dies, it seems to have become obligatory to "go through a mourning", and it is considered right to impose protocols for mourning which may work for some, but are not for everyone, and may even be harmful. Some mourning is simply impossible. For example, studies have shown that in some cases, it is absolutely necessary for the parents to be able to avoid contact with their dying baby in order for them to be able to mourn later on; according to these studies, visual and physical contact could have brought on post-traumatic stress disorder (PTSD) (Turton, 2009).

This birth, which was anticipated with joy, has become medicalised, complicated, and is now a source of anguish and grief. Not all parents will react in the same way to the death of a child. There is no system that can be applied in every case in the domain of the living. The only protocol we can apply routinely is the quality of our presence alongside the babies and their families. These families want us to be as human as possible in the way we care for them and their child. The transition to palliative care is not a "project of death", but a way of honouring and respecting little human beings and their families, by giving some meaning to their brief time on earth. It is for us to enable the families to make sense of this dramatic life event.

I recall Karim's mother, who said to her baby as he lay dying in her arms, "I shall never be the same again. You made me a mummy, and even if you leave me today, I shall still be different, and I shall talk about you to your brothers and sisters when they are born."

In that case, by making the baby real for the mother, the team had enabled her to inscribe Karim in her own history. Everything depends on the sort of reception the team have given the baby. For a long time now, we have made it our custom to welcome babies in a particular way, underpinned by the "supposition of subjectivity". Without this particular kind of reception, which is more or less routine in our service nowadays, the babies cannot have a sense of existing. In the early stages, contact between parents and babies is facilitated by the team. Without the team's active presence, the babies cannot exist for themselves or for their families. When babies are born, the world makes no sense to them at all. Peter Sloterdijk wrote on the subject of babies: "These little things without names are put into a situation in which they can expect nothing, and certainly nothing good, unless they encounter a mother or other human beings who can promise them a good and determined world" (Sloterdijk, 1989, p. 161 [translated for this edition]). When these babies are born, we too have to be determined. Receiving human babies into a world of human beings, taking account of all the changes their short lives will bring about, is an ethical position we cannot escape in a NICU. It is impossible to separate out the different registers—medical, ethical, psychological, and even philosophical; in the realm of palliative care all we can do is work together. Together, but also step by step, because each situation is different.

We cannot emphasise enough how important a "step by step" attitude is in this field. The way in which parents and medical teams think about the death of a baby is unlikely to be the same. In some cases, it will be necessary and desirable for the parents to accompany their babies through the process of palliative care. In others, it will not be, and we need to respect this. We need to recognise the prejudices prevalent in the team, and keep them well away from any decisions taken and any proposals put to the parents, once the transition to palliative care has been decided upon. The aim of seeing the parents several times—whether it is the doctor or the psychoanalyst who sees them, or both together in the case of joint consultations—is not to convince them to give their consent, or agree to take an active part in the palliative care programme; it is more to enable us to see what is going on for the parents, so that we can adjust our attitude to them accordingly. It takes time to try to assess the probable impact that palliative care will have on the parents, and, without judging them, to allow them either to protect themselves or to be completely present.

Following the implementation of the Kouchner and Leonetti laws in France, the question of the death of babies was no longer posed in the same way in neonatology services. Death was with us all the time, it was an ever-present threat hanging over us. Had the correct procedures been carried out, the right decisions made, the correct diagnosis given? But while death haunted the service, it was as if we were avoiding it, pushing it aside; we never spoke about it. To this day, some doctors can remember the difficulties they had at the moment of switching off the life-support machines, which they had to manage on their own, completely alone. Once the babies had died, they would be taken away immediately. Hardly time to turn around: the babies were taken straight down to the mortuary. We all know that there is a tendency in medicine to side-step death. Most hospital doctors rarely come across it nowadays, because once patients are on the point of death, they are transferred to a different service, and given palliative care. Other doctors than those who have been caring for them on a day-to-day basis will now tend these patients. Formerly, we did not have to look after dying babies, but nowadays this is no longer the case in a resuscitation service like ours; we can no longer avoid it. It is now up to us to work together to conquer our prejudices, our resistances, and our fears, so that we can stay alongside these little babies who are too small to live, as they approach death, in the most human and dignified way possible. And even if this way of working might seem more difficult for the team, there is every chance that ultimately, it will be more gratifying.

Breaking the news of abnormalities

Another difficulty doctors have, and something with which they often ask the psychoanalyst to help, is breaking bad news to parents. It is often said that spoken words evaporate, while written words remain. But when we listen to our patients, we hear a very different story. Spoken words do not evaporate, especially when they are spoken in a certain place or at a certain time. They may even come to be inscribed on the body of the person to whom they are addressed, and have effects on the body. They are inscribed, and develop over time.

The benign or maleficent words spoken over a cradle can change the course of a child's destiny. One mother said to me, "I always think of the male midwife who delivered my son. Before he laid him on my belly, he said to me, 'Look, he's making a face. He's hardly arrived in the world, and you could almost say he's already got it in for us. He's not in a good mood!'" For the last ten years, indeed, her son has been sulking. "Nothing's changed," his mother told me, when she came to see me on his behalf. "He's still angry." Another mother told me that on the day her daughter was born, a nursery nurse said to her, "You'll never have any problems with that one. She's an easy baby." Fifteen years later, this mother said that the prophesy had been accurate: "She's never given me any problems. You'll see," she told me, "she won't even give me trouble when she's an adolescent." Yet another mother, whom Maud Mannoni spoke about, said that just after she had given birth, a nurse found her by the window in her room, lighting a cigarette. The nurse rushed up to her and said, "But you're smoking! Are you trying to kill your baby?" Years later, she was able to realise that these words had had a significant and decisive effect on her relationship with her son. Those particular words, spoken to that particular mother, were heard with her particular ears. But how can we possibly know whom we are addressing?

This is precisely what makes breaking bad news so very difficult. And very often what happens to the child afterwards will depend on how this first moment is handled. Doctors are well aware of how difficult it can be to speak to parents. They often have to tell them that the diagnosis is extremely serious. What are the doctors telling themselves in those cases? All doctors fear these moments. They are afraid about the effects the news will have on the parents, but they also fear for themselves. They know that the violence that the news contains may well rebound on to them. From the parents' point of view, the doctors become responsible for the unhappiness, the death, or the disability of their child. In classical antiquity, messengers bearing bad tidings were killed, so that nothing they had announced could actually happen. This superstition has left its mark. Doctors, caught between the desire to flee and to do their duty, or rather to fulfil their obligation to give the information, are subject to the fear of finding themselves in the position of the accused: by the parents, if they do speak out, and by the law, if they do not. Often the temptation is to get rid of the problem as quickly as possible, and not to ask themselves the one question that is truly pertinent: what is the best thing to do in this particular case?

Saying the worst has become an economical and reassuring formula, because thinking case by case is considered to be too dangerous, too complicated, and above all, with some reason, too risky from their own point of view. However, the majority of doctors do not rid themselves of the problem so easily, even if they would like there to be a protocol, or a more or less scientific method—and that wish is understandable. But is there actually anything scientific in the encounter between doctors and patients? The doctors must surely know, even if they put up defences against it, that they are not entirely unlike priests, as Lacan pointed out, and that their words can take on the value of an oracle. Psychoanalysis is not in a position to offer a model doctor-patient relationship, but it may be able to allow doctors to recognise the effects of their speech, some of which may be unthinkable; for that is the very status of speech. Speaking or not speaking, both have unforeseen consequences. It cannot be left to the parents to make their own interpretations. Misunderstanding, which is rife among speaking human beings, is even more common at times when bad news has to be given. "They didn't understand what we were asking," say the parents. "They don't understand what I mean," the doctors complain, and they ask us about the iatrogenic effects of the bad news they have had to give. The lack of comprehension also stems from the fact that the illness as experienced by the family has nothing to do with the illness that the doctor is talking about. Upset by this lack of communication, the doctor asks, "How can we get rid of unwanted effects? How can we avoid a baby, who is suffering from a serious illness, suffering even more because the parents have been devastated by a diagnosis that's been given to them in a way that's too brutal, or too light-hearted, or explained badly?"

Breaking the news of Down's syndrome

Telling parents their child has Down's syndrome is always traumatic. However the news is broken, there is always a pervasive sense of guilt. It is the encounter with the Real that unleashes the trauma. Confronted with this dramatic news, the parents try to find explanations and give it some meaning. There is a force that drives every human subject to look for the causality of any event. All this serves to cover over the fact that absolutely anything can happen; it is impossible to admit that we are all at the mercy of the accidental. To avoid the anguish of facing up to the fact that anything can happen, we look for someone to blame, we look for causes. If a baby is a gift from God for some parents, then the promise of a child has not been kept. Is this failure a result of a malevolent force, or the revenge of the Other? Which Other, beyond all the lesser others, has been playing with our destiny, and why? Faced with the accidents that befall them in the Real, which are beyond their comprehension, and are by definition uncontrollable, the parents are overcome with panic. Sometimes the doctor will be blamed; in other cases, the mothers may use their own guilt as a way of coping with the trauma, as a means of making it possible to think the unthinkable. Violence and aggressivity are other modalities of defence, whether they are directed at others or turned inwards. Is the child a punishment for some wrong they have done? And what was it they did wrong? In the Middle Ages, abnormal babies were the Devil's children, or children of incest. There is nothing worse than being attacked through the medium of one's progeny. Think of the plagues of Egypt, the most terrible of which was undoubtedly the death of all the firstborn sons.

The parents are told the truth as soon as the doctors can confirm the diagnosis. But just because it is truthful, it does not make the news that "your baby has Down's syndrome" any less traumatic. Because however you wrap it up, those are the words that have to be said. And putting Down's babies into their mothers' arms for the first time is certainly going to affect the mothers. We may say that Down's syndrome is a different kind of disability from others, in that all mothers, even if they do not have the slightest knowledge of medicine, think that they know what it is. Down's babies, in their minds, are mongoloids, feeble-minded, children who will die young and be different from others. By the time they are seven, they will be being called "mong" in the playground, there's absolutely no doubt about it, there's no hope, and no dreams. Whose fault is it? Everyone in their turn is blamed. Was it the mother, who didn't go to all her appointments? Was it the doctors, who didn't take good enough care of her during pregnancy? In the past, it was much easier, because the answer was, it was God, it was His will. Once the news has been broken, the mothers will feel they can no longer be mothers, and the children will certainly feel the effects of this meeting with the doctor during which the news has been broken. The babies are hypotonic, very dependant, retarded in their psycho-motor development, in their acquisition of language, and will remain "little" for longer. This immaturity has repercussions for the mother. The sibling group, too, will have to adjust to the special status of this disabled newborn. All Down's children are similar, but the psychological development of each one is different. Some are very disturbed, psychotic or autistic; others are perfectly able to communicate, and go to school, even to mainstream primary schools, where they can begin to learn writing, reading, and arithmetic. They may develop some degree of autonomy, and find ways of more or less managing their disability as they grow up. Some are mad; some are not.

Let us return to the moment when a mother has been told that her baby has Down's syndrome. What happens to her ability to invest libidinally in her child? How can she feel proud of this child, be fulfilled, experience jouissance in relation to him, phallicise him? She knows the child does not look like her, nor the father, nor anybody; he is different. Separation, which is indispensable to the constitution of the subject, becomes problematic for these babies, because the symbolism of filiation is lacking. If there is no resemblance, filiation cannot be imaginarised, and as a result, nothing can be imagined for these babies. We know only too well what Down's babies look like. I recall one mother who said to me, "I was in despair. I didn't recognise him. Until one day, my husband's father said to me, 'Down's syndrome or not, he's my grandson, just like all my other sons' children; he's got my name, and he's part of our family. As far as I'm concerned, he's no different.'" This woman's relief came from the fact that her son had been given a symbolic inscription, which would enable her to separate herself from him and present him to her family, at the same time as "re-presenting" him to herself.

It is essential for babies to have a period when they are idealised in their parents' minds. Yet it is quite understandable that it is far from easy for parents to achieve this if they have just been told that their child has Down's syndrome. They are terribly upset, and their self-esteem collapses.

So what can we do?

The doctors, quite understandably, would like to have a protocol, a scientific method which would enable them to avoid the iatrogenic effects of giving bad news. In other words, they would like to avoid these Down's children becoming psychotic. They would like to avoid them having to suffer from parents who have been damaged by the diagnosis being given to them in too brutal a fashion or badly explained, or by words they could not understand properly, or by emotions the doctor could not hide from them. But then again, how can anyone know what parents will make of what they are told, at those particular times?

I remember a young woman with Down's syndrome who came to see me because she was severely depressed following cosmetic surgery: her cheekbones had been reduced, her jaw and nose had been refined, the skin around her eyes had been debrided; and she no longer looked as if she had Down's syndrome. She no longer looked like anyone or anything, and she had become delusional, and at the same time had forgotten everything she had learned from school and rehabilitation. We will leave aside the question of the responsibility of the cosmetic surgeons. The parents told me that when they had been in despair after the shock of their daughter's birth, the doctors had wanted to encourage and comfort them. "With a great deal of care and attention and love, you will see, there won't be any traces in a few years' time, and you won't even remember that she had Down's syndrome." In saying this, they thought they were doing a good thing. They were trying to be optimistic and consoling. A few years later, the parents had literally wanted to get rid of the traces of the syndrome that stigmatised their daughter's body. A series of operations had given her an image that was even more strange and disturbing, a terrifying image which she no longer recognised, and which caused her to become delusional. She, who knew the truth, could not succeed in wiping it out. So why had these apparently harmless words weighed so heavily on the rest of their lives? We only know that each individual reacts according to what has happened in his or her own history. And these are facts which are not available to doctors.

I also remember another mother who had been spoken to in a very religious manner, although she was not at all that way inclined herself. She had ended up leaving her baby with child social services, having been convinced that she was a monstrous mother, incapable of bringing up her child, because she was unable to understand that her son was absolute love, that he had a pure soul and that she had to love him just like any other baby. She had thought, "I will be a bad mother." And then there are the parents who experience the obstetrician leaving abruptly after saying very little, because he or she feels invalidated, overcome with anxiety and guilt at having failed to diagnose anything during the numerous scans during the pregnancy, which had nonetheless been carefully monitored in a high-tech service. Speaking produces effects which cannot be predicted. Each mother who is faced with the diagnosis of Down's syndrome is different, and so is each doctor. Some doctors think that Down's syndrome is unacceptable, and impossible to live with; others think that each child is different, and that these children are just a little more different than some of the others, and that the tendency towards eugenics which hovers over our modern world is becoming alarming. It is a question of conviction; a very intimate conviction, with all its subjective freight.

Some of the mothers of these babies will develop, given time. They need time to digest what has happened, and sometimes it is only much later that a bond can form between mother and child. In other cases, the child is accepted right from the start. We certainly see parents who refuse a therapeutic termination following amniocentesis, as well as infertile people who seek to adopt children with Down's syndrome. But we also know that some mothers will never be able to recover from this trauma. It is wrong for doctors to make judgements or to react according to their personal convictions. The best we can do is to be alongside this mother and father in their distress, accompanying them without prejudice. All we can do is respect their decisions, whether they refuse therapeutic terminations or decide to give up the child at birth, if the chromosomal anomaly has not been detected beforehand.

Adrien

Adrien was a premature baby with Down's syndrome, and had been admitted to our neonatal service. The Down's syndrome had not been diagnosed, in spite of the pregnancy having been monitored by doctors in the city. The mother was thirty years old, the scans had been normal, and there had been no problems during pregnancy. The shock when he was born had been terrible. At first, Adrien's mother did not want to see him. She and her husband had decided to give up the child. Adrien stayed in the neonatal service for almost two months. The whole team had listened to the parents, without insisting that they should come into the service, without judging them, just being alongside them. Some days, the meetings were punctuated by shouting and weeping; they were furious at this injustice, looking for someone to blame. There were some afternoons when the parents could not agree on their decision, and we were forced to be impotent witnesses to their endless rows. The whole team was shaken by their distress. Other days, they seemed calmer, and then they would ask to see their son. The team had recognised that we needed to be able to bear their changes of mind, their endless questions, their violence, their rows, their reconciliations, and their grief. We did not have an agenda we were trying to impose on them; we accompanied them on their journey as best we could, being attentive and present, but also keeping our distance. We could not make the decision for them, but they knew that, whatever decision they eventually made, we would support them and respect them. Gradually a bond was established between them and Adrien, and two months later, they finally left the service with Adrien in their arms. They had decided to keep him. The mother said to us as they were leaving, "It's funny, you call the mothers and babies 'patients'. But in your case, it's the doctors who've been the most patient."

All individuals react to bad news according to who they are, their structure, their history. It is true for patients, and also for doctors. They have to impart bad news which confronts them with the unthinkable.

Dmitri, a boy of thirteen, was suffering from mucoviscidosis. He had come to see me following a suicide attempt. From birth, he had been followed up and cared for in a quite remarkable way, both medically and psychologically. As soon as the parents had been informed of the diagnosis, the doctors had made time to have long discussions with them, to give them plenty of information, and to ensure that Dmitri was followed up. When the boy was five, they had spoken to him about the difficulties of being ill, but since then, no one had really spoken to Dmitri, and the follow-up had been more technical. The team thought they had done all they needed to do for the family. Ten years after he was born, the parents decided they wanted another child. Once again, the medical team was called upon, and did all they could for the family. There was a genetic consultation[4] involving pre-implantation genetic diagnosis, and a healthy boy was born. At this point, the doctors had not said anything to Dmitri. Four out of five embryos had had the faulty gene, and the mother had explained to Dmitri that they had thrown away the other embryos. Three years later, Dmitri threw himself out of a window. He survived with broken legs, but kept saying he wanted to die. In one session he said to me, "A boy like me isn't worth anything. If my parents had known about my illness before I was born, they would have thrown me away." Indeed, how can someone exist in those circumstances? What can we do so that, in spite of the bad news about the illness, the subject can come into being, and can grow up and continue to live?

An adult male, who suffered from a severe neurological illness which impeded all gestures and movements, but had left him with a lucid mind, once told me, "When an illness like this develops, it takes you over completely, it takes your body by storm, and all you as an individual can do is get the hell out." This annulment of the subject can also be recognised in the horror unleashed in the other by the spectacle of illness or its representation. The entourage, which is most attentive, acts as if it were nothing unusual, and the nearest and dearest also pretend they see nothing. But he knows that dogs bark when he passes them in the street, and that he frightens children. "Even the doctors talk about other things," he told me, "as if it was possible that anything else could matter to me these days." To be able to face up to a sick person, the healthy need to accept in themselves a zone of distress, of fragility, which unleashes a radical anxiety; and this is just as true if they are doctors. We cannot deny this part inside us; it is there in all of us, and it unleashes pure horror in us. Even if we try to seal it off, cover it up, put it into words, it still slips from our grasp, because it is beyond words. So in order not to let it make us mad, we try to familiarise ourselves with it. But it is impossible to familiarise ourselves with it; it is nameless. We can keep trying, but we never quite hit the mark; we try to find ways beyond words, to say what is both the closest thing to us and the most inaccessible: it is what psychoanalysts call "the Real". This inhumanity which is always present in the bosom of humanity unleashes a terrible fear in those who are close to a sick person, including the doctors, and no one is ever prepared for this. The longest and most erudite university studies will never enable us to master this phenomenon; and yet it is this Real that confronts doctors every day. It is also something that makes me admire the people who work in our service; the courage with which the doctors have ultimately decided not to dodge these issues, which force them so brutally to face up to themselves. Thinking in this way makes it easier to understand just how difficult it is to have to break bad news, and also how "saying everything" is not merely dangerous, but completely utopian. There are some doctors who, in response to the current way of thinking, have become veritable terrorists of transparency. However, psychoanalysis is there to remind us that the ideal of transparency is a trap, that the truth is never absolute, and at best can only be half-said. This ideal of transparency is an effect of science, a symptom, an aberration of our time.

A little boy aged six came to see me because he was suffering from insomnia and anxiety. He was refusing to go to school, and would not leave his mother, spending his days plying her with a thousand questions about death. When I asked the mother, who was a doctor, to tell me how she answered his questions, she said, "I tell him everything. I told him we can die at any moment, from a heart attack, or a ruptured aneurysm, anything can happen. When he asks me in the morning if I'm really going to pick him up from school, or if I'll be dead at four o'clock, I tell him, 'You never know. Anything can happen.'" When I expressed some surprise at what she had said, she retorted, "Surely you, as a psychoanalyst, are not going to tell me it's wrong to tell a child the whole truth?" That is really not what psychoanalysts say. I remember telling Françoise Dolto about this session. She simply replied, "This mother is mad. She thinks she is telling the truth, but all she is telling her child is about her own sadism."

As in this mother–child relationship, it is sometimes possible to recognise the link between truth and sadism in the words doctors use when speaking to their patients. Are the patients putting the doctors in a maternal position? Is it a sign that nowadays human beings are trying to reconnect with a type of support that was lacking for them? These days, we hear that the deficit in the welfare budget indicates a demand for maternal support of that order. It would not be entirely surprising if doctors were being made to pay for the disgruntlement of human beings towards their mothers. Doubtless, the problem rests on the fact that medicine and the science that underpins it have been placed in the position of maternal omnipotence. Science can do everything; the media are full of reports to convince us of that. And now, indeed, science and medicine are in a position to pay for a promise which, like mothers, they can back up, but which cannot be kept. Like mothers, medicine is not up to what it made us believe. It reminds me of the mother of a baby who had just died in the NICU, who said to me, "I really didn't think that a baby could die in a NICU, with all your science and technology." For this mother, medicine could not be allowed to fail.

The modern world gives us the illusion of being able to efface the unbearable aspect of castration. The role of modern medicine is therefore to cure illness and delay death. There is now talk of a life expectancy of one hundred and twenty-five years. Mothers, too, are expected by their children to protect them and ward off all dangers. Perhaps that is where the image of the doctor and that of the mother overlap.

But we know that it is vital for the child that the mother disappears, that she can show herself as lacking, that she can give up being motherly, and doing and saying everything on behalf of her child. Surely this is the case in medicine, too. Isn't it time that medicine stopped trying to be the omnipotent mother? It seems to me that it is the task of psychoanalysis to lead human subjects to believe that they can manage without this promise and allow themselves to face the unbearable aspect of castration, whether they are mothers, doctors, patients, or healthy individuals.

Parents who decide to put their children who are suffering from serious neurological illnesses into institutions are just as worthy of respect as those who decide to bring them up themselves.

What superegoic criteria would the team be using to make their judgements? How can we know what will happen to these disabled children in the future? Some children, who at first seem to be seriously disabled, will grow up reasonably well. Others, who seemed less severely ill, will turn out to be more severely disabled.

Old ideas must be constantly questioned afresh. The history and the development of each individual will be different. It is this difference that we have always to respect. Cécile, a young woman of twenty, suffering from cerebral palsy, had been born at thirty-two weeks gestation, and had severe complications resulting from resuscitation. "It's true," she told us, "I live in a wheelchair, I can't dance, or run, or walk. But when I see the sorts of problems some of the other girls have, I think I'm a lot less disabled than they are. At least I love life."

There can be serious problems linked with prematurity. Some of the complications can lead to death or severe cerebral lesions. Traditional psychiatry, which sometimes makes ideologies of its theories, has always linked organic problems with psychological disturbances; according to these ideas, there may be less serious, minor risks equivalent to smaller, hidden lesions, which are as yet impossible to detect, in spite of our sophisticated investigation techniques. The danger of such a supposition is that premature babies and their entourage could be labelled as a high-risk population.

And yet the majority of premature babies will not have problems later on, particularly if the care given in the NICU has also been possible at a level beyond the medical. "It would be easy to claim, according to the statistics, that prematurity is not an etiological factor except in a few cases of severely disturbed development, and that no role should be attributed to it in the field of child psychiatry" (Diatkine, 1977, p. 114).

Notes

1. The technique of aspiration involves clearing the babies' airways using suction.
2. D. W. Winnicott spoke of "primary maternal preoccupation" as a transitory "illness" that consisted in giving mothers the capacity to identify with their babies.
3. Child psychiatrist in an ICU for children, and lecturer at the University of Milan.
4. Pre-implantation genetic diagnosis (PGD) eliminates embryos which carry the gene for mucoviscidosis before implantation, so that the mother can be certain that she will not give birth to another child suffering from the same disease.

CHAPTER FIVE

Former premature babies

Who triumphs here? Clearly it is Desire,
Desire ... whose place beside the greatest laws,
Is, too, among the masters of the world.

—Antigone, Sophocles

The outcome for premature babies

What becomes of premature babies? How do they grow up? We have seen that research has indicated that social, emotional, or cognitive difficulties, as well as behavioural problems and learning difficulties, are more common than in the non-premature population (Anderson & Doyle, 2003; Chapieski & Evankovich, 1997; Wolke, Söhne, Riegel, Ohrt, & Osterlund, 1998).

At the same time, some rather alarmist results have been published on the link between extreme prematurity and ASD (autism spectrum disorder) (Bhutta, Cleves, Casey, Craddock, & Anand, 2002; Halsey, Collin, & Anderson, 1996). These early studies offer a rather pessimistic view of the development of extremely premature babies, even when there are no obvious organic lesions. But if neonatology specialists have not given up resuscitating very tiny babies, it is because their day-to-day clinical experience shows a different picture. Many premature babies grow up without problems, as we can see for ourselves, when they come to us for check-ups months or even years later. Scientists, some of whom do not like to be challenged, then proposed that the children who did well were those who did not have organic lesions. They put forward the hypothesis that the technical means for screening were inadequate. Our MRI scans[1] were not sufficiently sensitive to show up the lesions that must be present but could not yet be detected, which meant that the sample populations were skewed.

Of course, this hypothesis may have been reassuring to some, as is the hypothesis that everything is genetic in other circumstances; one day, thanks to science, everything will be explicable in terms of organicity. But a few years later other research came along to complicate the picture, whose methodology took into account environmental factors, and in particular the mother–baby relationship. At that point in time, we were developing a new approach to prematurity, based on the overlaps between the somatic, the parent–child relationship, and the doctor-patient relationship (Muller-Nix, Forcada-Guex, Borghini, Pierrehumbert, & Ansermet, 2009; Zelkowitz, Papageorgiou, Bardin, & Wang, 2009).

But beyond the field of prematurity, there are now many researchers and doctors who think it is vital to take psychogenesis into account as well as organogenesis. Currently, many scientists are seeking to explore the articulation between the two. Whether in the neurosciences or in genetics, studies have made considerable advances in this direction. The notion of "everything is organic" has been challenged. Researchers such as Bruno Falissard (1998) at INSERM (*Institut national de la santé et de la recherche médicale*) have worked to combine the two registers. In order to achieve this, their methodology has been rethought, statistics have been revisited, and ethical questions explored. For example, Jean-Christophe Thalabard (2010), a professor and researcher at CNRS (*Centre national de la recherche scientifique*), has investigated the ethics involved in methodology. Henceforth, studies are more complicated, and the questions have to be asked differently. The geneticists themselves have begun to speak about epigenetics, and have focused on changes that may be brought about by the environment, particularly methylome, which permits or inhibits the expression of genes. This new orientation for researchers allows us to hope that a great number of studies will also be initiated that will be of interest to psychoanalysts.

As early as 2008, in a study by Samara (Samara, Marlow, & Wolke, 2008), carried out under the aegis of the Epicure project on the outcome of former premature babies, the question of the relationship between parents and babies was explored. They noted that in extremely premature babies, there was a high incidence of attention deficit disorder: 33.3 per cent as opposed to 6.8 per cent in the non-premature population; difficulties in socialisation: 25.4 per cent as opposed to 5.4 per cent; and emotional regulation 13.5 per cent as against 4.1 per cent. At the conclusion of the study, the authors emphasised the impact of prematurity on the parents, and called for a broadening of our thinking on the complexity of the subject. In another section of the study, they note that 23.2 per cent of the premature boys had a positive score for pervasive developmental disorder compared with 3.4 per cent in the control group. While we do not yet understand the causes of autism, Samara had already deduced in 2008 that disturbances of socialisation and emotional regulation, and attention deficit disorder, cannot be explained solely on grounds of genetics or from a cognitive point of view. He therefore believes that we need to work on the question of the impact of stress on the parents of children who were born prematurely. Indeed, parents who have been overwhelmed by the premature birth then have to cope with babies who have suffered every day of their lives during the months since they were born (Golse & Keren, 2000; Golse, 2006), and this makes communication very difficult. Parental anxiety (Zelkowitz, Bardin, & Papageorgiou, 2007) and post-traumatic stress syndrome (Kersting et al., 2004) can also disrupt the bonding process. Many other studies have explored the role of the neonatal team, from the point of view of the babies (Pierrehumbert, Ramstein, Karmaniola, & Halfon, 1996; Vaivre-Douret, 2004), and from the point of view of the parents, with the aim of reducing the impact of this traumatic experience (Muller-Nix et al., 2004). From our perspective, then, what do we find when we see these children and their families at their follow-up appointments? And what about consultations in other settings, when the parents tell us, by the way, as if by chance, that their child was born prematurely.

An April morning in 2012: neonatal consultation at the hospital

The secretary told me that a little boy of six was waiting for me with his mother. Most children make use of the toys that are left out for them and turn the waiting room into a joyful and noisy playground; however, the secretary pointed to a child sitting absolutely still in the corner next to his mother, and looking very serious. It was quite clear he had not come here to play. When I went up to her, the mother said, "Do you remember us? Julien was born in your service, he was very premature. I've been looking everywhere for you, and they told me you were here. Can you possibly see us? He insists he wants to speak to you."

Julien had certainly not been born in our service. He had arrived in the maternity unit, three months before his due date. He had been transferred to our unit on a ventilator to ensure his best chances of survival. Yet his mother insisted, "He was born in your service." This conviction immediately made me think of the question mothers often ask us: "When is his actual birthday? The day he came out of my womb, or the day he was expected, or the day he came out of his incubator?" Symbolically, which is the "true" moment of birth for their child?

Julien had just turned six, and had recently started primary school. Having been born at twenty-nine weeks gestation, he was now a lively, intelligent, healthy boy. And yet, his mother told me, he had always been worried, and found it very difficult to be apart from her. Because he had been so fragile at birth, she had not been able to visit him in the nursery at first, because of the risk of contagion. He had only been separated from her when he went to nursery school, and the first year had been extremely difficult. He cried a great deal, isolated himself, and refused to let the teacher comfort him, or to let any other children near him. But when he started "pre-school", the mother told me that "everything changed"; he was no longer afraid, and had become one of the "leaders" in his group. What had happened during this year that his mother called "pre-school", which alludes to the preparation for going to a big school? It seemed he had made a significant developmental leap forward, and rather early at that. Since then, indeed, he had appeared much more independent and authoritarian, and would ask endless questions about everything around him, and would not tolerate evasive answers. Why was this little boy now so very curious? And why, asked his mother anxiously, was he suddenly refusing to go to school again, not wanting to leave her side, and unable to sleep on his own?

When I turned to Julien to ask him why he wanted to see me again, he said, "You know, don't you, where I was when I was born? And what about Mummy, where was she?" In fact this mother had found it very difficult to come in to the service and to have contact with her son. It seemed she had really lost her bearings, and was depressed. Julien's father had left her at the beginning of the pregnancy, and she had no family at all in France. In any case, she said, she had always been alone, she complained that her parents had rejected her and her mother had abandoned her at the time when she had married Julien's father. It was only a month later, when he heard from friends that his son had been born and was in hospital that he made contact with the mother and came into the service. When the baby was discharged, they started to live together again. We are quite familiar with the set-up where there is a mother who has problems with separation and suddenly finds she has an only son who cannot bear to be apart from her. Françoise Dolto reminded us that children are always in a position to be their parents' therapist. By never leaving her, Julien was clearly trying to reassure his mummy. At the end of the session, when the mother had asked for her coat at reception, she said to me, "It's difficult for me at the moment, all these questions my son asks me. I've just decided to separate from his father. Nobody knows about it, and I don't know what to say to Julien." Once again, faced with the enigma of the mother's desire, the child was looking for answers at the point where his father was about to leave, and Julien certainly knew something about this. This rather "classic" situation is similar to many others we encounter both in child psychiatry and in private practice.

So why had this woman, confronted with her current difficulties, decided to consult me? She had known me previously at a time of considerable disturbance and loneliness, and we had already discussed the question of separation and abandonment, so that she could eventually bond with her baby. The fact that Julien was premature had changed the situation. And the drama of his birth, with the baby hovering between life and death for a long time, had reactivated the dramas of the mother's past. We can doubtless imagine that retroactively, a new separation seemed insuperable, and she had wanted to come back to the place where another separation had been symbolised successfully. The "mark" of this difficult birth had certainly given a particular colour to her relationship with her son. This is often what we find in cases of children who were born prematurely. The birth remains with them years afterwards. I offered to see this woman to speak about her history, and Julien managed to go back to school. Why had this little boy wanted to come and see "the baby lady?" Was it simply at the mother's instigation, because she herself wanted to come back to the place where her son was born, and where separation had been possible? Or can we think that Julien too wanted to return to the place where everything had played itself out the first time, including his birth as a subject, and his father's return? But how could he possibly have remembered his time in hospital? Was it he who remembered, or was it his mother's memories that were having these effects on him?

Babies' memories

We have no memories at all of our lives as babies. So naturally, for many years, we thought that babies could not possibly have any sort of memory, and that they could not remember anything. The explanation given for childhood amnesia was purely functional—babies' brains were considered to be too immature to register information or carry out complicated mental processes. In those days, newborns were considered to be innocent and without consciousness.

And then Freud came along with the subversive idea that babies were not as naive as they seemed, and not quite so incapable of thinking and feeling emotions. The whole status of babies had to be revised in the light of infantile sexuality, which caused a great scandal. According to Freud, babies never forget anything. They are completely capable of registering impressions of childhood, and childhood amnesia was now explained in terms of repression. The reason why we do not remember anything is because these memories are repressed, pushed down into that obscure part of our being which he calls the unconscious, while at the same time leaving indelible traces. Clinical practice shows us the extent to which what happened when they were babies remains inscribed not only in children's minds but also in those of the adults who come to us for analysis. Infantile amnesia has certainly done its work, and the memories are no longer present; they have been symbolised, and cannot be recalled into memory. This limitation of recall does not prevent whatever is left from these earliest periods of life being recognised in terms of the traces, the marks or the scars which continually reappear throughout the lives of our patients, and become apparent in their analyses. For some adults, it is not a question of memories, but rather of symptoms, traces of a moment in the past that was rejected or repressed, and which can reappear in the form of the return of a traumatic past.

We often hear patients speaking about their feelings of insecurity, of their inability to be alone, of their feeling that there are "blanks" in their life, moments when they simply cannot think any more, moments when they find themselves suspended in an anguishing void. They may describe painful feelings which keep repeating themselves but cannot be put into words. These repetitions of acts or experiences which occur for no known reason lead them to fear that they will break down or go mad. It is often not until much later in the analytic work that we discover that they were born prematurely. This repetition of acts is the return of a traumatic past, and the "blanks" these patients feel evoke times of waiting alone in their incubators, left to their machines, hovering between life and death.

Jean-David Nasio tells us the story of Rachel, a young woman who had been born prematurely, and was suffering from periods of profound sadness, weeping uncontrollably and unable to explain why: "She gets her duvet, wraps herself in it, and weeps in the dark night of her solitude ... She had spent a long month in an incubator without her mother, who could not leave her bed to visit her ... Rachel needed to envelop herself in warmth, solitude and even darkness, to try to relive this ancient feeling of distress at being abandoned" (Nasio, 2012, pp. 15–25). It was a distress she could not remember, but which had left its traces.

As we have seen, since Freud researchers have spent a lot of time peering into babies' cradles, and while their field of research is in another register than that of the Freudian unconscious and its mechanisms of repression, they have been able to demonstrate the extraordinary capacities of the newborn. These days we know all the things babies can do, thanks to the various methods of study: recording the rhythm of their heartbeats, evoked potential, non-nutritive sucking rhythms, or their ability to focus their eyes. According to scientists, it is now possible to think that the period of pregnancy, the antenatal period, may also be a source of memories for babies, who are already bathed in language and sensations. From the age of three days, it is possible to reactivate their memories. If babies are confronted with a signal they are already familiar with, they will recognise it, as Carolyn Rovee-Collier (1999) showed.

These studies are of interest to psychoanalysts, and they are by no means at odds with the theories which underpin our work. For example, according to this latter study, we can accept that a signal is capable of reactivating sensations and impressions, even if we cannot speak of memories as events which we can represent clearly to ourselves. So now we can think that in the course of a child's life, events already experienced, or having a link with the past, can "reawaken" in the subject the very first traces laid down at a very early age, and which are certainly forgotten. Forgotten, yes, but they are still present. So we may speak of two forms of memory: the memory we refer to habitually, the memory of events, learning, memory that remains conscious and which, too, is subject to forgetting over time; and another type of memory which cannot be altered by time, the unconscious memory. This is what Alain Vanier (2011) calls "the memory of forgetting." "Since what is inscribed remains inaccessible to consciousness, appears as a forgetting in the subject's life, and remains unconscious while never ceasing to return in the formations of the unconscious: dreams, screen-memories, symptoms, the subject's acting out. This type of memory becomes inscribed by means of traces, and what gives it coherence and articulation is language." Certainly, at the moment when they were perceived, these things were not understood; they will not be made sense of until later, and they will only be used retroactively. The unconscious is a memory of what has been forgotten, and the subject's memory will be constituted on the basis of this forgetting. It is forgotten, but it has not disappeared. Indeed, we do not forget anything, since it is on the foundation of this ever-present forgetting that fantasy will be constituted. As they grow up, do these babies remember their time in hospital in the NICU? It does seem that we can discern these forgotten memories later on, in analytic treatment.[2] Of course, the parents' memories will have been added to these unconscious traces, and their memories are still conscious and living for them, and may give the child a different place from the one they would have occupied if they had been born at term. Their memories are very present, and may modify their relationship with their children.

Louis

Louis was four years old when he started to come to see me. He had been labelled "autistic" the previous year. He could not speak, and did not go to school. He showed no signs of attachment, nor any interest in anyone at all in his entourage. He banged his head, bit himself, had violent tantrums, which no one could understand the cause of, and when he was calm, he would spend hours on end rocking and singing the same notes over and over again. He would never let go of a piece of electric cable, which he passed back and forth between his hands with a gentle thwack, and this seemed to reassure him. His parents called this a "comforter", but it was more of an autistic object which fascinated him. During the first sessions, the parents explained that Louis had always been like that. He had been born very prematurely at just twenty-five weeks, weighing 500 grams. When he was discharged from the service, the doctors told the parents that the MRI scan was normal, and that Louis had no neurological sequelae. Yet he had never been a child like the others. When I asked Louis about his interest in the piece of electrical cable, his father explained: he was two years old when they had had some work done in their flat. The workmen left a reel of electrical cable lying around, and Louis had grabbed hold of it and insisted that they cut him a long piece. From that time on, he had never let go of it, day or night. Although they did not understand this sudden passion, the parents were quite relieved that their son, who seemed to be indifferent to everyone and everything, had become "attached" to something. And he certainly was attached to it. During those early sessions, I realised that he was not just playing with the cable by passing it from one hand to the other. He would hold one end carefully in one hand, and attach the other end very carefully to the leg of one of the chairs, or to the door handle, or anything else that was sticking out in the room. This activity could last for the whole session, but still it was impossible to make any sort of contact with him. He never reacted when I spoke to him, and he never looked at me. In one session, when I was trying as usual to speak to him about himself, his fears and his loneliness, it occurred to me, looking at the electric cable, to speak to him about his birth, and the long months he spent in the NICU. My intention was to put into words something about this period which he could not represent for himself. I knew from my experience in the NICU the sorts of difficulties these children had suffered, hooked up and plugged in with electric cables to highly sophisticated machines which kept them alive. Their difficulty was above all to feel that they existed.

Making use of this experience, and faced with this little Louis who, as the sessions went on, was becoming more and more absorbed in his rituals with the electric cable, it occurred to me to involve myself in the circuit, just as we do with babies in the service. So I took the cable in my hand, between him and the desk to which he had tied it, and as I spoke to him about the time he spent in the NICU, and what I imagined he had felt there, and saying I would not leave him all alone,

I wrapped the cable around my wrist. It was the first time Louis looked at me, furtively, full of fear, but really present—it was a real look that was meant for me. Session by session, he became more accepting of my presence, and would even come up to me and wrap the cable round my wrist, securing it to a fixed object, while carefully keeping the other end in his hand. A year later, Louis began to speak and gradually to take the risk of coming out of his autistic isolation. What were his memories of his time in the NICU? How could we not think that this autistic object was a remnant of it, a remnant that he could not forget?

Other former premature babies, those who can speak or draw, also bring material to their sessions which is evocative of these earliest times. They draw people surrounded by cables, characters who are tied up, with no mouth, shut inside boxes which evoke the incubators. And when they are asked what the drawings make them think of, the answer is always the same: "I don't know, it's just that, nothing else." "No comment," said a little girl to me one day. Because in fact there were no words available to her to speak about it.

Clémence

A young woman analysand, who had been born prematurely, told me that she had a recurring nightmare which she could not understand. She dreamt that she was enclosed in a concrete block and only her head came out of it. She could not move, and she would cry out for help throughout entire nights, but no one ever came to help. "And yet," she said, "there must be people around, because I can hear sounds, and I can see shadows moving around me." It is impossible not to think that this nightmare, too, has its roots in that earliest part of her life, a time she never mentions otherwise. The reason she came into analysis was, she said, to try to put into question why her love life was so full of distress. She could never become attached to any man. She said she could not trust them, and did not want to run the risk of being abandoned and being alone again. And yet she managed to get herself abandoned, time and time again. The repetition of her original state was implacable: her mother, who lived alone, and had herself been abandoned by the father who left her when she told him she was pregnant, was admitted to hospital for depression during the first two months of her daughter's life. These two months were also those during which she was in the NICU, and must have felt she had been abandoned.

In the analytic treatment of adults, we are often taken back to the time when they were babies—a time which, although it has been forgotten, has left its mark. Whether it is in dreams, slips of the tongue, bungled actions, or screen memories, it is often possible to recognise the traces of those times. There are traces which have been left at different times; astonishing memories which act as a sort of screen over the subject's history, and remain linked to a detail: a colour, a sound. These screen memories, even though they are reconstructions, all contain a fragment of truth, and this truth is sometimes linked with memories from baby-hood. This is why we have to make every possible effort in maternity units, SCBUs (special care baby units), NICUs (neonatal intensive care units), and services which deal with newborns, to pay attention to the way in which they are welcomed, and how we interact with them. Of course, things we found unpleasant are wiped out from our memories; and yet those unpleasant impressions are still, and always, present. This is how we understand why certain painful experiences keep on repeat-ing themselves right into adult life. Failures in love, for example, will continue to repeat in the same vein for any given subject. Neurosis is destiny. "It's always the same thing over and over, the story of my life," said one patient. "The reason I'm coming to you is so I can stop pressing the 'replay' button on my tape-recorder." This is what Freud called the "compulsion to repeat". It seems that there are memories of the earliest phase of life which are not memories as such, but which nonetheless keep on repeating themselves. We can spot the signs of these memories from babyhood in our daily life, and realise the impossibility of ever forgetting them. This memory of what is forgotten is constituted in the form of traces; it is both forgotten and ever-present; it constitutes the fantasy itself, but it is not intrinsically measurable, because it is articu-lated with the link to the Other. In other words, it is articulated with the way the Other addresses the baby, the way the baby is spoken to by the Other, articulated with the words that have been enunciated and which will mark the baby's body. It is a question of not only the presence of the Other, but also of the Other's absence and the moments when the Other is lacking. All these traces are associated with jouissance, and they are traces which will never be wiped out.

By taking these elements into account, we are in a better position to interpret the results of current research on the capabilities of babies, however exciting they may seem, and not just view them in terms of measures of performance or cognitive abilities. Babies' brains are not just computers which register, memorise, archive, or classify. What they do with these memories remains a mystery which is for us to unravel, case by case, and which is fundamentally as enigmatic as the status of this unconscious memory that no machine, perhaps fortunately for us, can measure.

Prematurity: the symptoms as they are currently classified

In France, the *Centre d'action médico-sociale précoce* (CAMSP), which is responsible for prevention and follow-up in cases of extreme prematurity, has recognised that in premature babies without neurological sequelae and without PDT (pervasive developmental disorders) there is an increase in the following symptoms:

- difficulties in falling asleep and sleep disturbance
- eating disorders (anorexia, vomiting, food phobias)
- difficulties in potty training
- fears, anxieties, phobias, and psychomotor disturbances (and the whole gamut of "dys-"—dyslexia, dyspraxia, etc.).

Once the child reaches school age, there are more frequently occurring problems of hyperactivity and learning disabilities, as well as difficulties with concentration, school phobias, and other symptoms. What are we to think of this?

Let us set aside the risks which certainly can make things worse in terms of "labelling" premature babies and giving the parents an alarmist prognosis, which is likely to make the parents see their babies as "disabled" even before they have been discharged from the service (they only need to consult the internet in order to be terrified by what the future holds for them!). We can then state the problem as follows: these various symptoms are actually those we encounter in our day-to-day practice with children, whether or not they are premature.

Symptoms are always a sign of suffering, a sign that something is wrong. Winnicott reminded us that the symptom was not to be "eradicated" as such, but that it was like a flashing warning light going on when children were calling out for help. Rather than "treating" the symptom, we need to understand what is making the child unhappy. When nothing is working anymore, children "cry out" through their symptoms, because they do not know how to speak about it. One symptom or another will be chosen according to the children's signifiers, their age, structure, or history, according to what is most fragile about them. We will need, as Maud Mannoni put it, to listen out for "the word encapsulated in the symptom".

From our point of view, if there are no organic sequelae, prematurity does not trigger "specific disturbances", of which premature birth would be the "sole" cause. There is no real relation of cause and effect, except perhaps that premature babies have most certainly lived through greater difficulties than others, and that this will very probably have repercussions for them. This is no doubt the reason why there is statistically a greater number of former premature babies who have "mental" problems.

During follow-up consultations after the discharge from hospital, we often note the extent to which former premature babies are "overprotected", they are "little princes and princesses", as they are called nowadays (even though these baby royals are actually in a rather greater state of weakness than the other children!) They make the rules at home. They tend to be very lively, agitated, and disobedient; they will never stay quietly in one place, because this is never enforced at home. They are at the centre of their parents' preoccupations (probably more so than other children), remaining "miracle" children who have survived the catastrophe of their birth against all odds. So of course, they are thought to be more fragile, in greater danger, and in need of closer monitoring than others. One mother came with her ten-year-old son for a consultation. He had grown into a fine young boy, tall and strong, and was a rugby fan; yet the mother told me, "It's terrible, I was so afraid he was going to die at birth that even now I get up several times a night to check on him and see if he's still breathing." Quite often the "former" premature babies can never become "former" for the parents. Their prematurity remains present, and whatever their age, their height, or their weight, this status seems to stick to them. It is difficult for them to find a way out of this bind, because the parents' anguish seems to be just as alive as it was when their babies were suspended between life and death, in the NICU. There are some memories that are so hard to get rid of! So it seems reasonable to suppose that premature children may have more reason than others to cry for help. The babies' history in the NICU will make things more complicated in some cases, as will the parents' histories, and the way these babies are taken up in the family following the circumstances surrounding their birth. We shall look at some examples from our clinical work which bear witness to this.

But at the same time it is important to point out that many former very low birth weight (extremely premature) babies do very well. There is no doubt that this will depend on what happened around the time of their birth, both for them and for their families. That is why we believe very strongly that the attention given in NICUs to the way babies and their parents are received and welcomed is of paramount importance, as is the work done in the precious time of the hospital admission.

Arthur

The psychologist at the crèche had advised Arthur's mother to bring him to see me. It was June, and Arthur, who was going to be three in October, was due to start school in September. He had only about twenty words in his vocabulary, and could not yet make them into sentences. His relationships with other children were difficult. He was overcome with fear whenever he had to face new difficulties. He seemed to be afraid of everything. "It may not take very much," the psychologist had said, "but if you don't do anything, he may find starting school is a real problem."

When I went to fetch him from the waiting room, Arthur leapt up and rushed out, pushed me aside and ran laughing into my office. He ran as far as he could go inside the room, and then finally turned towards me when he ran up against the wall. He was trapped, had run into a corner, and was staring at me fixedly. He had a strange expression on his face. He was smiling, yet it was an artificial smile, as if someone had painted it on to his cheeks, a smile that brought to mind the wide mouths of clowns: a cheery mask on a sad face. Above this fixed smile, Arthur's huge blue eyes reflected his distress and anxiety. This contradictory face evoked a feeling of disquieting strangeness. His smile remained absolutely fixed throughout the session, and did not flag for a single moment.

"Even if he falls over, even if he hurts himself, his smile never fades," said his mother, "you could almost believe he never feels pain."

The mother, who had followed her son into my office, seemed to "fade" a little as she collapsed on the sofa, looking exhausted. "It's like this the whole time, I never stop having to run after him, he escapes as soon as he can, he runs away."

Arthur, who had completed his run, sat down against the side of the desk. Without letting his smile fade for an instant, he listened very attentively as his mother spoke about his history.

He had been born at twenty-eight weeks, and was extremely premature, weighing only 980 grams. He was immediately transferred to the NICU in the town where they were living at the time. From the outset, the doctors, who were quite understandably worried, would not give any diagnosis as to his state of health. It would be impossible to say until he was three or four weeks old. The mother, who had gone into the NICU the same evening following the delivery, told me how she had been struck by his little old man's face, and by his extremely thin body. "I thought I'd given birth to a spider. It's awful, those long arms, and the legs with no flesh on them. It's unbelievable how ugly a foetus is. Maybe it'd be better if we didn't see them? That evening, I was really afraid of him."

The question of how the babies look often comes up for the parents of premature babies. The babies ought still to be hidden away in their mothers' womb. What sort of a transgression is it when these babies become visible, and what is it that the parents see? What is the prohibition that has been flouted? Making the transition from inside to outside in such a brutal fashion, the babies seem too "real". How can we preserve a space of imagination and dreaming for the mothers? They can no longer represent the babies to themselves, one day like this, another day in a different way. They have no time to allow their fantasy to "unfold", no time to talk about it. Children also need to be fed by their mothers' imagination, by the words they have spoken about them. They bathe in amniotic fluid, but also in the words spoken by those who surround them. It is a nourishing "bath" of language. But if mothers are prevented from dreaming by the realities of measuring and monitoring, it may also prevent them from nourishing their babies with speech. The babies they are carrying look nothing like the clichés that the scans show. And what is it they are "scanning" for anyway? "Whether it's a boy or a girl, it has nothing to do with the doctor," one mother said to me. "Even if I ask not to be told, he's going to write it in the file, I really feel he's got no right to do that, it's like he's robbing my baby of its secret." But not all mothers think like that.

"It doesn't look like anything, it's not a baby, it really makes me wonder what I've got inside me," said another mother, who had decompensated following a scan. These babies, "put on show" on the screen or in an incubator, may evoke violent archaic fantasies.

Arthur's mother recalled that she had not wanted to go back to the NICU for several days after he was born. "They were really kind, but the way they smiled, the way they made out that it wasn't serious at all, made me feel they didn't understand, and I felt useless and as if they wanted to make me feel guilty." So even then, she had found smiling disconcerting.

The team had certainly thought they were doing the right thing in welcoming Arthur's mother into the NICU in the most relaxed possible way. But this woman was not wrong. She knew how worried they were about the baby's future; she had overheard some of the doctors saying that there was a serious risk that he would die. She wanted her anxiety to be taken seriously, in the same way that they were taking her baby's condition seriously.

She had stayed in her room in the maternity unit. Her son was going to die, and she cried day and night, inconsolable at having lost this child. She really believed she had lost him, just as she had lost her brother, who was two years younger than her, two weeks before the baby had been born.

Arthur's second given name was the dead brother's name, Jean-François.

"Their names," wrote Freud, "made the children into revenants" (1900a).

Nurseries are full of ghosts, of good and bad fairies who lean over the babies' cradles and give their gifts, which may be marvellous or maleficent, and which will influence the children for the rest of their lives. The words spoken over their cradles are just so many spells, and will accompany the children throughout their lives in a good or bad way, depending on whether the fairies in question were invited to the baptism or not. Words and names. Children very often bear a name that belonged to another member of the family; this makes them bearers of the past. This is not always a bad thing, depending on the weight of the past represented in the family signifiers. In Senegal, the Oulof people give their children the name of a deceased grandfather or grandmother. They are reincarnations of those ancestors, and by making them live again, they appropriate their knowledge and some-times also their power. Then they can be beneficent and protect their family; but they can also become a threat, and a real danger to them-selves and others.

For Arthur Jean-François, it was no easy mission, and his premature arrival in the world had complicated matters further.

"When he was born, we were all in tears," said his mother, "the whole family was crying. We didn't know if we were crying for Jean-François' death, or for Arthur's imminent death—the midwife had told us we shouldn't get too attached to him."

Suddenly Arthur burst out laughing. He upended the basket of toys, and found a puppet of a wolf with sharp teeth which looked terrifying and aggressive. I leant towards him, and said, "Yes, Arthur, it's really not a very funny story, is it. It's like the wolf, he's really scary, so better laugh at him."

Arthur rushed over to his mother and pressed his head against her belly. "Arthur's just like that," she said, "he was born when we were all in tears, and now he laughs his way through life."

Arthur was the family clown; he made the others laugh. His mimicry, his liveliness, his way of tripping over the carpet all the time, caused a lot of merriment for everyone around him. He would pick himself up laughing, and everyone would applaud him.

Everyone—that is to say, his mother, her sister who was two years older, and the maternal grandparents. They all lived in the same flat; Arthur's father had left the family before the child was born. "It was a short-term relationship," said the mother, "he didn't know I was pregnant by him. I just wanted a child."

The mother continued to tell her story. When Arthur was two weeks old, she had returned to see him in the NICU. Really, nothing had changed. The doctors were no more reassuring than they had been, and nobody seemed to have noticed that she had not been there. "I'd have liked them to talk to me, because in those places, it's as if no time goes by at all."

Arthur had not really changed, either; though maybe he had put on a bit of weight, and was a bit less of a "spider".

"Good thing, really," observed the mother, "spiders are the only animals I'm really afraid of."

He was still being tube-fed and was still on a ventilator. He had put on some weight, but the nurses said that it wasn't that he was "nice and chubby". He was suffering from oedema, which often occurs in premature babies, and he needed to lose weight again. She would sit by the incubator and cry; day after day, she would sit there and cry the whole afternoon. One evening, the junior doctor asked if she would like to see the service psychologist. She refused. It was not a psychologist she wanted to talk to; she would have preferred it if the nurses had talked to her, at least someone who knew Arthur, and was taking care of him. She was already miserable enough as it was. She thought that if they now took her for a patient, a depressive, she would never come back. The team did not press her to make an appointment, so she came back and cried, sitting near her son. "I hadn't stopped crying since Jean-François died. I told myself that one day I would stop crying, not because I wasn't sad any more, but because my body would have dried out."

Little by little, Arthur came to life. He opened one of his eyes, then he held out one of his hands. He would now watch his mother as she came and cried by his incubator. Timidly, she slid one finger into the palm of his hand, and Arthur squeezed it so hard that for a moment she forgot to cry. "As the days went by," she said, "the only times I would stop crying were when I was with Arthur and he was squeezing my hand. He kept me alive."

This child, who had appeared to be stillborn, and had truly been resuscitated, had, only a few weeks later, become the one who was resuscitating his own mother. He struggled on his own behalf, but also on hers, trying to pull them both back from the brink, and to bring her back to life.

When the doctors decided it was time to take Arthur off the ventilator, he found it quite difficult for a time. His mother recalled her own panic. Sometimes, he would turn purple, he would be suffocating, the doctors would have to restart his breathing; and he would squeeze his mother's finger even harder as if to reassure her: "See, I'm still here." "I really thought I could hear him speaking to me, then he would become pink again, the scare was over, and I felt better because I knew he wanted to get through it."

Arthur, his mother's baby-therapist, also succeeded in reconciling her with the service. Little by little, she forged links with some of the nurses. She began to trust them, and felt somewhat reassured.

At this point in the story, Arthur moved away from his mother, whom he had not left until now, and turned back to the toys, still smiling. I spoke to him: "You had a lot of work to do, Arthur, when you were in the hospital. You had to try to survive, and you had to look after your mummy, who was so unhappy. So you were afraid and you were smiling, both at the same time." Arthur looked at me, and then tried to lift up a pot plant that was much taller than he was; he made a tremendous effort, but of course could not manage it. I spoke to him again: "Yes, Arthur, it's very heavy, you can't carry everything. I expect it was too heavy for you to carry, all that sadness; would you maybe like to have a rest from it now?" Arthur let go of the plant, looked at me again, and rushed back to his mother's lap. "It's absolutely certain," she said, "that the reason we didn't all go mad when Jean-François died was because Arthur was there and we had something to live for. But now his smile frightens me. Even if they hadn't said anything at the crèche, I would have come to see you."

When Arthur was discharged from the hospital, the doctors said that all the results of the tests were normal, and that Arthur would not suffer any consequences. And indeed, he had no medical problems from then on. He was still a little on the small side, and rather thin, but the paediatrician said he would soon catch up and be within the norms for a child of his age.

As a baby, he had been "perfect". He smiled all the time, with the same smile that he had given his mother very early on, when he was still in his incubator. It was the smile that had dried up her tears, but which now disturbed her.

He was very active, "maybe a bit too much so", she said. He ran around all the time, was difficult to control, and that was why he kept tripping up all the time, falling over, making everyone laugh. But he enjoyed clowning around, "especially when he's afraid", if people he didn't know came to the house, or when other children approached him. He was also afraid when people looked at him, or smiled at him. "He smiles all the time, why is he afraid of other people smiling at him?"

Children are sometimes afraid when people smile at them. These smiles that show the teeth, like the wolf in our first session, can be a threat to devour the child. Arthur knew just how important smiles were; he was afraid of other people's, but perhaps also of his own.

At the end of our first session, Arthur's mother scolded him: "Well, you didn't say much—you never stop talking usually!" Arthur turned towards me: "Wolf not frightened," he said to me as he threw the puppet out of the open window.

For the remainder of our sessions, I would first see Arthur with his mother, and then Arthur on his own.

I found out a few sessions later that he was a musician. That was one reason he was such a success socially. He could play the piano, he loved music above all else, and he loved to dance, said his mother. "I forgot to tell you that in the first session, but it's really important for him, I think we'll make a musician of him when he grows up." When I asked the mother where this particular gift came from, she explained to me that her brother had been a professional musician. She had been very moved by Arthur's early and obvious taste for rhythms and sounds. "Even when he was still in his incubator, he was alive to the sounds of the machines around him." Hooked up to those funny noises, Arthur was slowly able to construct himself; but his mother had interpreted it as a taste for music, and all of a sudden, Arthur was a musician. A musical clown.

As the sessions went on, the mother spoke about her childhood. She had been brought up in the provinces, in a calm and peaceful atmosphere. Her parents were both secondary school teachers, and lived a simple life, without problems. Her older sister loved dance, and her little brother loved music. She remembered that she had not loved anything. She waited for time to pass, walked around the little garden they had outside the house, and thought that one day she might like something, too. And indeed, when she was about thirteen, she decided that she liked children.

As a child, she had looked after her brother a great deal. How come she had not noticed the despair he was in? His suicide had been completely incomprehensible to the whole family. She, who had been so close to him in childhood, had not realised how bad he was feeling. She was convinced that because she was pregnant she had become selfish, deaf to her brother's unhappiness. She was expecting a baby, the whole family had accepted the pregnancy, and she felt fine. She no longer thought of anything but her belly, which was rounding out day by day: "The world could have fallen apart for all I cared." And then the world really did fall apart, blow by blow, with the death of her brother and the birth of a premature baby. At the time when he committed suicide, she was doing a course of haptonomy at the clinic where she was booked in for the delivery. She recalled how the haptonomy sessions became unbearable for her. "When Jean-François died, I couldn't bear to feel the baby inside me any more." She could no longer speak to the baby or make contact with him.

When she came in two weeks later to give birth, she was told that bereavement can sometimes bring on premature birth. She then felt doubly guilty: guilty of her brother's death, and guilty of having put her baby's life in danger, of having wanted to get rid of the baby from inside her body. At the moment of delivery, she had remembered the day she had "dropped" her little brother from the changing table, and how she had panicked. Her mother, in anger, had asked her, "But were you trying to kill him?"

The day of the delivery, she "dropped" Arthur, and her own mother's words were with her. Arthur's mother had been severely marked by those mortifying words. If this baby was alive, he would occupy the brother's place, he would be a ghost child, he would come to fill the gap. As a child offered up to death, he would become that loss in a concrete way.

If her own mother had lost her son because of her, how could she possibly have the right to have a child herself, unless he became the object she could restore to her mother?

What was this imaginary debt she was carrying?

How could she differentiate the baby she was carrying in her womb from herself? Who was more to blame for Jean-François' death, her, or the baby she was carrying? The foetus which the mother experiences as a part of herself becomes caught up in the play of identifications and introjections.

If she experienced herself as an object of horror, as a monstrous little girl, a spider with deathly powers, then when Arthur came into the world, he had no alternative but to become horrifying on his own account. He had the body of a spider. Was it guilt, then, disgust with herself at the moment of Jean-François' death, that pushed out this baby from her, the baby with whom she formed a unit? Because she could no longer bear to feel he existed, to the point of being unable to continue with the haptonomy sessions, which subjectified the baby too strongly for her.

Was it the deadly spider she had expelled from her womb? The spider of her childhood fear? Was it a phobia of herself, or of the baby she was carrying? How could she possibly differentiate between them?

As the sessions continued, Arthur's mother spoke about her fear, and gradually Arthur, who listened to her very attentively, stopped smiling.

When he was alone with me, he would only agree to play or speak after a number of detours, rituals which made him feel more secure. I was not allowed to look at him (perhaps he had been looked at too much in his incubator), I was not allowed to smile at him, but had to make an "impassive" face, and enable him to feel emotionally secure, which could only be achieved for him if there was a complete absence of seduction.

Day after day, he would enact scenarios with the wolf puppet he had chosen at the beginning of the treatment—the one he had thrown out of the window the first time we had met. Françoise Dolto pointed out that *"fenêtre"* (window) and *"faire naître"* (to create, to give birth) are neighbouring signifiers. It certainly was a second birth for Arthur, who gradually allowed himself to be in the world differently. He played the clown less and less, and spoke more and more, telling terrifying stories about animals devouring one another.

At the end of each session, he would go off to look for his mother, saying to me, "Mummy not frightened." The more she put her fear into words, and the more he started to come to life, the more he felt relieved of a weight that had been too heavy for him to carry.

One day in a session, the mother asked me, "Why didn't I want a father for my child?" Arthur, who was absorbed in drawing a house without a roof (*sans toit*)—or without you (*sans toi*)?—a black, sad-looking house, suddenly became angry. He tore up his piece of paper, and flew at his mother, shouting at the top of his voice and putting his hand over her mouth to shut her up. So we spoke at some length about the absence of a father. Arthur became calmer, and when he left the session, he said to me, "Tomorrow Arthur's going to school."

A few weeks later, Arthur's mother made an appointment to see a psychoanalyst, so that she could finally start treatment on her own account.

Perhaps a great deal of suffering, both for her and for Arthur, could have been avoided if they had been treated differently in the service, when he was born.

Notes

1. Magnetic resonance imaging.
2. See the case of Rachel, in Nasio (2012, p. 15).

CHAPTER SIX

A place for the psychoanalyst?

Finding one's bearings

Analysts need to "invent" their own place in a medical service. If the place is already there waiting for them when they arrive, the chances are they will find themselves in a closed system. They need to be free, not to be enclosed in a fixed way of functioning, knowing that in this particular case, the transference to the team will never be able to be analysed as such.

What is the relationship of the analyst to the medical world? There are several ways it can manifest itself.

Analysts may have a phobic relationship to the service. In other words, they will seek to have as little contact as possible with the medical team, and will not wish to know anything about the files or the children's state of health. This type of analyst will make sure they have an office well away from the rest, and will only ever speak to the parents referred to them by the doctors, outside the hospital context. But how can an analyst function in such a state of avoidance or disavowal? How can we pretend we are not in a hospital?

In other cases, analysts may consider the doctors to be their rivals, believing themselves to be omnipotent, and far better at "curing the symptom". "Unplug your machines," they will say, "this child's life depends on something beyond that!" Obviously the life expectancy of these analysts in a NICU is not likely to be very long.

Others may think that they represent a form of complementary medicine, or are being brought in like the latest medical gadget. "Put a shrink in your incubator," was a headline in a medical journal a few years ago. But is it really the role of the psychoanalyst to be the latest "must-have"? And yet it is sometimes what the teams ask for: that we should come in to help them guarantee a quality of care that would "bring something extra" on top of their medical care. But that "extra" is, ironically, the question of "less is more" that will be brought in to the unit. One day when Dr. Bolot and I had been invited to speak about our work at a symposium, a member of the audience asked, "Does having a psychoanalyst in your service mean you have the answers to all your questions?" Dr. Bolot replied, "You must be joking! It's much more the case that the presence of a psychoanalyst means we ask ourselves far more questions than we used to." Psychoanalysts certainly do not give answers to the doctors' questions. On the contrary, they raise new questions. And what is more, it is vital that they do not believe themselves to possess a supposedly superior kind of knowledge. If analysts are not capable of putting themselves in question, then no work can possibly be done. They will need continually to put into question the effects of their own transferences. It is only at that price that analytic work can be done, whatever the setting in which it takes place.

A few years ago another psychoanalyst, Sylvie Séguret, and I were both working in neonatology. We proposed setting up a working group for neonatal psychologists from Paris and the surrounding region, at the Robert-Debré hospital. This working group still continues to meet at Necker, where the "Clepsydre" (Clepsydra) association was set up on the initiative of Céline Ricignuolo, to allow psychologists working in NICUs to share ideas and experience, and to facilitate research. Working groups are organised regularly within this framework, and the place of the psychoanalyst can be explored there. So the torch can be passed on.

All the years of working in NICUs have led me to define the psychoanalyst's work within a team as follows: allowing a space to open up in which a certain type of listening and speaking can become possible. The analyst's place, which is different in each case, has to be recreated day after day. It has to remain flexible and supple. Analysts will situate themselves differently at any given time, depending on the people they are addressing, and on those moments when it is possible to speak about something. It can happen in a corridor, in an office, in the entry vestibule, it does not matter, as Daniel Oppenheim (1997) reminds us: "A psychoanalyst in a hospital is like a street psychoanalyst."

In order to find their own place within a team, the question of analysts' ethics has always to be more in the foreground than is otherwise usual. But while being part of the team, they also need to be at a distance, so that they can offer the caregivers and parents an image, or a way of listening, that is somewhat removed. At other times, if analysts find themselves beside an incubator when all the monitors start bleeping, then the best they can do is to support the team in so far as they can. In other cases, they may remain alongside the caregivers during the phase leading up to a baby's death. They need to move from place to place, and create spaces where something can be played out creatively on the basis of their availability.

For analysts, it is not just a question of "understanding", nor of systematic explanation. Their only *a priori* is to hold on to the status of interlocutor for the babies, however small, weak, and sick they may be. They need to help the parents to be parents to their baby in spite of everything, and to ensure that neither the caregivers nor the parents confuse the babies with the machines. Their role is to help everyone retain the capacity to speak and to think. That is what analysts are there for: this construction, this creativity, and this questioning is always at work, and can enable families and teams to listen differently to what is happening for them in their interaction with the babies. At the moment when a cut is imposed by the admission to hospital, the birth can be symbolised and an attempt can be made to start to reconstruct the family history. Perhaps on that basis, a corner of the veil can be lifted, and they can alter their route a little, and as we have seen in some cases, may choose to continue with some analytic work on their own account afterwards. During the period when the babies are in the NICU, for most parents, the situation is far too anguishing, they are too much caught up in the violence of the Real, and under permanent threat of death, for it to be possible for them to take analytic work any further.

In France, hospitals require analysts working in NICUs to have a degree in psychology or psychiatry; it is not possible for lay psychoanalysts to be taken on. On the other hand, many clinical psychologists and psychiatrists have undertaken a psychoanalytic training as well as their university degree. Through their university studies, they will have acquired knowledge of psychopathology, child development, and a certain amount of clinical experience, but their analytic training will offer them many other things in a quite different register. Their practice will have a particular orientation as a result, but the heads of service do not realise this, and often do not make any distinction between those who are analytically trained and those who are not. While they are obliged to employ some form of qualified "shrink" in order to make their (tertiary) service work according to protocol, they do not necessarily appreciate how much difference a psychoanalyst would make, by looking at things in a different light. The majority do not even realise that it is a different profession, and that work with a psychoanalytic orientation gives a quite different aim to any project that is put in place.

There is yet another dimension to a psychoanalytic orientation. Psychoanalysts, because they have been through a personal analysis, have undertaken many supervisions, and continually study psychoanalytic texts, will have a different way of looking at things. As we have shown, psychoanalysis is familiar with hate, and knows it is primary, even more so than love, and that it is not necessarily destructive. It is prepared to listen to mothers who say they resent their premature babies, without branding them "bad" mothers; it knows that ambivalence exists, that it is desire, mysterious and always unconscious, that leads the dance, and that there are inevitably conflicts within each and every one of us, and also that conflicts can arise within teams. It is not a question of "reassurance", or "adaptation", and certainly not of baby "observation" (if you consider that observation has to be carried out by researchers who are as neutral and detached as possible from what they observe). When psychoanalysts observe babies, it is not in order to translate their observations into graphs and statistics, but rather they agree to be involved in the experience, as Winnicott emphasised. What is more, thanks to their personal analyses, they will be able to be truly present in the service, whether alongside babies, parents, or doctors, without forcing them to bear the weight of their own projections, and with as few prejudices as possible. It will allow them to be there without feeling the need to protect themselves, without staying in an office separated from the others, far away from the service or the incubators, hiding comfortably behind their evaluation grids and their observation protocols. They can simply be there. Not to normalise the patients or the babies, or even to reassure the team, but to share everything with them—joys, sorrows, doubts, and the unexplainable. It is through this particular way of the analysts' being there that the caregivers can find, not answers to their questions, but different angles from which to approach their questions and to put into words what they are living through.

These services, which are constantly being revolutionised by advances in science and new technologies, and are both fascinated and terrified by the power over life and death that is given to them, would very much welcome the input of psychoanalysts. Because medicine is becoming more and more dehumanising, as much for the patients as for the doctors, the caregivers, who no longer feel they are involved as human subjects, also want, in their own way, to be brought back to life. There is good reason to believe that over the next few decades, medical teams will have more and more recourse to psychoanalysts.

But it seems there is a problem on the part of psychoanalysts these days, too. Those who see analytic patients in a traditional setting are often a little "scared" at the idea of venturing into a NICU, far from the couch and the armchair. And yet having this kind of experience is a great asset. Of course, there is no question of practising classical psychoanalysis in one of these services. We do not practise psycho-analysis in a NICU, and our place, which often rests solely on the teams' transference, is not an easy one to occupy and is constantly being questioned. But once you know how enriching this type of experience can be, such resistance on the part of psychoanalysts can only be deplored. Those who have agreed to take the risk have reported how much their practice, including their private practice, has been changed by the experience. Their relation to the archaic, to psychosis, to autism, and to their own bodies, has been changed by it. They have been led to question their theoretical presuppositions and to open up new paths of enquiry. The question of the Real has taken on new meaning for them. The work of "co-resuscitation" with a psychoanalytic orientation, which we set up at the Hôpital Saint-Denis, is real team-work, and could easily be set up elsewhere. It is truly not a question of working as an "extra" with the parents and babies, in parallel with the service, but of allowing the caregivers themselves to develop new ideas about the process of resuscitation in order to enable them to change their approach to it. Together, we have brought about a particular way of working that involves taking account of subjects and their desire, whether they are patients or doctors.

A research project

As we come to the close of this book, it is time to talk about the future. Over the past few years, in order to try to evaluate our rather "different" way of working (considering the ideas that are prevalent these days with regard to developmental care), we went to the lengths of suggesting a research project in our service on the outcomes of premature babies.

The project, which at the time of writing is taking place at the Centre de recherche psychanalyse, médecine et société (CRPMS) at the Université Paris-Diderot—Paris 7, is to be led by Professor Bernard Golse (Necker University Hospital) and Professor Alain Vanier. It will take place in the NICU in the Hôpitaux de Saint-Denis, with Dr. Pascal Bolot, our head of service, and myself as researchers. It will also take place in parallel at the Necker hospital for sick children, with Dr. Luis Alvarez and Dr. Lisa Ouss as researchers. Our hypothesis is that a psychoanalytically inspired approach to care improves the future chances of premature babies, and that this improvement can be measured as much in clinical terms (affective, cognitive) as in psychological terms.

This research is clearly ambitious, and the methodology is difficult to define. How indeed can we measure the effects of psychoanalytic care? We have been encouraged and helped by Professor Bruno Falissard and Professor Jean-Christophe Thalabard, who have agreed to take part in the research. We are highly motivated to carry out this research, which we expect to upset the status quo as much for the psychoanalysts, who for the most part refuse any kind of evaluation, as for the scientists, who do not believe that psychoanalysis is really a serious discipline. In addition, the thinking process which is ongoing in our service will be much strengthened by it. It is extraordinary that we have been able to work in this way at this particular point in time. Once again, we can understand the question in terms of transference, but it is also linked with the specificity of the Hôpitaux de Saint-Denis.

Hôpital Delafontaine

In this hospital, in a profusion of music and colours, we find Africa, North Africa, India, China, Eastern Europe, and other countries. The mix of cultures, traditions, and religions is astonishingly rich, and it means that the doctors and their teams have to be open to new ways of working. How can we receive and welcome these babies and their parents unless we are prepared to question the ways we function?

Twins, of very low birth weight, had just been born. The parents explained that in their village in Africa, twins had very great power in the family. In some cases the power was malefic, and in others it could be protective and healing. In order for everything to go well, they had to perform a particular ritual at the birth. It had to happen very quickly, the father said, but the team did not seem keen to have this ceremony. The family were very insistent, and after all sorts of questions regarding the safety of the babies, the father came and danced and sang around the incubators containing his sons, with his face painted with strange signs in bright colours, thus respecting the tradition.

On another occasion, a Haitian mother explained to us that her premature baby would die if he was not soaked in a bath containing plants with magic powers. His grandfather was a famous witch-doctor in their country, and he had sent by airmail the roots and herbs that, he said, were essential to save the life of the newborn. This mother was so worried that the team called a meeting to evaluate the risks, and to decide what we could do without harming this tiny baby. How, and to what extent, can we accept the prescriptions of other witch-doctors on behalf of these parents? We cannot avoid questioning our own belief on such occasions.

A little boy was born after a foetal illness so serious that it was assumed he would be severely brain-damaged. The doctors, who thought there were serious risks of sequelae, decided that it was time to speak to the parents about a possible transition to palliative care. The father was absolutely horrified. "But that's impossible. You can't do that. I had a dream in which God said that my son is the Messiah and that he'd been born to save all of mankind. That's why we've called him Christ. You can't kill Christ, or you'll be responsible for the collapse of the whole of humanity." Fortunately, a few days later Christ revived, he stopped having convulsions, and escaped palliative care. This father, apparently, had begun to suffer delusions at the birth of this child, his first, but what would we have done if the MRI scan had shown up something disastrous?

Both doctors and psychoanalysts need to rethink their attitudes and their diagnoses, and work differently. They need to be more flexible and more inventive, and face the fact that no pre-established protocol can be directly applicable at moments like these. The best they can do is to be available and open-hearted. It is just when doctors can no longer hide behind the norm, when they have to rethink their prejudices and their protocols, that work with psychoanalysts seems to become possible. It is during those moments of destabilisation and loss that they have the greatest need to speak with someone.

In neonatal resuscitation, the encounter between the hyper-sophisticated world of the most up-to-date technology and the patients, some of whom, prior to this premature delivery, had never seen a doctor, can produce the most astonishing effects. How can anyone who has suffered the trauma of premature birth not also speak of the trauma occasioned by their immersion in the high-tech world of the hospital? All these various parents with their different belief systems come up against ours, and force us continually to put ours into question. This extreme type of situation shows us in an amplified form what all patients are faced with when they come into contact with modern medicine. It is an encounter that is more or less traumatic for virtually everyone. The relation which the doctors necessarily have with the body as a machine that enables life to go on contaminates our own way of regarding our bodies. But the extreme cases we have considered in this book allow us to think about the effects *in vivo* through a magnifying glass.

There are mothers who have left their village and their family very shortly before arriving by plane and coming directly to the service. They are caught up in an incomprehensible whirlwind. This world, which is totally alien to them, may cause them to fall into a stupor, or may fascinate them and seem full of wonders. Some parents are actually afraid that the doctors will kidnap their babies for the purposes of experimentation; others will immediately adopt a completely submissive and trusting attitude, as if one terrifying power could replace another. We then need to ask ourselves questions about their docility.

One mother, who had just given birth to quadruplets, had upset the team very much. She showed no anxiety whatsoever, and was cheerful, smiling, and appeared to believe that everything was fine. Meanwhile, the team and the hospital's social workers, who surrounded her, were far from feeling that way. The woman, who had just arrived from Bangladesh, was alone in France, without papers, without anywhere to stay, did not speak French, and had absolutely nowhere to go when she was discharged. Of course, we first had to find people who spoke her language—we often have to find interpreters and caregivers who speak other languages. The nurses, auxiliaries, and doctors in the Hôpitaux de Saint-Denis come from many parts of the world. This linguistic and cultural abundance, among both the caregivers and the patients, gives our hospital a special feel, and creates a specific ambience. For this mother of quadruplets, it was one of the nursing auxiliaries who become our interpreter. If we can find an interpreter who is familiar with the team, it changes the relationship between the parents and the caregivers. We came to understand how reassuring our hospital was for this mother. In Bangladesh, she told us, the babies would not have been born, or they would have been stillborn, or would have died of hunger. So for her, the doctors and their machines were experienced as saviours, and the service as a place of beneficence and protection. She really was not concerned about what would happen next. What continued to amaze her, she said, was that she had been able to board the plane, and that they were all five alive, she and her four babies. Even if it only lasted one more day, it was wonderful.

Prematurity and precariousness

In Saint-Denis, you don't need to come from Bangladesh to know what it means to live in a state of precariousness. Many women are isolated; the family remains in their home country. Some of them are in France illegally, homeless and without papers. They are moved from hostel to hostel. In some cases, the father of their baby is there, in others he is not, having disappeared as soon as he found out about the pregnancy. The pregnancies are not always monitored as they should be, either through lack of resources or because of the fear that the mothers will be sent back home if they come to the prenatal clinic.

Among such families, the Hôpitaux de Saint-Denis are known as a place where they feel welcomed and safe. This is important, because many studies, such as the one carried out by the Paris hospital authority (AP-HP, 2005), show a high correlation between precarious social conditions, prematurity, and perinatal pathologies. The risk of acute illness, intra-uterine growth retardation, and infections is increased if pregnancies are either poorly monitored or not monitored at all. A report by Dominique Versini (2010), who was Children's Commissioner in 2010, showed that two million children were living below the poverty line in France at that time. Other studies show a significant correlation between the sociocultural milieu, precarious housing conditions, poverty, isolation, and risk of perinatal pathologies. At Saint-Denis, we very often treat women who live alone, without papers, without resources, and some of whom are homeless. When they leave our ultra-protective service, with babies who were born prematurely and now weigh 800 or 900 grams, they will find themselves back on the streets. (During 2012, we heard that in the course of the year, reception centres and hostels in our *département*, which were absolutely essential, were to be closed down.) How could our clinical work not be affected by this? Prematurity has become a symptom of the politics of healthcare, as if today's extraordinary technical feats were there to compensate for the injustice inherent in the distribution of care.

A psychoanalytically informed approach to care is not, as we too often hear repeated, the preserve of a privileged sociocultural milieu, any more than it is limited to the "couch and armchair" set-up. In the United States, the situation is even worse than in France. One study showed that for each dollar saved on care during pregnancy, additional costs incurred during delivery and follow-up during the first fifteen years of life amount to 4.63 dollars (Moore, Origel, Key, & Resnik, 1986).

It is impossible for us not to be concerned, as are all the doctors at the hospital, by these extremely worrying public healthcare problems. Perhaps if more psychoanalysts moved a little further away from the couch, it would help them, too, to realise how essential their engagement is, and, as Maud Mannoni put it, to agree to occupy the place where they are really needed—out in the world.

REFERENCES

Adams, R. J. (1987). Visual acuity from birth to 5 months. *Infant Behaviour and Development, 10*: 239–244.

Alexandre, B., & Bizos Kukucka, N. (1993). *Prévention de la prématurité et détresse maternelle: "Tombé du nid trop tôt." Un autre regard sur l'accouchement prématuré*. Paris: GERAL.

Als, H., Lawhon, G., Duffy, F. H., Emcanulti, G. B., Gibes-Grossman, R., & Blickman, J. D. (1994). Individualized developmental care and the very low-birth-weight preterm infant. Medical and neurofunctional effects. *JAMA, 272*: 853–858.

Anderson, P., & Doyle, L. -W. (2003). Neurobehavioural outcomes of school-age children born extremely low birth weight or very preterm in the 1990. *JAMA, 289*: 3264–3272.

(AP-HP) Assistance publique-Hôpitaux de Paris. (2005). Femmes en grande vulnérabilité et maternité. Study carried out by the Paris hospital authority.

Aubry, J. (2003). *Psychanalyse des enfants séparés*. Paris: Denoël.

Balint, M. (1964). *The Doctor, His patient and the Illness* (2nd edition, 1957). London: Pitman Medical.

Balogh, P., & Porter, R. (1986). Olfactory preferences in human neonates. *Infant Behaviour Development, 9*: 395–401.

Bentata, H. (2011). La voix des sirènes. *Essaim, 26*: 63–73.

Bergès, J., Lezine, I., Harrisson, A., & Boisselier, F. (1969). Le syndrome de l'ancien prématuré. Recherche sur sa signification. *Revue de neuropsychiatrie infantile, 17*: 719–779.

Bétrémieux, P. (2010). *Soins palliatifs chez le nouveau-né.* Paris: Springer.

Bhutta, A. T., Cleves, M. A., Casey, P. H., Craddock, M. M., & Anand, K. J. S. (2002). Cognitive and behavioural outcomes of school-aged children who were born preterm: a meta-analysis. *JAMA, 288*: 728–737.

Boukobza, C. (2003). La clinique du holding, illustration de D. W. Winnicott. *Le Coq-Héron, 173*: 64–71.

Bourgeois, L. (1926). Observations diverses sur la stérilité, perte de fruict, fécondité, accouchements et maladies des femmes et enfans nouveaux naiz. Cited in Duchatel, 1926.

Bowlby, J. (1969). Attachment. Attachment and Loss: Vol. 1. Loss. New York, NY: Basic Books.

Boysson-Bardies (de), B. (2001). *How Language Comes to Children.* Cambridge, MA: MIT Press.

Brazelton, T. B., & Cramer, B. G. (1991). *The Earliest Relationship: Parents, Infants, and the Drama of Early Attachment.* Boston: DaCapo Press.

Brazelton, T. B., Tronick, E., Adamson, L., Als, H., & Wise, S. (1975). Early mother–infant reciprocity, Parent–infant interaction. Ciba Foundation Symposium 33 (new series). Amsterdam: Associated Scientific Publishers.

Brun, D. (2011). *Mères majuscules.* Paris: Odile Jacob.

Busnel, M. -C. (1993). *Le Langage des bébés.* Paris: Jacques Granchet.

Bydlowski, M. (1983). Et si l'inconscient calculait la date de naissance? In: *Les Cahiers du nouveau-né, 6.* Paris: Stock.

Casper, A. J., & Fifer, W. P. (1980). Of human bonding: newborns prefer their mother's voices. *Science, 208*: 1174–1176.

Changeux, J. -P., & Dachin, A. (1974). Selective stabilization of developing synapses as a mechanism for the specification of neuronal networks. *Nature, 264*: 705–712.

Chapieski, M. -L., & Evankovich, K. -D. (1997). Behavioural effects of prematurity. *Semin. Perinatol., 21*: 221–39.

Damasio, A. (2007). *Descartes' Error: Emotion, Reason and the Human Brain.* London: Vintage.

De Casper, A. J., & Spence, M. J. (1986). Prenatal maternal speech influence new borns' perception of speech sounds. *Infant Behaviour and Development, 9*: 133–150.

Diatkine, R. (1977). *Le Devenir du prématurité.* Paris: PUF.

Dolto, C. (1995). Dialogue haptonomique pré- ou post-natal, sécurité affective et ouverture au langage. Conference on Haptonomy, November 1995.

Dolto, C. (2001). Dialogue haptonomique. In: R. Negri (Ed.), *Que savent les foetus?* Ramonville Saint-Agne: Érès.

Dolto, F. (1984). *L'Image inconsciente du corps*. Paris: Seuil.

Dolto, F. (1996). *Sexualité féminine*. Paris: Gallimard.

Druon, C. (1996). *À l'écoute du bébé prématuré. Une vie aux portes de la vie*. Paris: Aubier.

Duchatel, F. (1926). Histoire de la réanimation néonatale. Paper given at the Société française d'histoire de la médecine, 28 April 1979.

Eliacheff, C. (1998). *Á corps et á cris*. Paris: Odile Jacob.

Falissard, B. (1998). *Comprendre et utiliser les statistiques*. Paris: Masson.

Fernald, A., & Simon, P. (1984). Expanded intonation contours in mothers' speech to new born. *Developmental Psychology*, 20: 104–113.

Ferreira, S. (1995). De l'interaction mère-bébé, au dialogue mère-bébé: le premier pas. *La Psychanalyse d'enfant*, 16: 69–83.

Ferreira, S. (1998). Paroles et champ du langage chez le nourrisson. Paper given at the Journées d'études Association Freudienne-Espace Analytique, 22 March 1998 at the Sainte-Anne Hospital in Paris.

Field, T. M., Cohen, D., Garcia, R., & Greenberg, R. (1984). Mother-stranger face discrimination by the newborn. *Infant Behaviour and Development*, 7: 19–25.

Fonagy, I. (1983). *La Vive Voix*. Paris: Payot.

Fonagy, P. (2001). *Attachment Theory and Psychoanalysis*. London: Karnac.

Freud, S. (1900a). *The Interpretation of Dreams*. S. E., IV: ix–627. London: Hogarth.

Freud, S. (1905d). *Three Essays on the Theory of Sexuality*. S. E., VII: 125–245. London: Hogarth.

Freud, S. (1908c). On the sexual theories of children. S. E., IX: 207–226. London: Hogarth.

Freud, S. (1909d). Notes upon a case of obsessional neurosis. S. E., X: 153–249. London: Hogarth.

Freud, S. (1910c). *Leonardo da Vinci and a Memory of his Childhood*. S. E., XI: 59–137. London: Hogarth.

Freud, S. (1912d). On the universal tendency to debasement in the sphere of love. S. E., XI: 179–190. London: Hogarth.

Freud, S. (1912–1913). *Totem and Taboo*. S. E., XIII: vii–162. London: Hogarth.

Freud, S. (1913f). The theme of the three caskets. S. E., XII: 289–302. London: Hogarth.

Freud, S. (1914c). On narcissism: An introduction. S. E., XIV: 67–102. London: Hogarth.

Freud, S. (1930a). *Civilization and its Discontents*. S. E., XXI: 57–146. London: Hogarth.

Freud, S. (1931b). Female sexuality. S. E., XXI: 223–243. London: Hogarth.

Freud, S. (1940a [1938]). *An Outline of Psycho-Analysis*. S. E., XXIII: 144–207. London: Hogarth.

Freud, S. (1950). Project for a scientific psychology (1950 [1895]). *S. E., I*: 283–397. London: Hogarth.

Freud, W. E. (1989). Notes on some psychological aspects of neonatal intensive care. In: S. I. Greenspan, G. H. Pollock (Eds.), *The Course of Life: Psychoanalytic Contributions Toward Understanding Human Development, Vol. 1: Infancy and Early Childhood* (pp. 257–269). Madison, CT: International Universities Press.

Gazengel, J. (2002). *Vivre en réanimation*. Paris: L'Harmattan.

Gelis, J. (1996). *History of Childbirth: Fertility, Pregnancy and Birth in Early Modern Europe*. Cambridge: Polity Press.

Golse, B. (2006). *L'Être bébé*. Paris: PUF.

Golse, B. (2010). L'émotion dépressive et la co-construction des affects et des representations. In: A. Braconnier & B. Golse (Eds.), *Dépression du bébé, dépression de l'adolescent* (pp. 37–53). Toulouse: Érès.

Golse, B., & Keren, M. (2000). The pediatric team and the consulting child psychiatrist facing the hospitalized depressed infant: some clinical reflections. *Israel Journal of Psychiatry and Related Sciences, 37*: 197–204.

Goren, C. C., Sarty, M., & Wu, P. Y. K. (1975). Visual following and pattern discrimination of face like stimuli, by newborn infants. *Pediatrics, 56*: 544–549.

Granboulan, V. (1995). Prise en charge psychique de l'extrême prématurité. *Archives pédiatriques, 2*.

Granier-Deferre, C. (1994). Les compétences auditives prénatales. Doctoral thesis, University of Paris-South, Orsay.

Green, A. (1984). Pulsion de mort, narcissisme négatif, fonction désobjectal-isante. In: *La Pulsion de mort*. Paris: PUF.

Guérin, G. (1982). Introduction. In: G. Raimbault, *Clinique du réel: La psychanalyse et les frontiers du méadical*. Paris: Seuil.

Guillot de Suduiraut, S. (1998). La Vierge à l'Enfant d'Issenheim. Un chef-d'oeuvre bâlois de la fin du Moyen Age. In: *Dossiers du Museé du Louvre*. Paris: Editions de la La Réunion des musées nationaux.

Haag, G. (2005). Comment les psychanalystes peuvent aider les enfants avec autisme et leurs familles? In: B. Golse & P. Delion (Eds.), *Autisme, état des lieux et horizons*. Toulouse: Érès.

Halsey, C. L., Collin, M. F., & Anderson, C. L. (1996). Extremely low birth weight children and their peers: a comparison of schoolage outcomes. *Archives of Pediatrics and Adolescent Medicine, 150*: 790–794.

Humphrey, T. (1964). Some correlations between the appearance of human fetal reflexes and the development of the nervous system. *Progress in Brain Research, 4*: 93–135.

Kersting, A., Dorsch, M., Wesselmann, U., Lüdorff, K., Witthaut, J., Orhmann, P., Hörnig-Franz, I., Klockenbusch, W., Harms, E., & Arolt, V.

(2004). Maternal posttraumatic stress response after the birth of a very low-birthweight infant. *Journal of Psychosomatic Research, 57*: 473–476.

Klein, M. (1975). *Envy and Gratitude and Other Works 1946–1963*. London: Hogarth.

Lacan, J. (1951). Presentation on transference. In: B. Fink (Trans.), *Écrits*. New York: Norton.

Lacan, J. (1971). Séminaire XIX: Le savoir du psychanalyste, Lecture of 4 November 1971. Unpublished.

Lacan, J. (1975). Le Séminaire. Livre XXII: R.S.I. Unpublished.

Lacan, J. (1984). Discours de clôture. In: P. Gyuomard & M. Mannoni, *Enfance aliénée: L'Enfant, la psychose et l'institution*. Paris: Denoël.

Lacan, J. (1989). Geneva lecture on the symptom (1975). Translated by Russell Grigg. *Analysis, 1*: 7–26.

Lacan, J. (1991a). *The Seminar of Jacques Lacan, Book I: Freud's Papers on Technique (1953–1954)*. New York: Norton.

Lacan, J. (1991b). *Le Séminaire, Livre VIII: Le Transfert*. Paris: Seuil.

Lacan, J. (1997). *The Seminar of Jacques Lacan, Book III: The Psychoses (1955–1956)*. New York: Norton.

Lacan, J. (1998). *The Seminar of Jacques Lacan, Book XI: The Four Fundamental Concepts of Psychoanalysis (1964)*. New York: Norton.

Lacan, J. (1999). *The Seminar of Jacques Lacan, Book XX: Encore. On Feminine Sexuality, The Limits of Love and Knowledge (1972–1973)*. New York: Norton.

Lacan, J. (2003). *La place de la psychanalyse dans la médecine*. In: J. Aubry, *La Psychanalyse des enfants séparés*. Paris: Denoël, Espace Analytique.

Lacan, J. (2005). *Écrits* (Translated by Bruce Fink). New York: Norton.

Lacan, J. (2014a). *The Seminar of Jacques Lacan, Book IX: Anxiety (1962–1963)*. Cambridge: Polity Press.

Lacan, J. (2014b). *The Seminar of Jacques Lacan, Book IV: Object Relations (1956–1957)*. New York: Norton.

Laznik, M. C. (1996). Pourrait-on penser à une prévention du syndrome autistique? *Contraste, 5*: 69–85.

Laznick, M. C. (2010). Langage et communication chez le nourrisson. In: R. Frydman & M. Szejer (Eds.), *Naissance, histoire, culture et pratiques d'aujourd'hui*. Paris: Albin Michel.

Lebovici, S. (1960). La relation objectale chez l' enfant. *La Psychiatrie de l' enfant, 3*: 147–226.

Lessana, M. -M. (1993). *Malaise dans la procreation*. Paris: Albin Michel.

Lessana, M. -M. (2000). *Entre mères et filles: un ravage*. Paris: Pluriel.

Loux, F. (1991). *Une si longue naissance*. Paris: Stock.

Maguire, C. M., Walther, F. J., Sprij, A. J., Le Cessie, S., Wit, J. M., & Veen, S. (2009). Effects of individualized developmental care in a randomized trial of preterm infants <32 weeks. *Pediatrics, 124*: 1021–1030.

Malloch, S. (1999). Mother and infants and communicative musicality. In: I Deliège (Ed.), *Rhythms, Musical Narrative, and the Origin of Human Communication* (pp. 29–57). *Musicae Scientiae, Special Issue 1999–2000*. Liège: European Society for the Cognitive Sciences of Music.

Mannoni, O. (1969). *Clefs pour l'imaginaire ou l'autre scène*. Paris: Seuil.

Mathelin (Vanier), C. (1998). *Le Sourire de la Gioconde. Clinique psychanalytique avec les bébés prématurés*. Paris: Denoël.

Mehler, J., & Dupoux, E. (1995). *Naître humain*. Paris: Odile Jacob.

Mehler, J. et al. (1988). A precursor of language acquisition in young infants. *Cognition, 29*: 143–178.

Menès, M. (2012). *L'Enfant et le savoir. D'où vient le désir d'apprendre?* Paris: Seuil.

Mieli, P. (1999). Some reflections on medically assisted reproduction. In: J. Houis, P. Mieli, & M. Stafford (Eds.), *Being Human*. New York: Agincourt/Marsilio, Après-coup Psychoanalytic Association.

Misrahi, C. (1982). *Famille: travaux récents sur le père, la mère et l'enfant*. Paris: Encyclopaedia Britannica, Inc.

Moore, R., Origel, W., Key, T. C., & Resnik, R. (1986). The perinatal and economic impact of prenatal care in low-socioeconomic populations. *American Journal of Obstetrics and Gynecology, 154*: 29–33.

Moreau-Ricaud, M. (2000). Vers une histoire de l'homme entier. Histoire raisonnée des groupes Balint. In: M. Moreau-Ricaud & M. Balint, *Le Renouveau de l'école de Budapest*. Paris: Érès.

Muller-Nix, C., Forcada-Guex, M., Borghini, A., Pierrehumbert, B., & Ansermet, F. (2009). Prématurité, vécu parental et relations parents/enfants: elements cliniques et données de recherche. *La Psychiatrie de l' enfant, 52*: 423–450.

Muller-Nix, C., Forcada-Guex, M., Pierrehumbert, B., Jaunin, L., Borghini, A., & Ansermet, A. (2004). Prematurity, maternal stress and mother–child interactions. *Early Human Development, 79*: 145–158.

Nasio, J.-D. (2012). *L'inconscient, c'est la repetition*. Paris: Payot.

Negri, R. (1994). *The Newborn in the Intensive Care Unit*. London: Karnac.

Newman, A. (1995). *Non-compliance in Winnicott's Words*. London: Free Association.

Oppenheim, D. (1997). Lecture given at the Laboratoire du clinique, Espace Psychanalytique in Paris, 12 December 1997 (personal notes).

Paulme, D. (1976). *La Mère dévorante*. Paris: Gallimard.

Pierrehumbert, B., Ramstein, T., Karmaniola, A., & Halfon, O. (1996). Child care in the preschool years: attachment, behaviour problems and cognitive development. *European Journal of Psychology of Education, 2*: 201–214.

Raimbault, G. (1982). *Clinique du réel, La psychanalyse et les frontiers du médical*. Paris: Seuil.

Roudinesco, E. (2002). *La famille en désordre*. Paris: Fayard.

Rovee-Collier, C. (1999). The development of infant memory. *Current Directions in Psychological Science, 8*: 80–85.

Safouan, M. (1975). *Études sur l'oedipe*. Paris: Seuil.

Samara, M., Marlow, N., & Wolke, D. (2008). Pervasive behavior problems at 6 years of age in a total-population sample of children born at ≤25 weeks of gestation. *Pediatrics, 122*: 562–573.

Schaal, B. (1995). Responsiveness to the odour of amniotic fluid in the human neonate. *Biology of the Neonate, 67*: 397–406.

Seay, B., Hansen, E., & Harlow, H. F. (1962). Mother infant separation in monkeys. *Journal of Child Psychology and Psychiatry, 3*: 123–132.

Sloterdijk, P. (1989). *La Mobilisation infinite*. Paris: Seuil.

Soler, C. (1994). *L'enfant et le désir de l'analyste*. Toulouse-le Mirail: Presse universitaire du Mirail.

Spitz, R. (1993). *The First Year of Life*. Madison, CT: International Universities Press.

Stern, D. N. (1985). *The Interpersonal World of the Infant: A View from Psychoanalysis and Development Psychology*. London: Karnac.

Stern, D. N. (1992). *Diary of a Baby: What Your Child Sees, Feels, and Experiences*. New York: Basic.

Szejer, M. (1997). *Des mots pour naître*. Paris: Gallimard.

Tarnier, S., Chantreuil, G., & Budin, P. (1886–1901). *Traité de l'art des accouchements*. Paris: Stienheil. Cited in Duchatel, 1926.

Thalabard, J. -C. (2010). *Enjeux éthiques de la méthodologie des essais cliniques. Traité de bioéthique*. Paris: Érès.

Trevarthen, C. (2004). Intimate contact from birth: How we know one another by touch, voice, and expression in movement. In: K. White (Ed.), *Touch, Attachment and the Body*. London: Karnac.

Trevarthen, C., & Marwick, H. (1986). Signs of motivation for speech in infants, and the nature of a mother's support for the development of language. In: B. Lindblom & R. Zetterstrom (Eds.), *Precursors of Early Speech* (pp. 279–308). New York: Stockholm Press.

Turton, P. (2009). Long-term psychosocial sequelae of stillbirth. *Archives of Women's Mental Health, 12*: 35–41.

Tustin, F. (2003). *Autistic States in Children* (Revised Edition). London: Routledge.

Vaivre-Douret, L. (2004). Effect of positioning on the incidence of abnormalities of muscle tone in low-risk, preterm infants. *European Journal of Paediatric Neurology, 8*: 21–34.

Vanier, A. (1993). Autisme et théorie. In: *Hommage á Frances Tustin*. Saint André de Cruzières: Audit.

Vanier, A. (1995). Contribution à la métapsychologie du temps des processus psychiqes. Questions posées par l'observation et la clinique infanto-juvénile, Doctoral thesis (Dir. P. Fédida), Université Paris Diderot—Paris 7. Unpublished.

Vanier, A. (2000). Quelques remarques sur le 'Je' et le sujet. *Topique, 71*: 137.

Vanier, A. (2002). D'une dyade à plusieurs. Quelques remarques à propos d'un travail avec les mères psychotiques et leur nourrisson. *Psychologie clinique, 12*: 39–50.

Vanier, A. (2003). Principes du détournement. *Cliniques méditerranéennes, 68*: 23–35.

Vanier, A. (2010). *Une introduction à la psychanalyse*. Paris: Armand Colin.

Vanier, A. (2011). Mémoire freudienne, mémoire de l'oubli. *La Recherche, 344* [Special Issue 'La mémoire et l'oubli', July–August 2001].

Vanier, A., & Pelletier, N. (1989). Évaluation, soutien, orientation pour les enfants des mères marginales à la période périnatale. In collaboration with Dr. N. Pelletier, paper given at the fourth World Congress of the WAIPAD in Lugano, 20–24 September 1989.

Vanier, C. (2010). Prématurément mères. In: J. André (Ed.), *Maternités traumatiques*. Paris: PUF.

Vanier, C. (2012). Aux extrêmes limites de la réanimation. In: V. Estellion & F. Marty (Eds.), *Cliniques de l'extrême* (Ch. 2). Paris: Armand Colin.

Verlaine, P. (1895). *Poems of Paul Verlaine* (translated by Gertrude Hall). Chicago: Stone & Kimball.

Versini, D. (2010). Rapport annuel: Précarité et protection des droits de l'enfant. Published by the office of the French Children's Commissioner.

Werner, L. A., & Bargones J. Y. (1993). Psycho-acoustic development in human infants. In: C. Rovee-Collier & L. P. Lipsitt (Eds.), *Advances in Infancy Research, Volume 7*. Norwood, NJ: Ablex.

Winnicott, D. W. (1945). Primitive Emotional Development. *International Journal of Psycho-Analysis, 26*: 137–143.

Winnicott, D. W. (1949). Hate in the countertransference. *International Journal of Psycho-Analysis, 30*: 69–74.

Winnicott, D. W. (1965). *The Maturational Processes and the Facilitating Environment: Studies in the Theory of Emotional Development*. London: Hogarth.

Winnicott, D. W. (1971). *Therapeutic Consultations in Child Psychiatry*. London: Hogarth.

Winnicott, D. W. (1975). *Through Paediatrics to Psycho-Analysis*. London: Hogarth.

Winnicott, D. W. (1991). *The Child, the Family and the Outside World*. London: Penguin.

Winnicott, D. W. (2009). The newborn and his mother. In: *Winnicott on the Child* (pp. 32–42). Boston, MA: DaCapo.

Wolke, D., Söhne, B., Riegel, K., Ohrt, B., & Osterlund, K. (1998). An epidemiologic longitudinal study of sleeping problems and feeding experience of preterm and terms children in Southern Finland: comparison with a Southern German population sample. *Journal of Pediatry, 133*: 224–231.

Zelkowitz, P., Bardin, C., & Papageorgiou, A. (2007). Anxiety affects the relationship between parents and their very low birthweight infants. *Infant Mental Health Journal, 28*: 296–313.

Zelkowitz, P., Papageorgiou, A., Bardin, C., & Wang, T. (2009). Persistent maternal anxiety affects the interaction between mothers and their very low birth weight children at 24 months. *Early Human Development, 85*: 51–58.

INDEX